Myth
Conceptions

Tom Snyder teaches philosophy, aesthetics, social science, and film at National University in Southern California. He holds a Ph.D. in film studies from Northwestern University and has done post-doctoral research in Christian Apologetics at Simon Greenleaf School of Law.

Myth
Conceptions

Joseph Campbell
and
the New Age

Tom Snyder

Foreword by Bob and Gretchen Passantino

Baker Books

A Division of Baker Book House Co
Grand Rapids, Michigan 49516

Published by Baker Books
a division of Baker Book House Company
P.O. Box 6287, Grand Rapids, MI 49516-6287

Printed in the United States of America

Library of Congress Cataloging-in-Publication Data

Snyder, Thomas Lee, 1952–
    Myth conceptions: Joseph Campbell and the New Age / Tom Snyder; foreword by Bob and Gretchen Passantino.
        p. cm.
    Includes bibliographical references and index.
    ISBN 0-8010-8375-3
    1. Apologetics. 2. Myth. 3. Campbell, Joseph, 1904–87. 4. New Age movement—Controversial literature. I. Title.
BT1240.S68   1994
291.1'3'092—dc20   94-29907

Unless otherwise marked, Scripture quotations are from the HOLY BIBLE, NEW INTERNATIONAL VERSION®. NIV®. Copyright © 1973, 1978, 1984 by International Bible Society. Used by permission of Zondervan Publishing House. All rights reserved.

Scripture quotations identified NAS are from the New American Standard Bible, © the Lockman Foundation 1960, 1962, 1963, 1968, 1971, 1972, 1973, 1975, 1977.

To my wife, Jan

Contents

Foreword

Christians who have attended a secular college or university in the last twenty years have almost certainly heard of, if not enrolled in, a "Bible as Literature" or "World Religions" class. Many Christians attending public schools of higher education are eager to know more about the poetry, historical narratives, apocalyptic terminology, and parables of the Bible; or they want to see how the facts of Christianity stack up against the claims of Hinduism, Judaism, and other belief systems. Such classes became popular after the purging of prayer and religion from public schools in the '60s. Christians even viewed these new classes as opportunities to expose nonbelievers to Scripture through its literature, and to the belief claims of Christianity as a world religion.

Secular humanists seized the chance to promote a radically different agenda, however. "The Bible as Literature" and "World Religions" (and many sociology, anthropology, history, and other literature classes as well) became platforms for destructive higher criticism, skeptical mockery of Scripture, historical revisionism, and the transformation of Christianity into just another subjective, untestable, emotional experience. Literature and theology were largely ignored in favor of pseudo-intellectual Bible-bashing and faith-mocking.

In twenty years hundreds of thousands of young college and university students have been taught that the Bible is a fairy tale, Christianity is a myth, Jesus was a fictional flower-child, and God is an out-moded, irrelevant aberration of sick psyches. The impressionable students of the '60s, '70s, and '80s have become the journalists, television producers, educators, politicians, and New Age gurus of the '90s, repeating to us all these same prejudices about God, the Bible, Christianity, and Jesus Christ.

No author, speaker, or teacher has done more to promote this propaganda campaign than "master of myth" Joseph Campbell, author of the *Power of Myth* series, which dominates most popular American criticisms of Christianity. His books are the textbooks of choice in colleges and universities across the nation. His interview series with Bill Moyers is the one public television "religion" series that is rebroadcast time after time nationwide. Whether you have ever heard of Joseph Campbell by name or not, you have had his message of the myth of Christianity preached to you countless times in countless ways.

In *Myth Conceptions* Dr. Thomas Snyder openly challenges and refutes Campbell's complex but hopelessly skewed attack on Christianity. Through careful and thorough historical, literary, scientific, and theological research and argumentation, Dr. Snyder not only destroys Campbell's presuppositions and conclusions, but also presents a cogent, rational, reality-based worldview that validates the truthfulness of the Bible and Christianity.

Over the years that Dr. Snyder has worked with Answers In Action, he has argued consistently, persuasively, knowledgeably, and with passion and concern for truth—always sensitive to the light of knowledge rather than the darkness of prejudice. Whether he has been dialoging with a New Ager during our annual New Age Fair excursion or explaining Christian truth claims to an atheist during our weekly discussion group, Dr. Snyder's approach is always intellectually defensible and biblically responsible.

If you have wondered whether God exists, if Jesus is the Son of God, or if Christian faith is rational, this book will answer your questions. You can trust Dr. Snyder's comprehensive, meticulous research and his clearly and engagingly written text. *Myth Conceptions* is the book we turn to for answers to these questions, and it is with honor and pleasure that we recommend it to you, the reader, as well.

Bob and Gretchen Passantino
Directors, Answers In Action

Preface

oseph Campbell, author of *The Hero with a Thousand Faces* and many other books, died in 1987 but his ideas about religion, society, popular culture, and art still fascinate many people. His books are taught on many college campuses and displayed prominently in popular bookstores. The ideas in those books have been accepted by a wide cross section of the American public, including New Agers, neo-pagans, journalists, environmentalists, political liberals, and nominal Jews and Christians. Filmmaker George Lucas used Campbell's mystical ideas about hero myths to create his popular *Star Wars* and *Indiana Jones* films in the 1970s and 1980s.

Before Campbell died, PBS reporter and commentator Bill Moyers did a series of six one-hour television interviews with Campbell called "The Power of Myth," which aired on public television stations across the country. Since 1987, many public TV stations have rerun the series regularly, along with other shows featuring Campbell and his ideas. For example, the public TV station in Los Angeles reran "The Power of Myth" on March 1, 2, and 3, 1994, and again on March 5 and 6, 1994!

It is perfectly reasonable to assume, therefore, that even if you have never heard of Joseph Campbell, you probably have met or heard someone supporting one of his popular ideas. Unfortunately, however, most of Campbell's ideas are either irrational or factually false. Mortimer Adler, famous philosopher and editor of the *Ency-*

11

clopaedia Britannica, declared in the February 17, 1992, issue of *National Review* that Campbell's "understanding of the Christian creed and its theology [about which Campbell often spoke and wrote] was puerile. In that field he was an ignoramus." Adler also noted that Campbell's hedonistic philosophy of "follow your bliss," which Moyers found so wonderful, "represents the lowest debasement of twentieth century culture."

This book was not written only for people who know about Joseph Campbell and his ideas. It was also written for people who want to know some basic truths about religion, philosophy, ethics, science, aesthetics, the origin of mankind, western culture, Christianity, and the Bible. These are topics Campbell discussed and these are topics this book discusses.

There are at least seven major themes or ideas animating Campbell's work. These ideas are not new, but they have gained a major foothold in the social and intellectual spirit of this modern age. In America, we are engaged in a culture war over these ideas, which have become new sacred cows. Joseph Campbell, despite his death, is still a major figure in this battle. This book is my contribution against the spirit of this age.

Acknowledgments

irst and foremost, I want to thank God for giving me the opportunity to write this book.

Second, thanks to my professors at Northwestern University in Chicago, Frank McConnell and Stuart Kaminsky, for introducing me to mythological, or archetypal, criticism of popular culture. God used this endlessly fascinating topic to introduce me to comparative religion and psychology, which in turn helped lead me to Christ.

Next, I want to thank historian Paul Johnson for writing *Modern Times*, which began to show me how to unite Christianity with traditional conservative ideology. Together, they are the foundation of all that is good in western culture. I also want to thank the late Walter Martin, founder of the Christian Research Institute, who showed me that you don't have to put your brain on hold to be a strong Bible-believing Christian. Thanks also to C. S. Lewis for writing *Mere Christianity* and to Pat Robertson whose "700 Club" TV show, along with Lewis's book, played an important role in my conversion to Christ.

My editors, Gretchen and Bob Passantino, who are themselves excellent authors, deserve special thanks not only for working diligently on this manuscript but also for the guidance of their wonderful ministry, Answers In Action. Being their associate and friend has played a great role in my becoming a more mature and thoughtful Christian. Thanks also to all the other supportive friends I have met through their Mars Hill Club, especially Tracy, Jeff, Mike, and John, whom I knew previously.

I also wish to express my gratitude to all the folks at Baker Book House, especially Kin Millen, Dan Van't Kerkhoff, and Mary Suggs. My thanks to Alan Kindred, who created the cover for the original booklet I wrote on Campbell, a necessary step to having this book published.

Last but not least, thanks to my wife, Jan, for the patience, support, and love she has freely given me in spite of my irritating qualities. She has given further proof that we can only be saved by grace because we can only be truly loved by grace.

Love does not delight in evil but rejoices with the truth. . . .
Follow the way of love.

1 Corinthians 13:6; 14:1

Introduction: Storytelling and Mythmaking

Stories matter deeply to us. They make a profound difference in our lives. They stimulate our minds and stir our imaginations. They bring us laughter, tears, and joy. They help us escape our present lives for a while and travel to different times and places. They arouse our compassion, spur us toward love, and sometimes even incite us toward hatred or violence.

Why do we respond so strongly to stories?

Over the years, scholars have given us at least two basic answers to this question. First, different stories satisfy different needs. A comedy evokes a different response than a tragedy. A hard news story on page one affects us differently than a human interest story in the magazine section or a celebrity profile next to the movie listings. Second, although different stories satisfy different needs, many stories share common themes, settings, character types, situations, and other recurrent patterns. They possess a timeless, universal quality.

I like both these answers.

The first one helps us classify stories according to their *genre*. *Genre* means classification, used to aid people studying different kinds of stories, placing them in special categories depending on their distinct styles, forms, and content. A genre *is* a category. Using the genre approach, we can divide stories into broad categories like tragedy, comedy, epic, romance, and history and into more narrow categories like mystery, western, science fiction, horror, and farce.

The second answer helps us explore the unity behind all stories— their ability to paint the wonders of nature, to plumb the heights and depths of the human condition, and to discover the spirit of the imagination. By looking at this unity, we gain insights into truth and reality; we learn about human behavior.

For me, the most rewarding way to pursue the second answer is to view all stories as *myth*. In using the term *myth*, I do not mean the modern, most common definition of the word, which sees any-thing that is called myth as a lie or as something false. Nor do I define myth as only a story dealing with supernatural beings, deities, super-human heroes, and magical events having no basis in reality. Myths can be historical, scientific, or factual. Even an atheist can create or believe a story with just as many mythic qualities as any story that a religious person might tell. The definition that comes closest to what I mean by the word *myth* is "any real or fictional story, recur-ring theme, or character type that appeals to the consciousness of a people by embodying its cultural ideals or by giving expression to deep, commonly felt emotions."[1]

We can apply this idea of myth to both fiction and nonfiction stories, and to both religious and nonreligious stories. All four of these kinds of stories often portray cultural ideals and depict uni-versal concerns, hopes, and fears. A story may be firmly rooted in a historical time and place, yet at the same time express timeless qualities that transcend or go beyond a single physical location or cultural setting. Just because we call a particular story "mythic" does not mean the story is completely false and untrue, or even partially so.

For example, Abraham Lincoln, the sixteenth president of the United States, was born in a log cabin. Such a humble beginning for a major historical figure has a timeless, mythic resonance for many people because it suggests that greatness can come to any-one, even someone from the lowliest of beginnings. Lincoln's rise from log cabin to president of the United States is truly a heroic, mythic story, a story with many historical parallels. Does this mean that Lincoln wasn't born in a log cabin or didn't become president? Of course not.

It seems hasty, therefore, to automatically call all myths or all mythic elements in a story untrue, nonfactual, and unhistorical, even if they contain a religious content or assume the existence of the supernatural. Yet this is exactly what the late professor of literature and religion Joseph Campbell, author of *The Power of Myth, The Hero with a Thousand Faces,* and other popular books on myth and religion, constantly did throughout his long, almost fifty-year career, a career that changed the way many people think about religion and myth.

You may have seen Campbell giving lectures and doing interviews on your local PBS channel. Before he died in 1987, Campbell and well-known social commentator Bill Moyers did a series of six one-hour interviews, *The Power of Myth.* Doubleday published a book based on the television series. The book has sold nearly one million copies. Many PBS stations rerun the series regularly, supplemented by other shows featuring Joseph Campbell and his ideas.

In recent years, Campbell may have had more influence on American religious thought than any other contemporary writer, even though he never, to my knowledge, had any formal religious training beyond what he was taught in Catholic grade school. His books are placed in the religious sections of major bookstore chains. They are required reading in many college courses, especially in literature and comparative religion courses. They have become handbooks of spirituality to New Agers, neo-pagans, environmentalists, intellectuals, and nominal Jews and Christians. Some of Campbell's other books include *Myths to Live By, The Masks of God, Flight of the Wild Gander,* and *The Mythic Image.* Campbell's use of the term *myth* contrasts markedly with that already referred to. He said myths should never be mistaken for fact or truth. Campbell also said, "The myth does not point to a fact. The myth points beyond facts to something that informs the fact."[2]

Myths should also never be taken literally, he argued, and we should never try to make other people believe them literally. Instead, we should only experience every myth or mythic story as a psychological message to our inner selves—a message that leads us on an inward journey of self-discovery where each person can find his own internal "bliss."

This view of myth is much too limited. It contradicts the opinions of other well-respected myth scholars, including anthropologist Claude Levi-Strauss, historian Mircea Eliade, and literature professor C. S. Lewis. Campbell's view of myth also restricts the meaning of myth to a subjective, personal, and emotional level. In doing so, it dilutes the timeless, universal quality of myth.

Campbell's narrow view of myth overlooks the importance of genre to myth. Despite their many similarities, there are also many differences among myths. For example, some myths are grounded in pure fantasy while others convey a strong sense of realism. In the past, many scholars identified different kinds of myth, such as creation myths, initiation myths, captivity myths, and trickster myths. Each of these different kinds of myth does different things.

Finally, Campbell's view of myth is too limited because it completely separates myth from history and science. Other scholars, such as Levi-Strauss, Eliade, Lewis, and even psychologists C. G. Jung and James Hillman, whose views are closer to Campbell's, are not so quick to make an absolute distinction between history and myth or between science and myth.

Campbell's beliefs about myth and religion were hopelessly slanted by his own particular worldview, which was itself heavily influenced by his interest in Hinduism, Buddhism, and Native American folklore and mythology.[3] In this book I show how Campbell's worldview distorted his understanding of myth and religion. I also show how Campbell's work is filled with logical flaws and factual errors.

This is not just a book about Joseph Campbell, however. It's also a book about how we perceive truth. To view myth properly, we must be able to perceive truth correctly. A correct view of truth, including valid tests for truth, helps us divide reliable knowledge from unreliable knowledge. It shows us how to identify what is true and what is false. A good test for truth can help us tell when a politician is speaking nonsense. It can reveal whether a writer is presenting actual facts or just stringing us along with cleverly invented lies and innuendo.

Joseph Campbell's work displays his lack of philosophical training, which led him to have an improper view of truth. In this book I rectify that view so people can separate fact from fiction, see more clearly, and judge more fairly.

Finally, this is a book about stories. Like Campbell, I care about stories. Whether they are factually true or not, stories have a way of engaging our minds and grabbing our hearts. That's why it is so important that we interpret stories carefully and accurately, especially those stories that affect many people or that play a major role in shaping society. If you care about other people, if you care about what happens to your society and in your community, then you will think about the stories we tell each other and consider what are the best ways to interpret them.

Before exploring Campbell's handling of stories and myth any further, it will be helpful here to present a short biography of Campbell and then an overview of seven basic themes that run through his works.

A Short Biography of Joseph Campbell

Campbell's interest in religion, myth, and folktales began at an early age. Born in 1904 in New York City, he became fascinated with Native American culture, myth, and folklore as a child after making trips to Buffalo Bill's Wild West Show and the American Museum of Natural History. In grade school, he was taught the Christ story and Christian theology by Roman Catholic nuns. At this point Campbell began to see what he thought were profound similarities between the religious stories of Native Americans and the Bible.

As Campbell himself put it in *The Power of Myth:*

I was brought up in terms of the seasonal relationships to the cycle of Christ's coming into the world, teaching in the world, dying, resurrecting, and returning to heaven. The ceremonies all through the year keep you in mind of the eternal core of all that changes in time. Sin is simply getting out of touch with that harmony. . . . It wasn't long before I found the same motifs in the American Indian stories that I was being taught by the nuns at school.[4]

Although Campbell's description of Christian theology here bears little relation to the actual text of the New Testament documents, his early belief in the close resemblance between Christianity and Native American religion led him to the conclusion that both the Native American myths and the stories in the Bible are not historical and have no basis in fact. This early experience seems to have had an important influence on Campbell's later belief that all myths and all religions should never be taken literally because they have very little to do with truth, history, or physical reality. Campbell's notion of Christianity, the Bible, and Native American myths was based on false information.

Before graduating from Columbia University in New York in 1925, Campbell met a spiritual leader from India on a boat trip to Europe. He began to study Hinduism and Buddhism, and "again, he detected similarities" among different religious ideas, rituals, and stories.[5] Although he lost some of his admiration for Hinduism after making a trip to poverty-stricken India in 1954, Campbell never seems to have lost his attraction for Buddhism, which remained until his death a major part of his own publicly stated, personally held beliefs.

Campbell earned a master's degree in English in 1927 from Columbia University, where he studied medieval and Romantic literature, especially stories about the King Arthur legend and medieval courtly romances. He wrote his master's thesis on Sir Thomas Malory's *Le Morte d'Arthur,* which "won him a traveling fellowship from Columbia, and he spent the next two years, 1927–29, at the universities of Paris and Munich."[6] While in Europe, Campbell discovered the modernist art movement of painters like Picasso and Matisse, as well as novelist James Joyce's *Ulysses* and *Finnegans Wake,* and the work of German novelist Thomas Mann. In Germany, he also discovered the psychoanalytic theories of Sigmund Freud and especially Carl Jung, who had a similar fascination with religious stories and myth.

On returning to the United States in 1929, Campbell decided to abandon his pursuit of a Ph.D. because he found it too confining and irrelevant to his current interests. For five years, he spent his time playing saxophone in a band, writing short stories, reading, and studying. In 1934, he began teaching literature, comparative religion, and mythology at Sarah Lawrence College in New York, from which he retired thirty-eight years later.

After World War II began in Europe, Campbell met Heinrich Zimmer, a famous scholar of the art, religion, and philosophy of India. For a brief spell, Zimmer became Campbell's mentor, until Zimmer suddenly died in the second year of their friendship. From Zimmer Campbell derived, or at least perfected, his own particular worldview. Zimmer had an apparently unique ability to read all sorts of symbolism into art, religion, and everyday objects. This ability was not a systematic method of interpretation but rather was more like an intuitive sense of how people can create meaning. Campbell himself once said, "If I do have a guru . . . it would be Zimmer—the one who really gave me the courage to interpret myths out of what I knew of their common symbols."[7]

After his mentor's death, Zimmer's widow asked Campbell to edit many of her husband's lectures, notes, and manuscripts, a job Campbell didn't finish until the mid 1950s, although the first volume was published in 1946. Zimmer's work was reportedly in such disarray that it left Campbell with some unanswered questions. Campbell has said that he would often just close his eyes, ask the dead Zimmer the questions, and take down Zimmer's answers.[8] It is probably impossible to determine if this strange method of research constitutes an occult influence on Campbell's work. It speaks volumes, however, about Campbell's "ability" as a scholar.

In 1949, Campbell published what may be his best and most useful book, *The Hero with a Thousand Faces. Hero* investigates the pattern of "hero myths" around the world and interprets its meaning for us today. Campbell was not the first to do such work. Anthropologist Edward Tylor, folklorists Arnold van Gennep and Vladimir Propp, and psychologists Otto Rank, Freud, and Jung all did similar, previous works on which Campbell draws.

Hero became a popular book in the 1960s after Campbell published a huge, four-volume work on the world's religions, *The Masks of God.* George Lucas used Campbell's ideas about heroes in *The Hero with a Thousand Faces* to create his incredibly popular *Star Wars* and *Indiana Jones* films in the 1970s and 1980s.

To his credit, Campbell often spoke favorably of the religious and spiritual yearnings of human beings. He didn't spurn *all* religious ideas as many secular atheists, Marxists, and socialists do. His work, however, displays a strong bias toward Eastern religions, the occult, paganism, mysticism,[9] and pantheism,[10] coupled with an equally strong dislike for Judaism, Christianity, the Bible, and traditional western culture. Although he appreciated the kind of individualism America offers, his view of the individual was strongly colored by his attraction to Eastern religion, where the individual obtains enlightenment and fulfillment by losing individuality and achieving oneness with the Divine. Nowhere in his writings did he stop to think that the individualism America offers may be due directly to the theology of Protestant Christianity, or that the despotic systems of the East which Campbell found so loathsome in 1954 in India have been greatly influenced by the mysticism and pantheism of Eastern religions.

Campbell's Seven Basic Themes

There are at least seven major themes or ideas animating Campbell's work on myth and religion. They are the keys to understanding his worldview; they will be treated in chapters 1–10.

The first theme in Campbell's work is his idea of "truth," which I have labeled "intellectual relativism." It will be discussed in chapter 1. The second is his definition of myth and religious experience, linked to his method of interpretation (chapters 2 and 3). The third is his theology of mystical pantheism (chapters 4 and 5). The fourth is his view of ethics and morality, which is a crude and contradictory form of moral relativism (chapter 6). The fifth theme is his view on western civilization and its alleged problems (chapter 7). The sixth main theme in Campbell's work is his theory of the origin of man, myth, and religion, a theory that actually was disproved long ago (chapters 8 and 9). Finally, the seventh major theme running throughout Campbell's work is his constant attack on the historical reliability of the Bible and his often bitter and hostile assault on people who have a high view of the Bible's religious writings (chapter 10).

Campbell's presentation of these seven basic recurring themes or ideas is filled with logical flaws and factual errors. This problem would perhaps not be so bad were it not for the immense popularity of Campbell's work, even after his death, and were it not for the fact that many other people besides Campbell are trying to spread these ideas through society. Contemporary popular culture abounds with examples of Campbell's type of intellectual and moral relativism, mystical pantheism, religious emotionalism, and emotional, knee-jerk reactions against western civilization and its biblical heritage.

These ideas have gained a significant foothold in modern society. They have wormed their way to a prominent place in the spirit of the times. They have become the new sacred cows, the foundation of the politically correct thinking that is now rampant on many college campuses in America.

Throughout his many books, lectures, and interviews, Joseph Campbell urged his audience to follow their own personal "bliss." "What is it that makes you happy?" he asked in *The Power of Myth.* "Stay with it, no matter what people tell you. This is what I call 'following your bliss.'"[11]

It is too late to ask Campbell if this statement means it was okay for Adolph Hitler to follow his own personal bliss of mass murder and world conquest. We can, however, contrast Campbell's idea of bliss with the bliss that Jesus Christ and his apostles offer in the New Testament.

To Jesus and his apostles, God is the ultimate source of all true goodness, and people can only reach their best potential and find the fullest bliss by following Jesus Christ, who reveals the true nature of God to all people. Jesus offers the most holy and righteous kind of bliss, both in this life and in the life to come. He offers a bliss that promises to get people through bad times as well as good. "The servant of Christ is slave to no man," writes Dr. John Warwick Montgomery in *Where Is History Going?* "He is solidly grounded in an unchanging Christ, and therefore is free to develop his capacities to the fullest, under God."[12] "I am the bread of life," says Jesus in John 6:35. "He who comes to me will never go hungry, and he who believes in me will never be thirsty."

It is time to see if the bliss that Joseph Campbell offers can really measure up to the bliss of Christ. In today's society, we are surrounded by storytellers and mythmakers. Joseph Campbell was a master storyteller. Almost everyone likes to hear a good yarn now and then. The question is, which story are you willing to hear? Which story are you going to believe?

This book attempts to put these questions in perspective. Chapters 1 through 3 provide a foundation in critical thinking, myth, and the principles of interpretation with which to evaluate Campbell's seven major themes. They also give a response to Campbell's first two major themes. Chapters 4 through 10 look closely at Campbell's five other themes. Finally, chapters 11 and 12 provide a strong convincing defense of the Christian worldview, using the same criteria with which Campbell's themes were evaluated.

1

Tests for Truth

nce upon a time, there was a boy named Jack. One day Jack hiked into the forest. As he stooped down to examine a hollow log, he was startled by a big, booming voice behind him, "Hello there, young fellow, what are you looking for?"

Jack quickly turned around and there, directly in front of him, big as you please, with a smile on its face, sat a huge purple frog that must have been at least five feet tall! Jack was so frightened he ran out of the woods and didn't stop until he reached the front step of his house.

The next day, Jack screwed up his courage and began telling all his friends about the talking purple frog he met in the forest.

No one believed him. Everyone knew that there is no such thing as a talking purple frog. All of Jack's friends began to tease him horribly, and Jack went home crying.

When Jack's older brother Fred heard what had happened, he gently asked Jack to repeat the story to him. Although Jack's story seemed incredible, Fred was impressed by the details in Jack's story and the intense manner of Jack's description. Fred knew his brother seldom lied, especially about such a fantastic story as this.

The next day, Fred asked Jack to take him into the forest, to the exact same place where Jack had seen the talking purple frog. Sure enough, when they reached the hollow log, there was the purple frog, calmly munching on a carrot. Jack and Fred were so amused by the sight that they began talking to this unique creature.

"We've never seen a huge purple frog before," said Fred. "Much less one that could talk. What's your name? Where do you come from?"

"My name is Jerak," said the strange creature, "and I come from the third planet. I bring a message to your people."

"Wow!" said Jack. "He's an alien from Mars!"

"If you're an alien from Mars," said Fred, "where's your spaceship and how come you know how to speak English?"

"We have been monitoring your satellite transmissions for a long time now," said Jerak. "I have learned several Earth languages. As for my spaceship, I didn't need one. I used a molecular transporter device."

Fred and Jack looked at each other. "Wow!" they cried in unison. "Just like *Star Trek!*"

After another half hour of discussion, the three newfound friends walked out of the forest. Fred and Jack took Jerak to the local TV station, where they broadcast a worldwide interview with the frog from Mars. Pretty soon, the major governments of Earth sent ambassadors to see Jerak and to begin talks between his people and the people of Earth.

I can't say that everyone in this story lived happily ever after, but it is true that the lives of Jack and Fred changed drastically from that day forward, and that the people of Earth entered a new phase in history. Whether those changes were for the best or the worst, only time could tell.

Okay, back to reality now. What's the point of my little fantasy? What am I trying to prove?

Only this: that the believability of a story depends on how incredible it sounds when we first hear it and whether it conforms to the evidence we have amassed in our own view of reality. In the story, no one believed Jack's fantastic story until Jack took his brother Fred to the hollow log in the forest. Even then, Fred had trouble believing what was happening until the frog told a story that fit into

Fred and Jack's knowledge of science fact and science fiction. Fred and Jack had a "worldview" that allowed for a belief in strange creatures from another planet, no matter how incredible such a thing might seem.

This chapter is about the stories we tell, the truth claims we make. It explores the idea of evidence—how much evidence and what kind of evidence do we need in order to believe something?

One of the classes I have taught is an English class in which I try to help my students improve not only their writing skills but also their thinking skills. I do this partly because of the sorry state of intellectual thought in the humanities and the social sciences but mostly because I am convinced that everyone needs to know how to use critical thinking principles and how to weigh the evidence other people present to them. It is extremely important to be able to tell the difference between "good" thinking and "bad" thinking and between good evidence and bad. If we can't tell the difference, then how can we make judgments? How can a jury determine innocence or guilt? How can we decide which political candidates to vote for? How does a parent know when a child is telling the truth?

Sometimes I get into trouble when I mention the word *truth* to my students. Invariably, a student will say something like, "My truth isn't your truth," or "There is no absolute truth." Later in this chapter, I will try to show why such statements are not sound, but for now I would like to stress that the question of truth is one of the most important questions anyone can face. That is why this chapter, which explores the nature of truth, examines tests for evidence, and uses rational empiricism as a valid approach for determining truth, is the chapter I hope readers will take most to heart.

What Is Truth?

In John 14:6, Jesus Christ tells his disciples, "I am the way and the truth and the life. No one comes to the Father except through me." Later on, when he faces Pontius Pilate, the Roman governor, Jesus says, "Everyone on the side of truth listens to me." Pilate replies, "What is truth?" and immediately walks away (John 18:37–38).

Unlike Jesus, Joseph Campbell didn't believe that truth could be pinned down so easily. Before he died, Campbell told Bill Moyers, "The person who thinks he has found the ultimate truth is wrong."[1]

This statement contradicts itself. At the same time that Campbell denies the possibility of finding ultimate truth, he makes a statement that claims to be an ultimate truth—he says people who think they have found the ultimate truth are always wrong. If, however, Campbell's statement is *not* an ultimate truth, then the statement itself is wrong, and ultimate truth *does* exist somewhere and some people who think they have found the ultimate truth could actually be right. Either way, Campbell's statement is undeniably false.

The concept of truth is greatly misunderstood in today's society. According to many dictionaries, truth is whatever corresponds to "reality." We often confuse the word *truth* with the word *belief*. This can be seen by the frequency with which so many people claim, "My truth isn't your truth." To which we might reply, "Do you mean that your belief isn't my belief?"

Statements about truth are statements of *epistemology*. Epistemology is the study of the nature and justification of knowledge. It is a branch of philosophy. As such, it has a long history, beginning at least as far back as Plato, Aristotle, and Socrates, the three most famous ancient Greek philosophers.

Epistemology asks questions: What is truth? How do we know whether something is true or false? Can we ever really know whether something is true or false? How can we test for truth? How do we know that we know anything?

Perhaps you think we can't find the answers to such questions, or perhaps you think that asking such questions is a pointless game. Whatever you think, however, these questions are the most important ones we can ask ourselves. By asking these questions, we force ourselves to confront our own most cherished beliefs and to justify them before other people.

Tests for Truth

Many people today believe that science is the only valid test for truth, the only way to really know anything. Science has become such a sacred icon in our society that even people who study sociology, psychology, politics, anthropology, economics, and history are often called social *scientists.* Our courts and the halls of Congress are filled with "scientific" experts giving authoritative testimony about many important matters.

Is such a strong faith in science justified?

As a test for truth, science has several major problems. To begin with, neither scientists nor philosophers have been able to develop a clear-cut definition of science or the scientific method. Also, there is no clear line of division between science and non-science:

> Science is not an airtight compartment isolated from philosophy, theology, and other disciplines. It interacts with other fields of study in complicated ways. Only someone out of touch with the history of science could believe otherwise.[2]

Secondly, there is no one thing that could be called *the* scientific method. What we really find are *many different methods* used in *many different ways* in *widely different situations.* Biologists, chemists, astronomers, nuclear physicists, paleontologists, geologists, and even sociologists, psychologists, anthropologists, economists, and historians each use different methods in many different ways.

The existence of something called "the scientific method" is itself a philosophical question, as well as a historical one. Most scientists don't even think seriously about this subject, but every time a scientist sits down to determine a proper method for an experiment, he becomes involved in philosophical issues about physical reality and human knowledge. These issues raise questions about metaphysics,[3] as well as questions of epistemology, the study of knowledge. They also involve questions of intellectual values concerning truth and approximate truth, concerning theoretical simplicity versus theoretical complexity, and concerning internal consistency and clarity versus empirical accuracy and predictive success.

Finally, scientists cannot use science to test the truth of science itself. The goals, assumptions, and methods of science cannot be confirmed by those very same goals, assumptions, and methods. They must be rationally justified and confirmed by *philosophy.*[4] Philosopher Larry Laudan declares that we should just stop trying to justify or validate all scientific endeavors. Instead, we should simply ask ourselves what is *reliable* knowledge and what is *unreliable* knowledge:

> Our focus should be squarely on the empirical and conceptual credentials for claims about the world. The "scientific" status of those claims is altogether irrelevant.[5]

This comment from Laudan about "empirical and conceptual credentials" refers to what I believe are the two most reliable tests for truth: rationalism and empiricism. All science uses some form of rationalism and empiricism. Rationalism says that reason is the prime source of knowledge and truth, while empiricism says that experience, as filtered through our five senses, is the prime source of knowledge and truth. Empiricism relies on the use of observation and experiment, or trial and error; rationalism relies on the use of logic and common sense, or sound human judgment.

Although both rationalism and empiricism are very useful theories of knowledge or tests for truth, I personally favor rationalism over empiricism for one important reason: Empiricism is itself a rational, linguistic category that applies rational concepts and uses principles of logic. All empirical statements, e.g., "This is my dog Spot," use linguistic categories and logical principles which are not themselves empirical. For instance, when a scientist makes a distinction between two physical objects, say a section of bone and a section of cartilage, or between two different concepts like matter and energy or time and space, he is not only applying rational, linguistic categories to define his terms, he is also relying on the logical principle of noncontradiction to keep his ideas from running together or from becoming too confusing. No matter how hard we try to keep our facts and theories on the empirical or physical level, human reason and logic will always play a significant role.

Empirical facts without any preexisting ideas are meaningless. Philosopher Immanuel Kant believed that ideas must be applied to experience in order for both experience and ideas to have meaning:

> Experience alone is insufficient for belief or knowledge. Knowledge demands not only experience, but [also] a conceptual element. Kant

put it quite well when he said that sensations without concepts are blind.[6]

All knowledge, therefore, contains conceptual elements. We attach words and names not only to experience, but also to our knowledge of particular things, such as certain sounds or colors. The rational mind plays a crucial role in the process of knowing. Rationalism seems to be a more basic test for truth than empiricism, but it is not an exclusive test.

Consequently, the basic test for truth that I will use to evaluate Joseph Campbell's work is a modified version of rational empiricism. A description of this method and the specific principles it uses follows.

Rational Empiricism

Rationalism relies on the proper use of logic and human reason. The search for truth requires a proper understanding of logic and reason.

All language, and all thinking, depends on the three basic laws of logic: the Law of Identity, the Law of Noncontradiction, and the Law of the Excluded Middle. The Law of Identity says, "A is A." The Law of Noncontradiction says, "A is not non-A." The Law of the Excluded Middle says, "A is either B or non-B." Thus, apples may be compared to apples (A is A), but they are different from oranges (A is not non-A). Finally, apples are a kind of fruit or they are not a kind of fruit (A is either B or non-B).

Language and thinking would be impossible without making such logical distinctions as these. Empiricism would not be possible either because empiricism itself is a rational, linguistic category that depends on these basic laws of logic.

The Law of Noncontradiction is especially important. As atheist Antony Flew himself writes, "To tolerate contradiction is to be indifferent to truth."[7]

We can rely on this particular law because without it our words and even our thoughts would be in a constant state of discord and internal conflict. Without the Law of Noncontradiction, all communication between people, including Joseph Campbell's interviews with Bill Moyers, would collapse into absolute nonsense.

For example, suppose you ask me what the weather is like outside my house. I step out the door and say, "It's a cold, hot, cloudy, sunny, wet, dry day." My answer to you would not make any sense because it is full of contradictions. It is logically impossible to have a "cold, hot, cloudy, sunny, wet, dry day" at the same time and in the same place.

Likewise, it is logically impossible for an electric light to be on and off at the very same time. We can diagram this second example as follows:

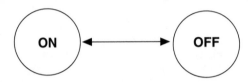

What about lights that dim, you ask? Aren't they neither on nor off? To accommodate this possibility, I would draw the diagram like this:

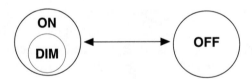

The diagrams should help to clarify that the concept "on" is a rational category, which *includes* the concept "dim." Conversely, the concept called "off" is a rational category that *excludes* the concept of "dim."

Using the Law of Noncontradiction and the Law of the Excluded Middle, we can classify other words and ideas into other rational categories. Notice in the diagram on the next page how some of these categories overlap, while others are mutually exclusive.

We cannot avoid using these kinds of rational categories. The very act of thinking and speaking depends on it. Let's say, however, that

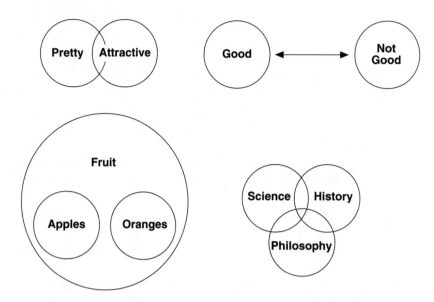

you still want to deny the existence of rational categories. Why can't you do it?

The answer to this question is simple. At the very same time that you deny the existence of rational categories, you set up your own rational category of intellectual skepticism. By doing this, you get stuck in a self-contradictory denial. Such a denial can't possibly be true.

For example, suppose you are having a conversation with your friend Bill the skeptic.

"Logic is not really a valid test for truth," says Bill. "For instance, logic can't tell me whether the light in my closet is on or off. It can't tell me what color your bedroom walls are painted. I have to go there and look."

"That's right, Bill," you reply, "but the concept of logic, the difference between on and off, the concept of color, and the location of your closet and my bedroom are all rational categories. Just now you used rational categories to deny the existence of rational categories and to attack the use of logic as a test for truth. Your argument was not consistent."

"That's what you say," pouts Bill. "But I say that you can't touch a rational category. You can't see it. You can't smell it. Therefore, it doesn't exist."

"Once again, Bill, you're using rational categories to deny the existence of rational categories. You're violating the Law of Noncontradiction."

"The Law of Noncontradiction is all in your head," Bill answers stubbornly.

"That's exactly right, Bill," you say.

"What?" Bill is now clearly perplexed.

"The Law of Noncontradiction, like all the other laws of logic, is not a physical thing. It's an abstract, nonmaterial, but rational category we use every day, every time we think a thought, and every time we open our mouths to speak. Just now, you unconsciously used the Law of Noncontradiction to say that the laws of logic are all in my head. But if they're all in my head, then they can't be outside my head. Remember, A is not non-A. Therefore, you cannot use rational categories to deny the existence of rational categories. You cannot use the laws of logic to deny the laws of logic. The basic laws of logic are themselves rational categories. They are universally applicable and undeniably true. Without them, knowledge is impossible and the search for truth becomes meaningless."

The first thing, therefore, that rational empiricism requires of any truth claim is that it follow the basic laws of logic. Any argument that violates the Law of Noncontradiction, for example, is false. That's why it is easy to reject the previously mentioned comment by Joseph Campbell that "the person who thinks he has found the ultimate truth is wrong." In making this statement, Campbell violates the Law of Noncontradiction. At the same time that he denies the possibility of finding an ultimate truth, he makes a statement that claims to be an ultimate truth.

The Law of Noncontradiction leads to two other rational tests for truth: the Law of Systematic Consistency and the Law of Undeniability. As with the Law of Noncontradiction, if you violate these two laws, the argument you are making becomes undeniably false.

The Law of Systematic (or Internal) Consistency is a test for truth *within* a system. It says that in order for a theory or a system of belief to be true, it must be internally consistent, especially in its basic premises or assumptions. If it isn't internally consistent, then it can't be true. Just because a system or theory is consistent, however, doesn't mean it is *factually* true. Any theory or system that violates this law, therefore, must be false, but any system that meets this test is not necessarily true.

For example, when a witness in a criminal trial gives the defendant an alibi, the prosecution lawyer will probably question the witness about his story. If the witness says that the defendant arrived at his house at 7:30 P.M., before the crime was committed, but later claims that the defendant arrived at his house at 8 P.M., after the crime was committed, he hurts the credibility of his story and the defendant's alibi. If on further questioning the inconsistency is not cleared up, then the prosecutor can probably make a good case that the alibi story is false. If, on the other hand, there are no inconsistencies in the alibi story, that does not prove the story is true.

We can use the Law of Internal Consistency to test the truth of political theories, scientific theories, sociological theories, or psychological theories. For example, Karl Marx, the father of modern communism, saw human beings as evil people who unfairly exploit their fellow men, but he also believed human beings are capable of an idyllic existence once socialists are able to usher in the new communist utopia. This view of human nature is false because it is not consistent.

Many people wrongly use the Law of Systematic (or Internal) Consistency to reject the truth of Christianity. In this book, I use this law to affirm the truth of Christianity and to reject the truth of Joseph Campbell's worldview.

The Law of Undeniability says that some statements are undeniably true or undeniably false because of the way in which they meet or fail the test of noncontradiction. For example, for me to say "I don't exist" would be an undeniable lie, because at the same time that I deny my existence, I also assert my existence by using the word "I." In other words, I must really and truly exist in order to say "I don't exist."

It is self-contradictory for me to say "I don't exist." Furthermore, since the statement "I don't exist" is undeniably false, then the opposite statement, "I exist," must be undeniably true. I can know for certain, therefore, that I do indeed exist. To quote Norman Geisler in *Christian Apologetics:*

> No one can deny his own existence without affirming it. One must exist in order to deny that he exists, which is self-defeating. But what-

ever is undeniable is true, and what is unaffirmable is false. Hence, it is undeniably true that I exist.[8]

To put it another way, it is *rationally inescapable* that I exist. The French philosopher Descartes was correct when he said, "I think, therefore I am." We might add to this, "I speak, therefore I am." Even a machine programmed to say, "I exist," actually does exist, even though it is not human.

Another undeniably false statement is, "I can't utter a word in English." If you can't speak English, then how did you just speak it? A third undeniably false statement is, "It's impossible to really know anything." If it's impossible to really know anything, then how do you really know it's impossible? Finally, another undeniably false statement is, "There are no absolute truths." If not, then is that statement an absolute truth and do you believe it absolutely? Because these statements are undeniably false, it logically follows that the following statements are undeniably true: "I *can* speak English. I really *can* know some things for certain. Absolute truth *does* exist somewhere."

Before we leave this crash course in basic logic, there is another category of logical tests for truth that we can use to refute Joseph Campbell's worldview. This category is often called "informal logical fallacies." Among these kinds of fallacies are the genetic fallacy, the categorical fallacy, the pragmatic fallacy, straw man arguments, guilt by association, and inappropriate appeals to authorities. Each of them is explained as it is used in this book.

Readers should note that committing only one, or even a few, of these informal fallacies does not necessarily invalidate one's entire argument, but it does damage at least part of one's argument. The more fallacies one commits, however, the more likely one's argument will be false.

Based on the above discussion, therefore, the first two tests this book uses to evaluate Joseph Campbell's work are:

1. Does Campbell at any point violate the Law of Noncontradiction, the Law of Systematic Consistency, and/or the Law of Undeniability? If so, then his argument at that point is automatically false.

2. Does Campbell at any point commit any informal logical fallacies? If so, then his argument at that point is probably false or, at the very least, highly doubtful.

Empirical Evidence—Just the Facts, Ma'am!

Although rational empiricism considers rationalism to be the foundation for empiricism and favors the laws of logic over observation, experience, and experimentation, it does not insist that we should use only logic and reason as a test for truth. Empiricism is itself a rational and linguistic category, but as a rational, linguistic category, it provides answers to many questions that the laws of logic alone cannot. For example, I cannot by reason alone know whether the light in my closet is on or off. I must go into the closet and observe or experience the "on-ness" or "off-ness" of the light for myself.

But what if I am unable to check out the light for myself? Chances are I would have to ask another person to check out the light for me. In other words, sometimes I must rely on the experience, knowledge, or *eyewitness testimony* of other people. How do I know, however, that the person I depend on really knows the true facts about a particular state of affairs?

Logically, a statement about a certain situation or state of affairs is verifiable only if you can state the conditions for disproving it. Thus, factual statements must be verified by checking the facts.

For example, in history, we can set the condition for disproving a historical statement: Does it fit the facts? Historians investigate particular facts. They must base their theories, conclusions, and interpretations on that investigation. They must make their theories, conclusions, and interpretations fit the facts. They should not try to make the facts fit their theories, conclusions, and interpretations. These are good basic rules for people in other fields, not just for historians.

Americans used to mock the communists in the old Soviet Union for rewriting history, for changing the facts of history to fit their own political theories. Today, however, on many college campuses and in our whole educational system, many supposed scholars and intellectuals do similar things. For instance, some of them claim that the Pilgrims were really thanking the Native Americans on the first Thanksgiving Day celebration, not thanking God, and that the Japanese were only responding to the American oil embargo when they bombed Pearl Harbor. Others try to demonize the European immigrants who formed the first colonies in America and sanitize the culture of the Native Americans who lived there. Such people change the facts of history to fit their political theories. Checking their facts is a good way to test the truth of their theories.

Besides looking at the facts concerning a particular situation or piece of testimony, we should also ask if the people giving the testimony are really in a position to know what they are talking about or "to observe, remember, or recount"[9] the situation or event they relate. For example, if a person testifies that he was able to see an event take place but our investigation of the situation shows that in reality his vision was blocked, then we would be right to dismiss his testimony as false. Also, if we read a psychology book by an expert who claims that his theories are based on hundreds of interviews with lots of patients but later we learn that no interviews took place, we would probably dismiss the "evidence" in the book, no matter how many Ph.D.s the expert held.

Another way to judge empirical evidence from other people is by looking at their personal credibility. For instance, what is their reputation for truthfulness? What are their qualifications as an expert or as a witness? If they have a reputation for lying or if we can show that their qualifications to give evidence are lacking, their testimony becomes more doubtful. Just because we prove that a person has a reputation for lying, however, or that his qualifications are bad, does not necessarily mean his evidence is actually or completely false. It only means that his credibility is questionable. He might be telling the truth on this particular occasion.

In addition to this, we should also try to discover whether the testimony or evidence a person gives reveals an obvious or undue bias that causes him to slant the testimony in some way. For instance, does his testimony or evidence demonstrate obvious or undue favoritism, prejudice, hostility, or self-interest? If so, then his credibility suffers.

The final test we should apply to empirical evidence is to ask, "Has anyone taken any action based on the evidence or testimony? What was the result?" This test is good because it asks for evidence, for facts, about the outcome of a situation or state of affairs. For example, if two people knock on your door with an old document that says fifty years ago your grandfather sold his land to their grandfather, you might want to go to the county title office to see who held the title to the deed of the property fifty years ago. To give another example, let's say you hear a politician who prescribes a solution for crime in your town or city. The politician gets elected and his or her solution is enacted. If, after a reasonable length of time, the solution fails to work, it is logical to believe that the solution was a false one and a bad one.

When all is said and done, any claim to knowledge or truth must also be based on *adequate or sufficient empirical evidence* and must contain *no rational contradictions or absurdities.* This is the essence of rational empiricism.

Judging whether there is sufficient evidence is hard. As a rule, however, one example can illustrate what you are talking about, but is usually not enough to convince anyone. Also, the more unexpected the conclusions, the more evidence must be supplied in order to persuade others.

Absolute certainty may not be possible in everything, but probability can be taken as sufficient proof for any truth claim until or unless new factual evidence or new rational arguments come to light. Although complete objectivity and fairness may not always be possible, objective standards of truth and goodness can be used successfully to test any truth claim.

Ultimately, the interpretations and value judgments we make should be based on both logical and factual evidence. People will judge our beliefs by the "breadth and soundness of [our] arguments."[10] We must always *weigh* the evidence before us with fairness. Most, if not all, systems of belief contain some unanswered questions. Even people who refuse to trust in any single system may sometimes wonder whether they aren't doing the wrong thing.

Using good tests for determining truth and applying critical thinking, we can evaluate Joseph Campbell's worldview and the seven major themes in his work. This evaluation should give us an adequate basis for accepting or rejecting Campbell's ideas. Therefore, this book uses the following seven tests to judge the truth of Campbell's work:

1. Is Campbell's work *internally consistent?* Does Campbell at any point violate the Law of Noncontradiction, the Law of Sys-

tematic or Internal Consistency, or the Law of Undeniability? If so, then his argument at that point is automatically false.

2. Does Campbell at any point commit any informal logical fallacies? If so, then his argument at that point is probably false or, at the very least, highly doubtful.

3. Is Campbell's work *externally consistent* with the factual evidence from other sources? Does it fit the facts? If not, then we have empirical grounds for rejecting his work.

4. Is Campbell really in a position to know what he is talking about? If not, then his work lacks credibility.

5. What are Campbell's qualifications? What is his reputation as a scholar? If it is not good, then why should we believe him?

6. Does Campbell's work contain an obvious or undue bias? Does it show obvious or undue favoritism, prejudice, hostility, or self-interest? If so, then it lacks credibility and is probably false.

7. If carried out to their logical conclusions, what are the possible results of the seven main themes in Campbell's work? When people hold beliefs similar to Campbell's, what have the results been? What does the factual evidence say?

Using these seven tests will show that Campbell's worldview, as expressed by the seven main themes in his work, is both logically false and factually untrue. His arguments are not rational and are full of factual errors.

At the end of this book, we will turn the tests around and apply them to the orthodox or traditional Christian worldview. By doing this, we will show that Campbell was wrong, that we can indeed believe in the ultimate truth of the orthodox Christian faith.

Joseph Campbell's View of Truth

To get a more complete idea of Joseph Campbell's view of truth, let us return to the quote from Campbell cited partially at the beginning of this chapter.

The person who thinks he has found the ultimate truth is wrong. There is an often-quoted verse in Sanskrit, which appears in the Chinese *Tao-te Ching* as well: "He who thinks he knows, doesn't know. He who knows that he doesn't know, knows. For in this context, to know is not to know. And not to know is to know."[11]

Interviewer Bill Moyers replied, "Far from undermining my faith [Moyers claims to be a Christian] your work in mythology has liberated my faith from the cultural prisons to which it had been sentenced."[12]

We saw earlier how the first part of Campbell's quote contradicts itself and is therefore illogical and false. Campbell violated our first test for truth, the Law of Noncontradiction.

The second part of this quote also contradicts itself because, at the same time that Campbell says it is better not to know than to know, he says "not to know is to know." The Sanskrit verse Campbell cites is illogical because it equates not knowing something with knowing something. If not to know is to know, then the distinction between knowledge and lack of knowledge becomes meaningless. If there is no real difference between knowing and not knowing, then why even talk about the difference? A difference that makes no difference is no difference at all.

This kind of intellectual confusion is typical of the way Campbell uses language and the way he talks about truth. To him, there is no "ultimate" or "absolute" truth, but this statement is itself a belief in an ultimate truth which Campbell believes absolutely. What Moyers calls profound, many others would call gibberish.

Like many people in today's society, Campbell believed in a kind of shapeless pluralism. Philosophically speaking, pluralism is the theory that ultimate reality consists of more than one thing or idea. These things or ideas do not have to be contradictory or mutually exclusive, although they may be depending on how they are expressed. Historically, the term *pluralism* describes a kind of society where people from different groups can participate in and develop their own "traditional culture or special interest *within the confines of a common civilization* [my emphasis]."[13] In recent years, however, pluralism has been expanded to mean that society should eliminate almost all beliefs in a common civilization that set limits on human behavior and instead should let everyone "do their own thing," or, as Campbell put it, follow their "bliss."

Under this new kind of pluralism, there is no ultimate truth; anyone who thinks he has found the ultimate truth is wrong. Under this new kind of pluralism, there is more than one way to God, truth, or goodness. Under this new kind of pluralism, the idea of God, truth, or goodness can mean whatever *you* want it to mean. Of course, if you refuse to accept this new kind of pluralism, then you are, almost by definition, an intolerant, irrational, and emotional extremist.

The real truth, however, is that this new kind of pluralism is itself a belief in only one way—a pluralistic way. In addition, it has been my experience that many of the people who spout this new pluralistic utopia can be just as dogmatic, irrational, emotional, and intolerant as those they rail against.

Campbell provides a perfect example of this. He frequently attacks the three major monotheistic religions: Judaism, Christianity, and Islam. For example, on page twenty-one of *The Power of Myth,* instead of citing all the good works throughout history that these three religions have done, he points to modern-day, war-torn Beirut, Lebanon, as an example of what these religions supposedly teach. In doing so, he not only neglects the fact that the terror in that city is due more to ethnic and political differences than to religious differences, he also fails to consider that the problems in that city may be caused by religious radicals and not by the actual teachings of those religions.

Conclusion

According to Campbell's worldview, objective facts don't matter as long as we are able to follow our own eccentric definitions of happiness, as long as we follow our "bliss." According to Campbell, ultimate truth is impossible to know, and anyone who tries to find ultimate truth is fooling himself.

As we have seen, however, this kind of belief is illogical and undeniably false. Absolute, ultimate truth does exist somewhere; we can really know some things for certain.

Let's be honest with ourselves. Everyone makes a truth claim of one kind or another. Truth matters. Seeking truth is a noble thing to do. We shouldn't be afraid of having firm convictions about what is true and what is false. Even Campbell himself believed he had found the truth. Otherwise, he wouldn't have written so many books, nor made so many dogmatic statements.

It's not a crime to affirm what we truly believe, even if we are truly wrong. But it would be a crime if we simply threw up our hands in exasperation and withdrew from the search for truth. For if we allowed ourselves to do that, the next seeker might not be as charitable or as intelligent as we, and we might become unwilling victims of someone else's "truth."

2

Close Encounters
with the Sacred

One of the strongest precepts in today's secular society is the idea that religious beliefs are irrational, that faith and reason are mutually exclusive categories. Many people believe that because belonging to a religion involves a personal decision, all religious decisions are purely subjective. Therefore, they argue, we should just let people believe what they want—we shouldn't challenge anyone's personal religious beliefs, no matter how strange or absurd they seem.

This chapter explores this important issue by examining Joseph Campbell's view of myth and religious experience. It also begins to outline my own view about these subjects, based on scholars other than Campbell.

Campbell's View of Myth and Religious Experience

Joseph Campbell's view of truth, refuted in chapter 1, is related to his subjective view of God and his method of interpreting religious stories (or myths, as he called them). In his view, it is wrong and decidedly foolish for people to get any kind of ultimate truth out of religious stories. Religious stories should never be taken as fact or truth, he often declared. Instead, they should be looked at as "provinces of one great system of feeling . . . an energy-evoking sign that hits you below the thinking system . . . enormous poems that are renditions of insights, giving some sense of the marvel, the miracle, and wonder of life."[1]

According to Campbell, religious stories like those in the Bible, or like those in religions outside of Judaism and Christianity, are nothing more than ways in which individuals can personally get in touch with the "transcendent." *Transcendent* is a term with several different meanings. Campbell derived his own concept of the transcendent partly from the work of philosopher Immanuel Kant and partly from his lifelong interest in Eastern religions, especially Buddhism.

To Campbell, the transcendent is beyond human personality. It is thus impersonal or transpersonal. As such, "the transcendent is unknowable and unknown."[2] Consequently, said Campbell, the existence of God, or any other supernatural beings or forces, is not a truth or a fact that can be known by the mind of man. The existence of God is only a thought or an idea that refers to the transcendent, which is beyond all thoughts, ideas, and personalities:

> "Transcendent" properly means that which is beyond all concepts.
> . . . The transcendent transcends all of these categories of thinking.
> Being and nonbeing—those are categories. The word "God" properly refers to what transcends all thinking, but the word "God" itself is something thought about. Now you can personify God in many, many ways. Is there one God? Are there many Gods? Those are merely categories of thought. What you are talking and trying to think about transcends all that. . . . whatever is ultimate is beyond the categories of being and nonbeing. Is it or is it not? As the Buddha is reported to have said: "It both is and is not; neither is, nor is not." God as the ultimate mystery of being is beyond thinking.[3]

Also, said Campbell, although people "always think in terms of opposites," the idea of God is beyond such thinking and refers to something that lies "beyond all categories of thought."[4]

Campbell's comments contain at least five basic errors. Whether you consider these errors individually or all together, each one of them seriously weakens, if not defeats, Campbell's whole argument. Moreover, since Campbell's comments here are very crucial to understanding the rest of his work, these five errors cripple his work as a whole and undermine his basic worldview.

To begin with, Campbell's definition of the word *transcendent* is too narrow. Transcendent does not always mean something that exists "beyond all concepts" or "beyond all categories of thought." It can simply mean something that exceeds or surpasses certain limits. For example, the power of parents to discipline their own children in their own home transcends that of their neighbors. We can describe the God of the Bible as being transcendent because he exists outside the material universe and because he has infinite or unlimited qualities. Something can also be "transcendent in a religious sense if it is believed to be ultimate" in some way, such as God.[5]

Historian of religion Mircea Eliade, in *Rites and Symbols of Initiation*, describes the experience of transcendence that shamans (a religious leader who uses magic) and other religious mystics undergo in "primitive" societies. He says they not only experience a special kind of ecstasy and freedom, they also can become "a contemplative, a thinker."[6] Eliade even compares them to philosophers.

Eliade was at least as good a scholar in religion and myth as was Joseph Campbell. His comment here suggests that Campbell was wrong when he said that the transcendent always lies beyond all categories of thought.

In the second place, although Campbell claims that the transcendent lies beyond all concepts, categories, and thoughts, at the same time he uses concepts, categories, and thoughts to define and describe the transcendent. In fact, the word *transcendent* is itself a concept, a category, and a thought. Campbell contradicts himself when he uses concepts, categories, and thoughts to define and describe the transcendent, while at the same time denying the validity of such concepts, categories, and thoughts. This contradiction alone is enough to disprove his definition of God, his idea of transcendence, and his view of religious experience.

Third, it's not true that we always think in terms of opposites. The idea of time, for example, can be divided into three distinct, but not opposite, categories: past, present, and future.

When Campbell tells Michael Toms in *An Open Life* that "the rational is always stressing I-Thou opposites"[7] in order to support his view of the transcendent, he makes another factual error. It is not true that our rational minds only think in terms of I-Thou. They also think in terms of We-Them, These-Those, He-She-It.

It simply is not true that human reason always stresses opposites. Even if one quality of the transcendent is to go beyond thinking in terms of opposites, that does not mean that in doing this, it leaves all rational thought and logic behind. In fact, in orthodox Christianity, the transcendent Creator-God is actually the foundation of rational thought and logic. In Christianity and other forms of ethical monotheism, perfect rational thinking is one of God's most important abilities. If reason and logic are not rooted in a transcendent Creator-God, that is, a God beyond our universe or realm of existence, then as part of the system, reason and logic cannot judge the system.

Fourth, if the transcendent is "unknowable and unknown," then how does Campbell *know* this? Since it is unknowable, he doesn't really know it for a fact, he only feels that this is true. But why should anyone else accept his feeling? By his own admission, he can't really give any rational reasons to support his feeling, because the transcendent is supposed to lie beyond all categories of rational thought. Frankly, this particular point by Campbell makes no sense.

Finally, it's true as Campbell asserts that religious stories are full of emotion and poetry, but does that totally exclude rational thoughts and factual statements? Emotions and poetry are themselves rational categories or concepts that can occupy our thoughts. We apply thought and reason to them whenever we think about them or discuss them. Campbell's writings are themselves filled with intellectual discussions of religious literature and poetry. Campbell often tried to apply science and logic to his reading of myth, poetry, and religion. For example, in *The Power of Myth,* when he says that "the great realization of the Upanishads of India in the ninth century B.C. [is that] heaven and hell are within us, and all the gods are within us,"[8] he is applying rational categories ("within"/"without"), the Law of Noncontradiction (A is not non-A; i.e., apples are not non-apples), and the rules of empirical truth to the religious teachings of the Upanishads.

Why do we have to put our minds on hold when we think about religious ideas? Why do religious ideas have to be exempt from the rational principles of logic and experiential relevance? Jesus Christ quotes the Old Testament in Mark 12:30: "Love the Lord your God with all your heart and with all your soul and *with all your mind* and with all your strength [emphasis mine]." Using our minds to approach the transcendent is not a sin in the Bible—it's a divine command!

Christian philosopher Stuart C. Hackett doesn't believe that religious claims should be exempt from the use of reason, logic, or rules of empirical evidence. He says that if we make such an exemption, our decision will either be totally arbitrary or it "will in the end rest on the very sort of principles and categories"[9] that are used to exempt religious claims. Such an argument thus defeats itself, says Hackett.

Furthermore, to even make a claim that we have actually had a "religious" or "spiritual" experience is "to presuppose a structure of interpretive principles, logically prior to the experience...."[10] How do we define "religious" or "spiritual" experience anyway, asks Hackett, and how do we decide which experiences are valid and which are not? Unless we appeal to reason and rational categories, Hackett declares, any judgment we make will be arbitrary.

You cannot use the Law of Noncontradiction to deny the universal truth of the Law of Noncontradiction. Even a person like Campbell, who believed that myth, religion, and logic are mutually exclusive categories, should have admitted that the Law of Noncontradiction is a universal, ultimate truth. If during his life he had denied this, he would then have defeated his own argument because he would have had to justify his argument on the universal validity of the Law of Noncontradiction.

Sometimes, however, people try to avoid the laws of logic by appealing to subjective experiences or other empirical evidence, but they fail to realize that all empirical statements use categories and principles that are not themselves empirical. Empirical truth is itself a special logical category, as I pointed out in chapter 1.

Frequently, people claim we can't look at religion in an objective manner, without letting our personal, subjective feelings, experiences, and biases distort the truth in some way. But if this claim is true, how do we know that the claim itself isn't purely subjective? For if it's not a purely subjective claim, then objective decisions about religion are possible. On the other hand, if it is a purely subjective claim, then the claim itself is a distortion and why should I believe a distortion? Either way, this oft-repeated claim is easily refuted. As Dr. John Warwick Montgomery writes in *Where Is History Going?* "If God cannot be looked at objectively, then God can't be looked at—period."[11]

Truth must be objectively independent of limited, fallible human beings. Otherwise, all knowledge of any kind is completely unreliable. Truth must also be unchangeable and "fully true and relevant at every point within space-time."[12] Otherwise, there would be no absolute truth and that statement is totally absurd, itself being either an absolute truth (disproving itself) or a relative "truth," which isn't truth at all.

All of this means that we can completely reject Joseph Campbell's basic notion of truth, myth, and religion, as well as his whole contradictory system of interpretation. This alone is enough to refute the other five major themes in his work. If the foundation of one's teachings crumbles, then the rest of the edifice surely will not stand.

Campbell's View of the Hero

Not everything Campbell wrote or said was wrong. For instance, he actually said some profound things about the human condition and about the role of heroes throughout human history. His book *The Hero with a Thousand Faces* was one of the primary inspirations for my Ph.D. thesis, *Sacred Encounters: The Myth of the Hero in the Horror, Science Fiction, Fantasy Films of George Lucas and Steven Spielberg.*

In *The Hero with a Thousand Faces,* Campbell divides "the standard path of the mythological adventure of the hero"[13] into three stages: separation, initiation, and return. Although these three stages are very similar to folklorist Arnold van Gennep's three stages of initiation rituals or rites of passage (separation, transition, and incorporation) in *The Rites of Passage,* originally published in the early 1900s, Campbell uses them to develop a very interesting narrative structure of stories about heroes.

I have found Campbell's structure about the hero very helpful in my own interpretation of many stories. For example, in the popular story *The Wizard of Oz,* Dorothy travels through at least three stages. In the first stage, she is *separated* from her home in Kansas and travels to the Land of Oz, where she undergoes a series of trials or *initiations* that test her character. At the end of the story, she *returns* to Kansas. Of course, there are a lot of nuances to Campbell's three-stage structure that we can't go into right now, but at least we get the picture.

Some scholars have accused such structures as Campbell's of not fitting many stories, but I have usually found that such critics are often guilty of trying to apply such structures in a ridiculous or rigid fashion. I even found one scholar who complained that he seldom found stories that depict all three stages. His complaint was utterly ridiculous because there are many stories that focus on only one or two of the stages heroes can endure, but which reflect all three. The film *Alien,* for example, mostly takes place within the initiation or transition stage.

One profound statement from Campbell's book on the hero is the very last sentence where Campbell talks about the "supreme ordeal" that heroes often face and that the average human being faces as well. "Every one of us shares the supreme ordeal," writes Campbell, "not in the bright moments of his tribe's great victories, but in the silences of his personal despair."[14]

The greatest battles we face, Campbell seems to be saying, are those battles we fight within ourselves, apart from other people. Although Campbell often interprets such insights in terms of his own narrow religious beliefs, I think he has hit here upon a fundamental truth of the human condition which, at least for me, carries a deep intellectual, spiritual, and emotional impact, in the best sense of those words.

In his first interview with Bill Moyers, Campbell notes that one of the greatest acts a hero does is to sacrifice himself for another person, a people, or an idea. This is a very important idea that we can apply to the life of Jesus Christ in the New Testament. In that historical collection of books and letters, Jesus becomes the ultimate hero because he is the first and only person in history who sacrifices himself to redeem the whole human race from the bondage of sin. Using Campbell's own ideas about heroes, we can actually affirm the unique, comprehensive quality of Christian theology.

Campbell's Method of Interpretation

Even so, despite this kind of dividend from Campbell's work, his basic method of interpretation leads him to make false statements and unsound arguments that many Christians and other discerning people find offensive. This problem seriously damages the credibility of even what he says that may be true, good, or enlightening.

One of the worst faults of Campbell's system of interpretation is his pervasive tendency to limit all myths and religious stories to the purely symbolic or figurative level. By doing this, Campbell has made all religions, including Christianity and Judaism, purely subjective as well as unscientific and unhistorical. By completely separating myth and religion from all notions of historical truth, Campbell stacks the deck unfairly in favor of his own theological worldview and against orthodox Christianity. Other scholars in myth studies, including historian Mircea Eliade and even psychologist Carl Jung, aren't so biased against Christianity, so why is Campbell?

The answer is that Campbell has an ax to grind. And that ax is aimed directly at the head of the historical Jesus!

As a foundation to our examination of Campbell's worldview and truth, we must first turn to appropriate ideas about myth, comparative religion, archetypes, and the proper principles of interpretation. Since 1974, I have done my own research into these areas and verified it with other authoritative sources. My research contradicts Campbell's work in many places.

Religion and Myth: Close Encounters with the Sacred

Many great thinkers and philosophers have asked what makes human beings tick. In giving an answer to this question, they have often tried to arrive at a general description of the human condition. These are some ideas they have put forth:

1. Man has physical needs. He must search for food, water, and shelter.
2. Man has a need to communicate with other persons, to establish personal relationships, to form personal attachments.
3. Man has a thirst for knowledge.
4. Man has a need for personal pleasure, recreation, comfort, and relaxation.
5. Man has a need to procreate himself.
6. Man is self-destructive.
7. Man enjoys hurting other people.
8. Man has a need for meaning and purpose in his life.
9. Man has a desire to experience and communicate with the transcendent. This desire serves as the basis for man's religious behavior.

All of these ideas affect the mythmaking and storytelling human beings do, but our focus now is primarily on the last one: man's desire to experience and communicate with the transcendent.

First, however, we need to recall the definition of myth in the introduction. According to that definition, myth is "any real or fictional story, recurring theme, or character type that appeals to the consciousness of a people by embodying its cultural ideals or by giving expression to deep, commonly felt emotions."[15] Myth has deep significance for both the particular society in which we live and the human condition in general. It has a timeless, almost universal quality.

We can apply this idea of myth to fiction and nonfiction stories and to religious and nonreligious stories. Any one of these different kinds of stories can portray cultural ideals and depict universal concerns, hopes, and fears. A myth may be rooted firmly in a historical time and place, yet at the same time express timeless qualities that transcend a single physical location or cultural setting. A myth gives substance to cultural aspirations and evokes deep, commonly felt ideas and emotions.

Myth is also one way man can attempt to satisfy his desire to experience and communicate with the transcendent. According to Norman L. Geisler and Winfried Corduan in *Philosophy of Religion,* "something is transcendent if it goes beyond or is more than one's immediate consciousness. . . . Second, something is transcendent in a religious sense if it is believed to be ultimate. The Transcendent is the object of a total commitment. . . ."[16]

Man's desire for the transcendent engages his whole person. His desire for the transcendent involves a total dependence on the object of his ultimate commitment. Myths, even nonreligious, atheistic, or scientific ones, can express this desire. Reading, hearing, or watching myths is one way people satisfy this desire.

Mircea Eliade's description of myth has greatly influenced my own definition. Therefore, it is important to consider some of his other ideas on myth.

According to Eliade, myth involves our whole being, including our religious, intellectual, philosophical, social, emotional, biological, and ethical life. A myth "becomes a model"[17] for the whole society, and even the rest of the world. It serves as an eternal and universal example, an ideal people can admire and emulate.

Myth, adds Eliade, divides the world into two different realms: a sacred world and a profane world. His definition of the sacred is derived from Rudolph Otto's 1917 book *The Sacred.* For both men, the sacred is a *numinous* (or supernatural and holy) power that manifests itself as "wholly other."[18] The sacred is fundamentally religious and supernatural, and is often mysterious and powerful. Essentially, however, it is defined by its contrast with the profane world, which is the worldly, everyday existence that human beings experience in their regular lives. When we encounter the presence of something sacred, we may often express a special reverence or profound respect for it. This reverence may include intense feelings of admiration, devotion, peace, love, awe, or even fear. Most myths, religions, and religious rituals are filled with such encounters with the sacred, says Eliade.

Myth works with religion and ritual, states Eliade, to take us to sacred times and places that transform our profane world. Anyone who has attended a powerful religious ceremony, or even visited an exciting New Year's Eve or birthday party, or visited a beautiful sunset at the ocean, can see how such times and places become somehow sacred in our eyes, giving our lives a spiritual dimension.

I have three important observations or additions to Eliade's vision of the sacred.

First, although many myths and religions in fact may view the sacred as something "wholly other," many others may not. For example, the first book of the Bible, Genesis, says that God made man in God's "image." This means that man in some ways shares the divine attributes of God. For instance, man has personhood and God has personhood. God is infinitely self-aware, man is self-aware in a limited way. God knows all things, we can know many things. God has a perfect rational mind, man has a limited rational mind. God has emotions, and we have emotions.

If we include this traditional Christian frame of reference, then we can define the sacred not only as something that may or may not appear as wholly other, we can also define it as something that may or may not appear unlimited and infinite or "wholly transcendent." Any definition of the sacred must be able to incorporate this Christian view of the supernatural and holy.

Christians do not believe that God would create other personal beings who could *never* relate to him because he is "wholly other." *Sacred, supernatural, numinous,* and *holy* are words that describe transcendent qualities. These qualities are at least partly accessible to us, no matter how limited or fallible we may be.

Second, besides being supernatural, transcendent, holy, and infinite, the sacred may also appear as something bizarre, terrifying, apocalyptic, or evil and demonic. For instance, there is both apocalyptic and demonic imagery in Revelation, the last book of the New Testament. In that prophetic book, probably written between A.D. 65 and 66 by the apostle John,[19] the wrath of God comes to destroy the demon-possessed "beast," the great and evil Roman Empire, which has slaked its thirst on the blood of Christian martyrs. This apocalyptic vision is seen as a great victory for Jesus Christ, whose followers will rule "for a thousand years" (a figurative number that signifies a long period of time). They will rule until the final day of judgment when all the dead throughout history will be resurrected to receive their eternal rewards or punishment.

In many myths and religions, there is a dark side to the supernatural world of the sacred. Any definition of the sacred must therefore account for this possibility.

Finally, sometimes in myth and religion, especially in pagan societies, there is a shadowy middle world that seems destructive on the surface but can actually have some positive effects.

Psychologist James Hillman is one scholar who takes this approach toward myth. Hillman says that myth actually undermines the concrete reality of the everyday world. It does this by creating images of death, darkness, burial, concealment, madness, terror, anxiety, distortion, fragmentation, and loss of control. The goal of the mythic imagination, says Hillman, is to seek out and to travel into the depths of the psyche or soul. In Hillman's worldview, the soul is pathological or abnormally sick, but to him this is good, not bad.

For Hillman, myth is a pluralistic or polytheistic phenomenon, something that can't be pinned down into one idea. He is opposed to both organized religion and to all forms of monotheism, or belief in one God. Thus, for him, the sacred is something that is, more often than not, fragmented, diverse, and erratic. This means that, as far as he is concerned, all mythic encounters with the sacred lead us to tear down the ruling ideas limiting our conscious lives and to make a deep, but dark and even terrifying, journey into the sickness of our soul. We are all neurotic, says Hillman, but our own neurotic behavior is what makes us different from each other: "a pathologized awareness is fundamental to the sense of individuality."[20]

Consequently, here is how Hillman views myth:

Myths offer the multiplicity of meanings inherent in our lives, while theology and science attempt singleness of meaning. Perhaps this is why mythology is the mode of *speaking* religion in polytheistic consciousness, and why monotheistic consciousness *writes* down theology. Polytheistic consciousness is ever reminded by myth of the ambiguity of meanings and the multiplicity of persons in each event in each moment.

Despite their graphic description of action and detail, myths resist being interpreted into practical life. They are not allegories of applied psychology, solutions to personal problems. This is the old moralistic fallacy about them. . . . Living one's myth doesn't mean simply living *one* myth. It means that one lives *myth;* it means *mythical living.* As I am many persons, so I am enacting pieces of various myths. As all myths fold into each other, no single piece can be pulled out with the statement: "This is my myth. . . ."

Myths do not tell us how. They simply give the invisible background which starts us imagining, questioning, going deeper.[21]

Although Hillman's unique vision of myth adds to our overall concept of myth and the sacred, Hillman carries his vision too far. For example, Hillman believes it is better to live many myths rather than one myth, but to live many myths is also to actually live one myth: the myth of polytheism or pluralism. This is where Hillman clearly contradicts himself. His idea that people should not be pinned down to one myth or one mythology is itself an attempt to confine people to one idea and to one way of thinking about myth.

This is why I firmly believe that, while Hillman's ideas can be applied to some myths and to some depictions of the sacred, they cannot be applied to all. Like Campbell, Hillman tries to make his theory do too much.

In addition, Hillman's idea that "myths resist being interpreted into practical life" is simply not true. It contradicts Eliade's finding that myths often serve as a model for us, as an ideal toward which we strive. Here, I believe we should bow to Eliade's knowledge as a historian of religious ideas.

Hillman's theory also fails to take into account the stories of the Bible. Whether or not you accept them all as true, it would be irresponsible to adopt a theory about myth that doesn't consider them, yet this is exactly what Hillman eventually does.

Summary and Conclusion

Although there are good things we can say about some of his ideas, Joseph Campbell's basic view of myth and religious experience is limited by his narrow, illogical definition of the transcendent. Contrary to what Campbell said, the transcendent is not beyond all categories of thinking. The transcendent is itself a rational category that is subject to the Law of Noncontradiction. Something is transcendent if it seems to go beyond our immediate experience or if it seems to be unlimited or ultimate. By creating or telling myths, man tries to satisfy his desire to experience and communicate with the transcendent. Man's need for the transcendent engages his whole person. His desire for the transcendent involves a total dependence on it.

One of the most useful descriptions of myth's connection with the transcendent is Mircea Eliade's concept of the sacred, which he developed from Rudolph Otto's work. We have added a few things to Eliade's concept, however, to make it more comprehensive.

To sum up, the sacred is a supernatural, numinous world that reveals itself as something wholly other, transcendent, infinite, unlimited, or deeply mysterious. As such, it may appear to be holy, good, and worthy of admiration or even worship, or it may appear to be something dark, hidden, evil, demonic, fragmented, disruptive, and even terrifying, yet sometimes still positive in some way.

Myth "relates a sacred history."[22] It narrates the eruption of the sacred into the profane world and provides a model for various activities and rituals. By doing so, it infuses the profane world with sacred energy from the sacred world. This energy can give us a powerful sense of transcendence, peace, love, and renewal or bring us intense feelings of despair, loss of control, loathing, and terror. By looking at how various stories describe these encounters with a sacred world, we can begin to judge their religious and mythic character and content.

In the next chapter, we look at different kinds of myth in order to create our own myth models. We also briefly examine the issue of interpretation in order to develop objective principles of interpretation we can apply to the stories Campbell discusses. In doing these two things, we have an even better set of criteria by which we can evaluate the rest of Campbell's work.

3

Kinds of Myth and Principles of Interpretation

I n the introduction I mentioned that there are many different kinds of myth—creation myths, captivity myths, and so on. Of the many different kinds of myth or mythic story, one of the most important is the myth or story of initiation. What do myth scholars say about this kind of myth? How can it enlarge our understanding of myths in general?

Mythic Initiation—Time of Testing, Time of Change

In his book *Rites and Symbols of Initiation,* Mircea Eliade describes rites and myths of initiation and the "profound need" people have for the renewal, regeneration, and "spiritual transformation" this type of ritual and myth still gives us today.[1] According to Eliade, "The term initiation . . . denotes a body of rites and oral teachings whose purpose is to produce a decisive alteration in the

religious and social status of the person to be initiated."[2] Most of
the initiation myths and rituals "imply a ritual death followed by resurrection or a new birth . . . symbolizing the death of the novice and
his return to the fellowship of the living. But he returns to life a new
man, assuming another mode of being."[3]

This is the spiritual transformation Eliade describes. Modern
man's desire for the renewal that initiation brings "would appear to
represent man's eternal longing to find a positive meaning in death,
to accept death as a transition rite to a higher mode of being. . . . It
is only in initiation that death is given a positive value. Death pre-
pares the new, purely spiritual birth, access to a mode of being not
subject to the destroying action of Time."[4]

Despite the secularization of modern society, myth survives not
only in our cultural art forms but also in some of the most materialistic behavior and philosophy. For example, among many scientists and environmentalists today, there is a deep reverence, almost
a kind of worship for "Mother Earth" and "the universe that spawned
her." Even an atheistic philosophy like Marxism can't resist the creation of apocalyptic and utopian visions. Marxism envisions an apocalyptic world where one class of people, the working class, revolts
against another class, wealthy capitalists, and eventually produces
a communist paradise without God.

Popular culture preserves "the structure of myths" even though
it often drains them of their religious significance, adds Eliade.[5] Take
a look at popular films like *Terminator 2,* which is partly about the
initiation of a boy and his android, or a classic TV show like *Happy
Days,* which is about the initiation of teenagers in Milwaukee during the 1950s. Or consider a film like *Schindler's List,* which tells
the story of Oscar Schindler's initiation from an uncaring cad to a
sympathetic hero.

The myth of initiation is important in Mircea Eliade's research on
religion, and it is crucial to the late anthropologist Victor W. Turner's
writings. Initiation is central to Turner's description of the "liminal"
quality of myth, religion, ritual, and even art.

Liminal is a term first employed by folklorist Arnold van Gennep in 1909 to describe rites of passage or rites of initiation, such
as puberty rites, marriage rites, childbirth rites, and funeral rites in

primitive societies. Van Gennep reasoned that we should look at the dynamics or structures of such rituals. He suggested that rites of initiation have three stages: separation, transition, and incorporation. Each initiation ritual contains rites of separation, rites of transition, and rites of incorporation, in that basic order.

Rites of transition are liminal, said van Gennep, because they often emphasize both separation and incorporation in one single symbol or one single action. For instance, the circumcision ceremony in the transitional phase of many male puberty rites is an act of separation that also stresses the initiate's incorporation into and unity with the adult male group. Van Gennep adds that in many transition stages, something is cut off, such as a lock of hair or a part of flesh. This permanent separation leads to a permanent incorporation because it is also a sign of union with other people and a mark of membership in a new community, which the person going through the ritual is joining.

Rites of transition are also liminal, said van Gennep, because the initiate symbolically exists in a position where he is part of two worlds yet belongs to neither. Anthropologist Victor Turner describes this transitory position as a place that is "betwixt and between."[6] Within this liminal state, the individual seeks, through the myths, ceremonies, and symbols in the initiation ritual, "the power to transcend the limits of his previous status, although he knows he must accept the normative restraints of his new status."[7] Turner coins the term *liminality* to describe this process and says that it happens in many myths, not just those that stress initiation. Liminality removes us from the particular structure of our individual society, adds Turner, and teaches us about "the deep structure of culture and indeed of the universe."[8] This returns us to the metaphysical and philosophical underpinnings of myth.

Crossing over or under a threshold is an important rite of transition, says van Gennep, because thresholds are a liminal place of great sacred power and "to cross the threshold is to unite oneself with a new world."[9] The word *liminal* itself derives from the Latin word *limen*, meaning threshold. Carrying your bride over the threshold is a liminal experience. So is the idea of being on "the threshold of adventure."

Not only do we get a power of liminality when we undergo a special initiation ritual or experience an initiation myth, according to Turner, we also experience a feeling of community, or an emotional bonding with other members of society or with the human race as a whole. Such a feeling sounds similar to the kind of fellowship the New Testament encourages Christians to demonstrate among one another.

The Seven Dimensions of Myth

We can now expand on our original definition of myth: Myth is any real or fictional story, recurring theme, or character type that appeals to the consciousness of a people by embodying its cultural ideals or by giving expression to deep, commonly felt emotions. A myth has at least seven dimensions: spiritual, philosophical, social, psychological, biological, ethical, and aesthetic. These dimensions may at times overlap, but they generally manifest themselves in the following ways:

1. The Spiritual Dimension

Myth narrates a sacred history filled with personal encounters with the sacred. The sacred reveals itself as something supernatural, wholly other, transcendent, infinite, unlimited, or deeply mysterious. As such, it may appear as holy, good, and worthy of admiration or worship, or it may appear as dark, hidden, evil, demonic, fragmented, disruptive, and terrifying, yet sometimes still positive in some way.

2. The Philosophical Dimension

Myth expresses philosophical concerns about the nature of reality and about the fundamental and eternal issues facing human beings. It leads us to various ideas and viewpoints about the "deep structure" of life and the universe.

3. The Social Dimension

Myth is a liminal experience that can promote a change in social status, provide a sense of community, and direct people to "the generative power underlying human life, a power that from time to time oversteps cultural limits,"[10] but can also help people create new social limits.

4. The Psychological Dimension

Myth explores psychological issues surrounding our mental and emotional life, as well as those concerning our sense of personal individuality and our personal relationships with others.

5. The Biological Dimension

Myth focuses on issues of biology—issues concerning the major biological stages, changes, and events that take place in our lives, such as birth, childhood, puberty, adulthood, marriage, sex, parenthood, sickness, aging, and death.

6. The Ethical Dimension

Myth addresses questions and issues about ethics and morality, both our duty to the sacred world and our obligations to other people.

7. The Aesthetic Dimension

Myth tells stories. These stories bring us aesthetic pleasure, even when they deal with painful or horrible subjects and situations. Mythmaking and storytelling are essential for the creative energies of all human beings. They are the stuff that dreams are made of.

This model of myth dimensions is valuable for two reasons: It is comprehensive in its range of interests, yet it is also flexible enough to let other scholars, coming from different viewpoints, make their own personal contributions. Because of this, it is more objective than Joseph Campbell's basic approach to myth. Therefore, it is more useful and accessible to, as well as more open-minded and tolerant of, those people who don't share one's own worldview. This model of myth can be used by both Christians and non-Christians. Compared to my model, Campbell's approach to myth is much more narrow. That is why I and other scholars reject most of what Campbell says about the subject.

Archetype and Culturetype

In our definition of myth, there are two important concepts deserving special mention. The first is the idea that myths embody a people's "cultural ideals." The second is the idea that myths express "deep, commonly felt emotions." These two ideas are similar to the concept of "archetype" developed by psychologist Carl Jung and the concept of "culturetype" espoused by communication scholar Michael Osborn. In his writings, Jung discusses the role archetypes play in myths. Osborn also discusses archetypes and myth in his work, but he adds the theory of culturetype as a "counterpart"[11] to the archetypal theory.

According to Jung, archetypes are basic metaphors, patterns, paradigms, images, and concepts exerting strong influence on our intellectual and emotional behavior. Archetypes are transcultural; that is, they appear in at least more than one and often in many different societies throughout history. Archetypes are what give stories their timeless, universal quality, as well as their intellectual and emotional power. Any time we see many different myths or many different stories sharing common themes, settings, character types, situations, and other recurrent patterns, chances are we are seeing something working on an archetypal level. Some examples of archetypes are the hero, various images of motherhood and fatherhood, or the idea of the sacred.

Although archetypes often carry a strong emotional impact, this doesn't mean that they are completely irrational, as many scholars have claimed. After all, the very idea of archetype or emotion is itself a rational category that we can apply to some of the phenomenon occurring in the lives of human beings. As I noted in chapter 1, all of our language and all of our thinking depends on making such basic, fundamental, rational categories that can be applied to human experience. Thus, all rational categories are, in one sense, archetypes—basic metaphors, patterns, paradigms, images, and concepts exerting a powerful influence on our intellectual and emotional behavior. Without these archetypes, we could not think thoughts, speak to one another, or tell stories and myths. Therefore, to believe in the existence of archetypes and to believe in the existence of transcendent rational categories is rationally inescapable. Their existence is undeniable.

Culturetypes, according to Michael Osborn, are "culture-specific symbols that resonate important values,"[12] such as Valley Forge,

President Franklin D. Roosevelt's New Deal, the neon glitter of Las Vegas, or the idea of the American Dream. They

> receive their charge of special symbolic meaning through narratives that are heavily freighted with social significance. It is also possible . . . that archetypes and culturetypes brace and complement each other, archetypes anchoring the cultural system in enduring mean-ingfulness. Culturetypes remind us of what it means to be American, archetypes of what it means to be human. Successful myth, I strongly suspect, must include both in harmonious combination. And while archetypal symbols alone may not be a sufficient condition for the presence of myth, the constellation of archetypal and culturetypal symbols, as well as the narratives that sustain them, may well be essential to the mythic presence.[13]

Jung's and Osborn's basic notions of myth, archetype, and cul-turetype enrich our definition of myth and its seven dimensions. They are useful tools in interpreting and judging myths.

The Myth of the Hero

Anthropologist Victor Turner names two types of stories myth often tells: creation stories and trickster stories. Perhaps even more widespread than either of these is the myth of the hero. The mythologies, religions, and popular cultures of the world abound with tales of heroic journeys and quests. These mythic tales have formed an extensive group of story conventions and formulas that seem to crop up everywhere.

Vladimir Propp in *The Morphology of the Folktale* and Joseph Campbell in *The Hero with a Thousand Faces* each develop their own narrative structures of heroic journeys and quests. Propp's book centers on the fairy tale hero and heroine while Campbell's concen-trates on the myth hero and heroine. Even so, Propp's fairy tale hero has his origins in the mythic hero and thus shares many qualities with the myths Campbell discusses in his book. For instance, the hero in both fairy tales and many myths often receives a specific "call to adven-ture" before he embarks on his archetypal journey or quest. This call often comes in the form of a request, to which the hero must respond.

Both Propp's and Campbell's structures match Arnold van Gennep's structure for rites of passage. Both structures contain a stage of separation where the hero departs, a stage of transition where the hero is tested and undergoes an ultimate confrontation, and a stage of incorporation where the hero returns from his journey or quest. Campbell describes the three stages as "a separation from the world, a penetration to some source of power, and a life-enhancing return."[14] Of course, not every story follows these stages to the letter, but however far each individual fairy tale or myth follows or fails to follow these three stages, each story may run the gamut from tragedy to comedy.

Using these three stages, the heroic myth becomes a dynamic narrative process from which deep meaning can be derived. It also becomes a strong metaphor for the stages of life and rites of passage all human beings can undergo in their lives. The mythic hero is a model for society and a symbol of the archetypal individual. His story is constantly being told and re-told by many cultures.

In general, the archetypal hero myth contains three main elements: 1) a hero, the protagonist with whom we may identify or sympathize; 2) an environment in which the hero acts; and 3) a narrative that describes the interaction between the hero and his environment.

Narrative is another word for story. A narrative is a detailed description or account of a series of events and incidents. An event may be defined as "an occurrence of some importance and frequently one having antecedent cause." An incident may be defined as "an occurrence of brief duration or secondary importance."[15] Propp's and Campbell's books are valuable precisely because they give a detailed description of the typical kinds of events and incidents that take place in fairy tales and myths.

In the hero myth narrative, two events generally occur. First, the hero undergoes a rite of passage or initiation that ultimately, but not always, leads to a change in status for the hero; and second, during this rite of passage, the hero encounters various archetypes and culturetypes, which test his courage, stamina, and strength, and which can affect his personal development in the following seven different ways, which mirror the seven dimensions of myth on pages 64 and 65.

The Myth of the Hero

First, spiritually, the hero encounters a sacred world—metaphors, images, symbols, etc., of something supernatural, wholly other, transcendent, infinite, unlimited, or deeply mysterious that appears either as holy, good, and worthy of deep admiration and even worship or as dark, hidden, evil, demonic, fragmented, disruptive, and even terrifying, yet sometimes still positive in some way. This encounter takes at least two forms:

    a. The hero leaves his profane world to venture forth into this sacred world, or

    b. The sacred world erupts into the hero's profane world, sometimes through another party who needs the hero's help.

Eventually, the hero may discover that everything has a sacred purpose or meaning, and he must learn how to properly knit together both the sacred world and the profane world.

Second, philosophically, the hero may learn something new about the nature of reality or about the fundamental and eternal issues facing the human race. He may also learn about the "deep structure" of life and the universe.

Third, socially, the hero's experience is a liminal one that can often change his status in the world, provide him with a sense of community, or give him the power to transcend cultural limits and create new limits or new social structures. Of course, his experience can also be a negative one in these areas, but whatever happens, the hero usually has some kind of social role in the community to fill, even if it's the role of an outsider.

Fourth, psychologically, the hero faces challenges to his intellectual or mental states and to his emotional state. This challenge affects his sense of personal individuality and his personal relationships with other people or beings. During his experience, the hero may learn how better to integrate his emotional life with his intellectual life.

Fifth, biologically, the hero undergoes an actual or symbolic encounter with different biological stages, changes, and events, such as birth, childhood, puberty, adulthood, marriage, sex, parenthood, sickness, aging, and death.

Sixth, ethically, the hero faces questions and issues about morality, including both one's duty to the sacred world and one's obliga-

---

The Myth of the Hero (continued)

tions to other people or lesser beings. The hero will often have
to make some difficult moral choices. The particular challenges
he faces may influence how he makes those choices.

Seventh, aesthetically, the hero confronts issues pertaining to his
sense of beauty and to his sense of aesthetic or creative pleasure.
His experience affects his creative abilities, the life of his imagination, and his ability to dream.

As I have already noted, these seven dimensions often overlap.
For instance, the hero's moral or ethical development may concern
questions involving his sense of duty to the sacred world. Thus, a
particular myth or story may link together the hero's spiritual development and his ethical development. Likewise, a particular story
may connect the hero's social development with his psychological
and biological development.

For example, in the popular *Batman* movies, hero Bruce Wayne
is a millionaire who masquerades at night as the caped anti-crime
crusader Batman. This peculiar social status has a strong psychological implication for his character's development. It also affects his
biological development and his romantic relationships in the films.

This model of the hero myth is a useful, valuable tool. As shown
by our *Batman* example, we can easily apply the model to a wide
variety of stories, from high tragedy to low comedy, from epic to
romance, from *Batman* to Shakespeare. To quote Frank McConnell
in *Storytelling and Mythmaking: Images from Film and Literature,* "Storytelling . . . is always the story of the individual in
some sort of relationship to his social, political, or cultural environment."[16] Since the hero is himself an individual, it makes perfect sense, therefore, that a good model of the hero myth should
be able to reveal such relationships in many different kinds of stories. It also, however, should be able to give meaning and purpose
to the personal lives of individual audience members. After all, as
McConnell points out, "You are the hero of your own life-story."[17]

Of course, sometimes a particular story or myth will tell the
tale of a whole cast of heroes. For example, in many of American
film director Howard Hawks's movies *(The Big Sleep, Red River,*

Rio Bravo, To Have and Have Not), the story is really about a small community or group of people facing some kind of dangerous challenge. Although Hawks usually focuses on one or two characters in the group, each person often gets a chance to become the hero for at least one brief moment, or to perform a heroic deed that helps the group fight the darkness surrounding it. For a more modern example, consider George Lucas's *Star Wars Trilogy.* In those three films, we have at least seven heroes: Luke Skywalker, Princess Leia, Han Solo, Chewbacca, Lando Calrissian, and the two comical robots, R2D2 and C3PO. Although Luke is the main hero, each of these other characters adds a special heroic dimension to the group and to the films. Thus, even a collective group of heroes can serve as a model for the individual lives of the audience members.

By giving us such vivid heroes, stories give us a deep intellectual and emotional outlet for all the forces that shape our lives. By way of the imagination, they help us enter the spiritual, philosophical, social, psychological, biological, ethical, and aesthetic dimensions of the human condition.

Different stories present different kinds of heroes. One story may present a positive hero whom we admire and wish to emulate, but another story may present a hero whom we look down on or even pity. Still another story may give us a hero who appears to be our equal. Even if the image of a particular hero is negative, however, the portrayal of such a character may still leave us with a positive experience.

For instance, Macbeth's soliloquy when he finds out his wife has committed suicide is one of the most poignant cries of despair ever penned, yet it comes from a negative character who has been betrayed by his own evil lust for power and blood. Not a very nice guy, Macbeth, but he remains one of the greatest tragic heroes of the theater. Shakespeare's play is an icon of western culture and a provocative symbol of the human condition. It gives us a truly mythic story.

For these reasons, I believe this model of the hero myth gives us a good structure for interpreting almost all kinds of stories, including fiction and nonfiction. Using this model is not the only method we have of interpreting stories, however.

Principles of Interpretation

I wish I had a nickel for every time I heard someone say, "You can interpret the Bible any way you want. There are so many different interpretations. There's no such thing as the right interpretation."

This is one of those tired clichés many people blindly accept as absolute truth, incapable of being challenged. But are such statements really true? Can you really get any meaning you want out of the Bible? Can you interpret any story any way you want? Is there such a thing as a right interpretation and a wrong interpretation?

The science of interpretation, called hermeneutics, gives us rational principles and guidelines to explain the actual meaning of a piece of literature like the Bible. According to Peter Cotterell and Max Turner in *Linguistics and Biblical Interpretation,* "Meaning can be attributed only to *people,* not to texts."[18] Thus, coherent meaning "is a consequence of purpose, and . . . it is the author who gives a stamp of coherence through his organization of the material,"[19] while it is readers or audience who *infer* the meaning by looking at the text.

Of course, our understanding of the author's intended meaning may never be exhaustively complete, but this does not mean no one is able to determine the *basic* meaning of a particular passage. Likewise, although people may disagree about the meaning of the text, we can go back to the text, apply the principles of interpretation, and arrive at the most likely meaning.

Limited space precludes a complete study of the science of interpretation. Many people have written whole books about the subject, and some of them are listed in the bibliography. For the purposes of this book, I will focus on the following eight basic principles.

The first principle of interpretation is to *study each passage in its grammatical and historical context,* "the historical and linguistic situation in which it was originally recorded."[20] If the meaning of a passage is designed to be historical and factual, it should be interpreted historically and factually. If the meaning is designed to be symbolic and figurative, the passage should be interpreted symbolically and figuratively. For example, the New Testament documents present Jesus Christ's bodily resurrection as a physical, historical fact, but they present Jesus Christ's parables as the moral fables they are intended to be—fictitious stories illustrating moral and religious principles. The goal of interpretation is exegesis, reading meaning *out of* the text, not reading meaning *into* the text.

The second principle of interpretation is to *look at the immediate context of each particular passage or block of text.* According to Dr. A. Berkeley Mickelsen, "The meaning of any particular element is nearly always controlled by what precedes and what follows."[21] In order to truly understand the meaning of a particular passage, we must study the words, sentences, and paragraphs immediately preceding and following it. Only after we study the immediate context of a passage can we proceed to the larger context of the text *as a whole.* In the case of the Bible, we can also look at the other books in the Bible. For instance, when we study one of the apostle Paul's letters, we may want to read his other letters in order to help us determine the meaning of a particular passage.

The third principle is to *use the text to interpret the text.* In other words, use the clear passages in the text to interpret the meaning of the unclear or obscure passages. Give the text the benefit of the doubt and "assume the work to be a coherent whole"[22] whose coherence was intended by the author. Never assume, because the text seems unclear at one point, that the author was contradictory or confused.

The fourth principle of interpretation is that *"Main points [in the text] are clearer than details."*[23] Thus, although orthodox Christians may often disagree about what a particular passage in the Bible means in detail, they usually agree on the essential teachings and basic moral values the New Testament writers support.

The next principle tells us to *look at the historical, cultural, and geographical background of a text to help interpret its meaning.* For example, many people today laugh at the kind of acting depicted in most silent films and call it "melodramatic," but at the time the movies were made, the acting was considered reasonably "realistic." Only by understanding the historical, cultural, and geographic background of these films can we truly understand the meanings within them.

The sixth principle of interpretation tells us to *be aware of special formulas, genres, and categories the author uses.* For instance, many Christians try to interpret the Book of Revelation literally. In reality, however, since Revelation is apocalyptic in nature, it is full of unique symbols and strange images. As such, its meaning should be interpreted in a figurative manner. Thus, when Revelation 20:4 says that some souls "came to life and reigned with Christ a thousand years," we are probably not talking about a literal thousand years.

Understanding the difference between general hermeneutics and special hermeneutics is helpful to the sixth principle. According to Milton S. Terry in *Biblical Hermeneutics:*

> General Hermeneutics is devoted to the general principles which are applicable to the interpretation of all languages and writing. It may appropriately take cognizance of the logical operations of the human mind, and the philosophy of human speech. Special Hermeneutics is devoted rather to the explanation of particular books and classes of writings. Thus, historical, poetical, philosophical, and prophetical writings differ from each other in numerous particulars, and each class requires for its proper exposition the application of principles and methods adapted to its own peculiar character and style.[24]

When approaching a book like the Bible, therefore, we should not only apply general principles of interpretation, we should also apply special methods that consider the unique formulas, genres, and categories of each individual book, letter, or poem.

The seventh principle of interpretation tells us that *when comparing two or more passages or texts, we must not neglect the differences between them.* For example, Moses' brother Aaron in the Old Testament is a type of Jesus Christ in one sense because he presents the sacrifice on the Day of Atonement. Despite this comparison, however, there are many other things that render Aaron's example on the Day of Atonement completely different from the meaning of Jesus Christ's death on the cross.

Finally, the eighth principle of interpretation is to *be aware of the logical flow of thought in the text.* For instance, Paul's intended meaning in chapters 5–16 of Romans will become more clear after we carefully examine Paul's basic argument in the first four chapters of Romans. Jesus Christ's intended meaning in John 14:6 when he says, "I am the way and the truth and the life," is easier to understand when we study Jesus' words in John 14:1–14.

We can use these basic principles to help us explain the meaning of any story, both factual stories and fictional stories. When we couple these principles with the seven dimensions of myth given earlier and the structure of the hero myth above, we can objectively interpret any story.

Conclusion

Joseph Campbell's theories about myth and religious experience are woefully inadequate. In their place I have proposed my own ideas about myth and religion, based on the work of other scholars. The principles of interpretation presented in this chapter are more objective and more exact than Campbell's. Campbell, after all, is the one who said, "To me, all mythologies are provinces of one great system of feeling. I think of the mythological image as an energy-evoking sign that hits you below the thinking system."[25]

Unlike Campbell, I don't think emotion and intellect are so easily separated. In fact, in my discussion of archetypes and culturetypes, the building blocks of myth, I said the very ideas of archetype, culturetype, and emotion are themselves rational categories that make a profound impact on our lives. As a Christian, I believe emotion and intellect are two related functions of the spirit-body dualism of which human beings are made. Viewed in this light, feeling and thinking become complementary abilities all human beings share. They are basic, fundamental, rational categories or archetypes the existence of which is undeniable. Joseph Campbell may wish to stress emotion at the expense of rational thought, but in doing so, he is using rational thought to deny rational thought. This idea is self-contradictory and therefore automatically false, but almost all of Campbell's work is based on it! By putting all his intellectual marbles in this flimsy bag, Campbell fatally undermines his basic worldview.

Not only does Campbell violate basic tests for truth, some of which are described in chapter 1, he also often violates our eight basic principles of interpretation. For instance, he often ignores the historical and grammatical context of a story or myth. He also often fails to look at the immediate context of particular passages and frequently pulls passages out of context in order to read his own biased meaning into the text of a story. Finally, he frequently distorts the meaning behind a particular author or character's argument and seldom examines in detail the logical flow of thought in many passages. In subsequent chapters we will see many examples of these mistakes.

4

Campbell's Pantheism: All Is One, One Is All

oseph Campbell "didn't have an ideology or a theology," claimed reporter Bill Moyers in the introduction to his TV interview with the late mythologist. During the next six hours of intense interviews, however, Campbell proved Moyers wrong.

Joseph Campbell did indeed have an ideology and a theology. At one point in the interview, he ridiculed the Judeo-Christian belief in a bodily resurrection of Jesus Christ by calling it "a clown act, really."[1] He then said that immortality instead should be seen as an "identification with that which is of eternity in your own life now. . . ."[2] At another point, he said, "We have today to learn to get back into accord with the wisdom of nature and realize again our brotherhood with the animals and with the water and the sea."[3]

If this isn't an ideology or a theology, what is?

Not only did Campbell often bitterly attack the historical theology of orthodox Christianity and its accompanying moral code, he also advocated a mystical, pantheistic view of God and religious experience. This view caused him to take a peculiar attitude toward human perception, nature, logic, and God.

Pantheism is the belief that the whole universe and everything in it are part of a divine, impersonal force or consciousness. Mysticism is a religious, often intellectual, discipline or belief that tries to make an immediate contact with ultimate reality or with God. This contact often, though not always, involves trying to achieve complete union with ultimate reality or the object of belief. Mysticism can be pantheistic, monotheistic, or polytheistic, but it is often associated with pantheism.

In order to determine whether Campbell had an ideology or a theology, even if it was a pantheistic ideology or a theology of no-ideology or no-theology, consider the following quotes from his books:

> What was proper fifty years ago is not proper today. The virtues of the past are the vices of today. And many of what were thought to be the vices of the past are the necessities of today. The moral order has to catch up with the moral necessities of actual life in time, here and now.[4]

> There is no "Thou shalt" anymore. There is nothing one *has* to believe, and there is nothing one *has* to do.[5]

> There is no divinely ordained authority any more that we *have* to recognize. There is no appointed messenger of God's law. In our world today all civil law is conventional. No divine authority is claimed for it; no Sinai; no Mount of Olives. Our laws are enacted and altered by *human* determination, and within their secular jurisdiction each one of us is free to seek his own destiny, his own truth, to quest for this or for that and to find it through his own being.[6]

> You can see it in the Bible. In the beginning, God was simply the most powerful god among many. He is just a local tribal god.[7]

> The wonder of the universe that is being developed for us by our scientists surely is a far more marvelous, mind-blowing revelation than

anything the prescientific world could ever have imagined. The little toy-room picture of the Bible is, in comparison, for children. . . .[8]

The transcendent is unknowable and unknown. . . . The mystery of life is beyond all human conception. . . . Eternity is beyond all categories of thought. . . . God is a thought. God is a name. God is an idea. But its reference is to something that transcends all thinking. The ultimate mystery of being is beyond all categories of thought.[9]

There are two ways of thinking "I am God." If you think, "I here, in my physical presence and in my temporal character, am God," then you are mad and have short-circuited the experience. You are God, not in your ego, but in your deepest being, where you are at one with the non-dual transcendent.[10]

There's a transcendent energy source. . . . That energy is the informing energy of all things. Mythic worship is addressed to that.[11]

I have a feeling that consciousness and energy are the same thing somehow. Where you really see life energy, there's consciousness. Certainly the vegetable world is conscious. And when you live in the woods, as I did as a kid, you can see all these different consciousnesses relating to themselves. There is a plant consciousness and there is an animal consciousness, and we share both these things.[12]

We are a natural product of this earth, that is to say; and, . . . if we are intelligent beings, it must be that we are the fruits of an intelligent earth. . . . We may think of ourselves, then, as the functioning ears and eyes and mind of this earth, exactly as our own ears and eyes and minds are of our bodies. Our bodies are one with this earth. . . .[13]

When you see that God is the creation, and that you are a creature, you realize that God is within you, and in the man or woman with whom you are talking, as well.[14]

[Your life comes] from the ultimate energy that is the life of the universe. And then do you say, "Well, there must be somebody generating that energy?" Why do you have to say that? Why can't the ultimate mystery be impersonal?[15]

That old man up there has been blown away. You've got to find the Force inside you.[16]

If there is no divinity in nature, the nature that God created, how should there be [divinity] in the idea of God, which the nature of man created?[17]

These quotes show how Campbell's theology of mystical pantheism permeated his thinking. They also show his worship of nature.

Campbell believed we are one with the material universe and one with the planet, and our personal identities are one with an impersonal divinity. At the same time, he believed that the wonders of the material universe shown to us by science are more magnificent than the wonders depicted in the Bible. This in turn led him to validate secular culture, a world without religion, where all people are free to pursue their own happiness, or "bliss" as he calls it, but only if their bliss does not include religious or moral dogmatism.

Theology is "the study of the nature of God and religious truth." It also is the "rational inquiry into religious questions," or "an organized, often formalized body of opinion concerning God and man's relationship to God."[18] Finally, Webster's defines theology as "the study of religious faith, practice, and experience; especially the study of God and his relation to the world."

Ideology is "the body of ideas reflecting the social needs and aspirations of an individual, group, class, or culture."[19] Ideology also is "a systematic body of concepts especially about human life or culture" or "the integrated assertions, theories, and aims that constitute a sociopolitical program."[20]

In his books, Campbell talks about the nature of God, religious experience, and spiritual truth. He takes strong positions on these issues and is very dogmatic about them. In reality, therefore, he really did have a theology.

We can also see from his writings and interviews that Campbell had definite opinions about social needs and aspirations, and about human life and culture. He also had a sociopolitical program consisting of a strong belief in globalism and ecology. He did indeed have an ideology.

The question arises: What is so terribly wrong with having a strong, even dogmatic, theology or ideology? And why should we be afraid of adopting a particular system of belief, so long as we are able to support it with sound arguments and solid evidence? The problem is that people who hate dogma like Campbell are usually very dogmatic about their hatred, and therefore they contradict themselves.

Joseph Campbell fails to give sound arguments and solid evidence for his theology and his ideology. In fact, Campbell hypocritically condemns other people for being dogmatic and narrow-minded about truth, God, religion, and morality, but he himself is guilty of doing the same thing.

As I noted earlier, Campbell says that people who believe they have found the ultimate truth are wrong, but his own statements about this are themselves a belief in only one truth. Thus, Campbell's beliefs about truth and religion lead him to do the same thing he accuses conservative Christians and other people of doing.

In trying to rid the world of one dogma, Campbell simply invents a new one. Although he claims to support an "open," pluralistic approach to religion and morality, he strongly disagrees with those people who don't share his own narrow ideas. He berates others for being dogmatic, but he himself is very dogmatic.

This attitude is a clear violation of the first test for truth listed in chapter 1, the Law of Noncontradiction. It also demonstrates that Campbell had a clear and obvious bias against ideas that don't agree with his own theology and ideology. This is a violation of the sixth test for truth listed in chapter 1, which asks whether an author or eyewitness has an obvious or undue bias that distorts his testimony.

Joseph Campbell's Pantheistic, Mystical Worldview

Joseph Campbell not only had strong opinions about the nature of God, the nature of religious experience, spiritual truth, human life and culture, and social issues, he also had a specific worldview.

A worldview is a comprehensive theory of reality or of the world/universe. It is "a way of viewing or interpreting all of reality... an interpretive framework through which or by which one makes sense out of the data of life and the world."[21] Examples of some world-views are theism, atheism, deism, pantheism, and polytheism.[22]

Worldviews are closely related to philosophies. According to Webster, a philosophy is "the most general beliefs, concepts, and attitudes of an individual or group." A person's worldview and philosophy can affect his overall vision of, or attitude toward, life and the purpose of life.

Although Campbell apparently didn't believe people have a spirit or soul, his worldview is one of pantheism. As mentioned before, pantheism is the belief that the whole universe and everything in it are part of a divine, impersonal force or consciousness. In pantheism, the universe flows out of an impersonal "god." Miracles are impossible and man's goal is to unite or achieve oneness with this divine force, often after being reincarnated countless times in numerous physical bodies throughout history. Unlike the ethical monotheism of orthodox Christianity or Judaism, which says that people should *do good and avoid evil,* pantheism says that people must eventually *transcend good and evil,* especially when they unite with the divine force or consciousness, from whom both good and evil originate. Until that time, people are encouraged to live moral lives to attain ever higher levels of spiritual growth. Despite this last common belief, not many pantheists have a highly developed view of what is good and what is evil, so it's often difficult to know exactly how they know to live a moral life.

In his brand of pantheism, Campbell postulates "a transcendent energy source" that is impersonal, yet conscious in some way. Our own life energy and consciousness flow from this energy source, which is transcendent because it exists beyond all thought and beyond all rational concepts or categories. According to Campbell, one can't apply reason and logic to the transcendent. As we quoted above, Campbell also believes that people are "a natural product of the earth," "the fruits of an intelligent earth." We are one with nature and with the cosmos, which are themselves just a part of the transcendent, divine, and impersonal energy source. Nature includes an animal consciousness and a vegetable consciousness, and human beings share in these two types of consciousness. Finally, since people are a part of the divine transcendent, the ultimate goal is to become one with the transcendent. At the same time, however, since we ourselves are also divine, each one of us has a right "to seek his own destiny, his own truth, to quest for this or for that and to find it through his own being," but not to seek those things through external realities or through some "old man up there."

Campbell's pantheism seems to be a cross between an eternal, "permeational pantheism" and a changing "modal pantheism." Permeational pantheism claims that "a oneness like a Life Force underlies and permeates all that is real,"[23] while modal pantheism "teaches that each individual thing [or person] is a mode or modification of God,"[24] or the transcendent energy source, as Campbell puts it.

As this chapter argues, Campbell's worldview is false for several reasons. First, it violates basic laws of logic and commits several logical fallacies. It is therefore irrational. Second, it ignores many important facts. This means it is factually untrue. Finally, Campbell's worldview is superficial at best because it fails to even mention, let alone answer, any of the objections many scholars and philosophers have raised against mysticism and pantheism through the centuries. Why should we accept the worldview of a scholar who doesn't make at least some attempt to answer criticisms against his worldview? Many Christian scholars try to answer major arguments against Christianity. Why didn't Campbell answer objections to his own worldview?

This last point, though important, isn't enough to *invalidate* Campbell's worldview, however. In order to refute his worldview, we need to give evidence for the first two points. My argument against Campbell's basic worldview is divided into four areas: 1) his explanation of mysticism; 2) his view of man's relationship to his environment; 3) his attack on reason and logic; and 4) his concept of God.

Campbell's Explanation of Mysticism

Throughout his work, Campbell contends that the highest form of knowledge is by direct, mystical experience. For example, in *The Power of Myth* Campbell discusses his idea of "peak experiences" that transcend language.

"Words are always qualifications and limitations," says Campbell, "and that's why it is a peak experience to break past all that, every now and then, and to realize, 'Oh . . . ah . . .'"[25] It is in such moments of silent, inexpressible bliss that we begin to find a touch, and see a glimpse, of the divine energy source that transcends language and goes beyond all rational thought, says Campbell. Such an experience puts us in touch with the eternal, a place beyond time, according to Campbell.

"The peak experience refers to actual moments of your life when you experience your relationship to the harmony of being," explains Campbell. "My own peak experiences, the ones that I knew were peak experiences after I had them, all came in athletics."[26] When having such an experience, says Campbell, we should realize our essential oneness with "the non-dual transcendent" existing deep within us but also beyond our limited, rational mind and the categories it establishes.

This description of mystical experience plays a big role in Campbell's pantheism. The problem with such a description is that it blurs the line between the knower (the person having an experience) and the object or situation being experienced. Within Campbell's worldview, there is no true subject, there is no true object, there is only experience. And because there is no real distinction between subject and object, experience begins to lose all connection with human personality and all connection with the material world. The result is that experience becomes everything and everything becomes one.

This view of experience and reality has many faults.

First of all, if there is no real, transcendent difference between subject and object, then how do you know that you have even had one of these "peak," mystical experiences Campbell wrote and talked about? How could you even describe such an experience to another person? Why would you even be interested in sharing your experience with another person or trying to convince him that your experience gives you a particular view of life that is valuable? How could you even argue rationally for mystical pantheism? Yet this is exactly what Joseph Campbell tries to do!

Also, Campbell provides no way to test whether or not a person has had a mystical experience. There is no external way to verify this kind of experience. What is the difference between saying "I am one with God" and saying "I am one with Abraham Lincoln"? According to Campbell's worldview, there is no difference, but a difference that makes no difference is no difference at all.

Another problem with this view is that it contradicts Campbell's other statements, cited above, that the "non-dual transcendent," with which we become "one," is "unknowable and unknown" and "beyond all categories of thought." Despite this claim, Campbell's work is filled with discussions about how to define mystical experience and descriptions of mystical experiences that he or other people have had. This is a clear logical contradiction in Campbell's work. It undermines his worldview.

Furthermore, when Campbell talks about mystical experiences that "transcend language" and are indescribable, he again contradicts himself. At the same time he denies the use of language in approaching these experiences, he also affirms the use of language because he uses language to describe them. In telling Bill Moyers they transcend language, he has in reality failed to transcend the very language he finds inadequate. Such comments are inherently illogical and should be dismissed as irrational.

Campbell's description of mystical experience is thus fundamentally flawed. It does not really transcend language, nor is it beyond the reach of the rational thought processes of human beings, in spite of their faults and limitations. As David Clark and Norman Geisler point out in their book *Apologetics in the New Age: A Christian Critique of Pantheism,* "Mystics do not lack for words. How can they claim initially that the object of their experience is beyond words and then turn around and write about it page after page? . . . Mystics effectively describe their experiences, and non-mystics clearly understand those descriptions."[27]

We can level this same charge against Joseph Campbell's description of mysticism. Look again at the many quotes from him already cited. Despite what Campbell said, we can use language to describe ultimate reality, even if that reality is supernatural.

As for Campbell's claim that the non-dual transcendent is unknowable, the following quote from Norman Geisler and William Watkins's *Worlds Apart* is instructive:

The very claim that "God is unknowable in an intellectual way" seems
to be either meaningless or self-defeating. For if the claim itself *cannot* [authors' emphasis] be understood in an intellectual way, then it
is a meaningless claim. If the claim *can* be understood in an intellectual way, then it is self-defeating, since it affirms that nothing can
be understood about God in an intellectual way. In other words, the
pantheist expects us to know intellectually that God cannot be understood intellectually. But how can he make a positive affirmation about
God that claims only negative affirmations can be made about God?
Even the pantheistic philosopher and mystic Plotinus admitted that
negative knowledge presupposes some positive awareness. Otherwise, one would not know what to negate.[28]

Replace the words "God is unknowable in an intellectual way" with
Campbell's statement that "the transcendent is unknowable" and
you will see that the quote from Geisler and Watkins refutes
Campbell's worldview.

In chapter 1, I argued that all experience and all knowledge contain "a conceptual element." I also said that all language and all
thought would be impossible without applying rational concepts or
categories and without using basic principles of logic. These statements apply equally to Joseph Campbell's belief in "peak" mystical
experiences and to his statement that the non-dual transcendent is
unknowable.

For example, Campbell's brand of mystical pantheism provides a
conceptual background, an "interpretive context,"[29] that gives meaning to the mystical experiences and attitudes he advocates in his
books, lectures, and interviews. Thus, Campbell's description of mystical encounters with the non-dual transcendent depends on the concepts and categories of his own philosophical concerns. It requires
a conceptual element. Therefore, his claim that these experiences
are beyond rational thought and beyond language is patently false.

To expand this point further, let's reconsider the idea of the sub-
ject/object distinction. Philosopher Stuart C. Hackett says that the
idea that there is no real distinction between subject and object,
between my personal experience or idea of a thing or object and the
actual physical existence of that thing or object, is highly dubious.
Our experiences and ideas are separate from the objects they represent, he says. For instance, an idea can be clear or confused and

experiences can be distinct or vague, but an object has indisputable physical properties.

In addition, our visual perceptions of objects are separate from our tactile perceptions. The object has an existence separate from our perceptions of it, and our perceptions can change. If there is no difference between our perceptions and the object, Hackett asks, then how do we explain different perceptions and how can we account for error? Even if we admit that only some things or objects are identical to our ideas, experiences, and perceptions, says Hackett, how do we decide which ones are identical and which ones are not?

"Knowledge arises," says Hackett, "only through the application of a structure of interpretive principles" to our ideas, experiences, and perceptions which, in one way or another, are "distinct from, and normally extraneous to, the principles themselves. . . ."[30] These ideas, experiences, and perceptions are also distinct from the things or objects they describe or encounter.

"There are always two distinct aspects to every knowing situation," says philosopher Warren C. Young in *A Christian Approach to Philosophy:* subject and object.[31] If there were no real difference between them, he adds, then we couldn't account for error in the knowing process. And, if we couldn't account for error, then how could we ever correct an error when we saw one?

For these reasons, we must reject Campbell's belief that people can have a set of experiences that actually make them "one" with the "divinity" in nature and "one" with an eternal, impersonal "non-dual transcendent," the source of "the ultimate energy that is the life of the universe." Campbell's belief in mysticism is illogical and does not correspond to the true facts of how people actually experience reality.

Campbell's View of Man and His Environment

Another problem with Joseph Campbell's worldview is reflected in his comments that "we are a natural product of this earth" and, therefore, "if we are intelligent beings, it must be that we are the fruits of an intelligent earth." These comments fit in well with his other statements about life energy and consciousness and about different kinds of consciousness, such as "plant consciousness" and "animal consciousness."

Once again, Campbell is guilty of confusing different words with different meanings and coming up with unclear, vague, or ambiguous definitions, enabling him to wrongly validate his own personal worldview. This is an informal logical fallacy that damages the validity of Campbell's argument.

Campbell equivocates on the words *intelligence* and *consciousness*. For example, there may be some sense in which animals are said to have consciousness, but that evades the question of whether animal consciousness is qualitatively the same as human consciousness. Even more confusing, however, is Campbell's use of the term *plant consciousness*. It's hard to see in what context a plant can be said to be "conscious."

Contrary to what Campbell seems to claim in his books, lectures, and interviews, the terms *intelligence* and *consciousness* definitely include the idea of "personality" or "personhood." Thus, although the words *life energy* can perhaps refer to something impersonal, the terms *intelligence* and *consciousness* cannot. Animals do seem to have some kind of "personality" analogous to human personality, but plants do not (unless, of course, you want to count science fiction stories about alien vegetables from outer space).

The words *intelligence* and *consciousness* refer to something nonmaterial and nonphysical while the term *earth* refers to something material and physical. The phrase *intelligent earth* is thus an oxymoron.

If you doubt that the words *intelligence* and *consciousness* refer to something nonmaterial and nonphysical, consider the following argument.

Our conscious, intelligent thoughts are not identical to the electrochemical activity in our physical, material brains. Although I can "see" the color green, there is nothing green in the physical organ that is my brain. In addition, not only do I have direct, personal experience of my mental thoughts, I can also interpret and think about my thoughts.

Colors, sounds, tastes, and smells "exist as sense data (mental objects or images) in the mind," says Dr. J. P. Moreland, who holds an undergraduate degree in chemistry and a Ph.D. in philosophy from the University of Southern California. "Mental states point beyond themselves to other objects even if those objects do not exist."[32] For example, Dr. Moreland says you can think about the car you really own or you can think about owning a spaceship that doesn't exist. Both thoughts point to external objects separate from your individual identity.

"If I am just matter," adds Moreland, "then my actions are not the result of free choice. They are determined by the laws of chemistry and physics. . . ."[33] Moreland believes this kind of materialistic determinism or physicalism is false and irrational:

> In sum, it is self-refuting to *argue* that one *ought* to *choose* physicalism *because* he should *see* that the *evidence* is *good* [author's emphasis] for physicalism. Physicalism cannot be offered as a rational theory because physicalism does away with the necessary preconditions for there to be such a thing as rationality. Physicalism usually denies intentionality by reducing it to a physical relation of input/output, thereby denying that the mind is genuinely capable of having thoughts about the world. Physicalism denies the existence of propositions and nonphysical laws of logic and evidence which can be in minds and influence thinking. Physicalism denies the existence of a faculty capable of rational insight into these nonphysical laws and propositions, and it denies the existence of an enduring "I" which is present through the process of reflection. Finally, it denies the existence of a genuine agent who deliberates and chooses positions because they are rational, an act possible only if physical factors are not sufficient for determining future behavior.[34]

Thus, the words *intelligence* and *consciousness* refer to mental properties or characteristics which are nonphysical and nonmaterial. It is hard to see how such properties are "the fruits of an intelligent earth" as Campbell claims. How did they emerge from a planet that appears, on the surface at least, to be only physical? Does this mean that all matter has the potential to produce mental properties?

"Are these potential properties conscious?" asks Moreland. "If so, then why do we have no memory of them when they emerge to form our own minds? Does it really make sense to say that my mind is composed of several particles of mind dust . . . ? If these potential properties are not conscious, how are they still mental?"[35]

Campbell wrongly tries to equate human beings with plants and animals or with the whole planet. This belief has important consequences for his ideology, as we shall see in the next two chapters.

When we experience a tree, we do not become identical with it. We establish a special *relationship* with the tree. Such a relationship may have a positive effect on us. We may even want to treasure that effect and seek more positive relationships with the organic environment around us. But why do we need to treat the tree and the rest of nature as a divine object in order to do this?

Joseph Campbell's pantheistic view of man and his organic environment, the planet on which we live and the universe we inhabit, has serious difficulties. He takes words like *intelligence* and *consciousness*, mixes them with his own pseudoscientific, mystical ideas about evolution, and twists them into a strange theology that is linguistically, scientifically, and philosophically unsound.

Campbell's Pantheistic View of Logic

To Campbell, the concept of God refers to an unknowable, transcendent "something" beyond all rational thought and logic. According to him, all experience of this mysterious "non-dual transcendent" is also beyond rational thought and logic. In effect, however, Campbell has used rational thought and logic to deny rational thought and logic when it comes to describing this ultimate reality and our experience of it.

Essentially, here is how his thinking goes: 1) If I accept the truth of logic concerning the transcendent, then I need to resolve any contradictions in my description of the transcendent; 2) If I deny the truth of logic concerning the transcendent, then any contradictions do not need to be resolved; 3) I do not accept the truth of logic concerning the transcendent; 4) Therefore, I can ignore the truth of logic concerning the transcendent, and contradictions don't need to be resolved.

Campbell posits a difference between reason and mystical experience of his pantheistic transcendent, but in doing this he sets up basic logical distinctions. For instance, he sets up a distinction between personal consciousness and impersonal consciousness and between duality and non-duality. This is clearly an inconsistent, absurd thinking pattern. To quote Geisler and Watkins again:

> Denying that logic applies to [ultimate] reality involves making a logical statement about [ultimate] reality that no logical statement about [ultimate] reality can be made. To deny that logic applies to [ultimate] reality, one must make a logical statement about [ultimate] reality. But if no such logical statement about [ultimate] reality can be made, how can the pantheist even explain his view?[36]

As I noted in chapter 2, Campbell's idea of the transcendent is itself a linguistic category subject to the laws of logic. To say that such an idea is beyond rational thought and logic is to make a complete mockery of the process of communication between human beings. It is sad so many intelligent people have fallen for Campbell's fuzzy-minded rhetoric. It is hard to believe our society's critical thinking skills have fallen to such a low state of affairs.

Campbell's Theology Is Incoherent

Campbell's idea of God and God's relationship to man is incoherent. It is also vague and shapeless. Campbell claims people shouldn't try to define God, but then he says God is a concept referring to something both indescribable and transcendent, both impersonal and conscious. At the same time he denies we can apply concepts to the idea of God, he tries to apply his own concepts to the idea of God. As noted before, this is clearly a contradiction.

If God is an *impersonal* energy force transcending all categories of human thought, then God transcends even that description, and the idea of God becomes empty of all meaning whatsoever. Campbell tries to get away from the Judeo-Christian idea of a personal God, but he sets up his own categories of impersonal consciousness, energy, and transcendence at the same time he rejects the use of such categories. It is illogical to say God transcends categories like personality, but then to claim God is an impersonal but transcendent energy source or consciousness.

If God is the ultimate mystery lying beyond all categories of thought, then why does Campbell use his own human reason to defend his pantheistic view of God? If the transcendent is unknowable, as he claims, then how does he know it is unknowable? To call God a transcendent mystery, which cannot be grasped by the human mind, is an evasive tactic that avoids the responsibility all writers and scholars have for defending their viewpoints with reasonable arguments.

In spite of his vivid description of the non-dual transcendent, Campbell's theology is vague and shapeless. Although he is quick to use words like *energy*, *divinity*, *consciousness*, and *bliss*, his apparent definitions of these words are so broad and vague that they become nearly meaningless. Campbell's arguments are filled with such pleasant-sounding but empty words and phrases. He doesn't give his audience rational reasons for belief; he gives them emotional rhetoric. Furthermore, since Campbell uses broad and vague terms, it is easy for him to persuade people like Bill Moyers, who obviously has had no training in orthodox Christian theology.

As with all pantheists, Campbell believes, deep down, that all human beings are divine and we share this divinity with the whole physical universe. "When you see that God is the creation," says Campbell, "and that you are a creature, you realize that God is within you, and in the man or woman with whom you are talking."[37]

There are numerous problems with this. At this point, let me deal with two.

First, how can we be God when we go through changes, but God, if he exists, does not? Perhaps Campbell means that God actually changes, but this isn't clear from reading his writings and hearing his interviews and lectures. Second, if God changes, then God can't really be God, because *God* is a word referring to a supernatural being who is ultimate and infinite. If God can change, he is neither ultimate nor infinite, and thus it's hard to see how God can be transcendent, even if we accept Campbell's definition of this term. "To say that God is infinite and yet somehow shares its [sic] being . . . with creation," say Geisler and Watkins in *Worlds Apart,* "is to raise the question of how the finite can be infinite."[38]

The Christian View of God and Christian Mysticism

Compared to Campbell's theology, the traditional Christian view of God makes more sense. It is logically consistent and coherent.

As Clark and Geisler point out in their book on pantheism, applying specific attributes to God (such as love, power, knowledge, and personality) does not limit God's infinite and transcendent nature if you believe that those attributes are themselves infinite and transcendent because they stem from God's nature. This is exactly what orthodox Christianity teaches.

Christianity also teaches that God is a person whose existence is *outside* the space and time of the material universe, but who can act *within* it. Viewed as such, God is separate from his creation. He is also the divine foundation of all the rational categories Joseph Campbell tried to do away with. Campbell may have wished to deny the universal validity of these rational categories originating from the divine mind of God, but without them he defeats the rational plausibility of his own arguments. In doing so, he proves that his worldview is false.

You don't need to be a pantheist to accept the validity of mystical experiences with God. Christianity teaches that when we confess Jesus Christ as our divine, personal Savior, God begins to change us by the power of the Holy Spirit, the third person of the Triune God. This change gradually helps us turn away from evil and become like Christ, who was sinless.

> The union is not one of merging essence which destroys personality, but the biblical one of union of human love and will with God, which does not lose the subject-object relationship. Such mysticism was contemplative, personal, and practical: action on the plain followed retreat to the mountain.[39]

This kind of Christian mysticism can have many stages. These stages vary depending on the individual person. There are, however, three stages common to all orthodox Christian mystics: "awareness and confession before God, life lived totally under God, and a most personal experience of God."[40] Although a person may not achieve the last stage often, "it is the most intimate of divine relationships and therefore is usually not expressed in words."[41] A good example of a Christian mystic is Bernard of Clairvaux, who lived from A.D. 1090 to A.D. 1153 and was strongly orthodox in his belief and practice.

Christian mysticism avoids the excesses of pantheistic mystics
like Joseph Campbell because it allows for and can even encourage
rational statements about God and about mankind's relationship to
its Creator. It also retains a high view of God as the Divine Creator
who exists apart from the material world and who is the source of
all good things. As Christians, we can identify with Christ and feel
unity with the Creator. That doesn't mean that we become infinitely
divine, transcendent beings in some way, nor does it mean that we
can become wholly and permanently divine after we die. It means
that, when we establish a proper relationship with God, God will
share some small portion of his divine attributes with us, without
having us lose the best parts of our personal, but finite or limited,
identities. Even the apostle Peter writes in 2 Peter 1:3–4 that we
can "participate in the divine nature" through the power of Jesus
Christ's "glory and goodness."

We don't have to become God in order to be *like* God. We don't
have to become God in order to find true bliss.

Summary and Conclusion

Contrary to what interviewer Bill Moyers said, Campbell did have
a theology and an ideology. His theology and ideology reflected a
worldview of mystical pantheism. That worldview was self-contradictory, unduly biased, factually wrong, and too vague and ambiguous. It also contained a self-defeating mysticism that fails to match
reality, a contradictory viewpoint of man and his environment, a wrong
view of logic, and an incoherent view of God. Compared to Campbell's
mystical pantheism, the Christian concept of God is far superior. It
also allows for a moderate, but thoroughly monotheistic mysticism.
Such a Christian mysticism has a high view of logic. It corresponds to
the way human beings truly perceive reality because it retains sub-
ject-object dualism, something Campbell's worldview denies.

The next three chapters show the moral consequences of Campbell's pantheism. They also examine his tendency to wrongly insert
pantheistic concepts into nonpantheistic religions, including Christianity. Finally, they discuss his veiled attacks on western civilization and its Christian heritage rooted in the worldview of the Bible.

5

Myth Interpretations

oseph Campbell's pantheistic worldview not only affects his view of myth and religion, it also has other ramifications. It influences his statements about morality. It guides his negative attitude toward western civilization and its biblical roots. It causes him to find mystic and pantheistic ideas where there are none. In order to truly understand the problems in Campbell's work, we need to recognize and evaluate these assertions.

Campbell Sees Mystical Pantheism Everywhere

According to Campbell, all myth and religion, even the story of Jesus Christ, eventually leads to "the ultimate, transcendent yet immanent ground of all being . . ."[1] and "to the mystery dimension of being . . . [which is] at one with itself."[2] To him, this is the "deeper meaning" behind all myths and religions. We must get away from all local, ethnic expressions of myth and religion, declares Campbell. Instead, we must focus on this deeper meaning, which is, of course, pantheistic and mystical. It is pantheistic because one of its main messages is the idea that man is "an organ of the living cosmos."[3] It is mystical because it teaches all of us to find enlightenment and bliss by becoming one with nature and one with the "non-dual transcendent."

This idea that all myths and religions have a deep, pantheistic meaning is one of Joseph Campbell's strongest beliefs. It is a major message in Campbell's *Power of Myth* interview with Bill Moyers. It also is a major topic in his *Flight of the Wild Gander* and his four-volume *The Masks of God.* Unfortunately, this belief is so strong that it clouds his vision of religion in general. It makes him see mysticism and pantheism where there is no mysticism and pantheism.

In Volume 1 of *The Masks of God,* Campbell compares the religious temples in ancient Sumeria (ca. 3000 B.C. in Mesopotamia) with the Greek idea of Mount Olympus (home of the gods), with the Aztec temples to the sun god, and with Hindu-Buddhist ideas of the "world mountain." He then says that all of these religions and mythologies create "the image of man's destiny as an organ of the living cosmos."[4] He also claims that this image appears to have begun in Sumeria and, through a process of cultural "diffusion" or dispersal, spread to Greece, North America, India, and the Orient. Ultimately, in all of these religious systems, "the microcosm of the individual is brought into relation to the macrocosm of the all."[5] What starts as a psychological and social need to unite the members and groups of society into some kind of ordered relationship becomes for Campbell simply another example of impersonal pantheism, the one true religion.

Campbell claims that the idea of a city state with a priesthood class "first emerged as a paradigm"[6] in Sumeria, about 3200 B.C. The idea spread to the East and the West, says Campbell, first to Egypt, around 2800 B.C., then to Greece and India, around 2600 B.C., then to the Orient around 1500 B.C., and finally to Mexico and Peru, as long ago as 1000 B.C.

By giving us this scheme, Campbell tries to show there is a link between the city state and religious temples of Sumeria and the image of Mount Olympus from Greek mythology, as well as with Hindu-Buddhist images of the "world mountain," where paradise and immortality is, and with Aztec temples of the sun. If that's all Campbell tries to show, I might not have an objection to his scheme.

Unfortunately, however, Campbell also contends that there are two main meanings to all these religious ideas and images.

First, he says these ideas and images are an attempt to bring all the parts of society "into an orderly relationship to each other." Second, he says these ideas and images suggest that the whole cosmos, or universe, has "a universal order" and is subject to "a higher, all-suffusing, all informing principle or energy." Ultimately, these ideas and images set up a system of myths and rituals "through which the microcosm of the individual is brought into relation to the macrocosm of the all." They also suggest that man is "an organ of the living cosmos."[7]

There are three problems with this fanciful construction by Campbell. First, he shows a naive, one-sided, and somewhat outdated understanding of the process of cultural diffusion, which was first extensively discussed by ethnologist Leo Frobenius (1873–1938) in the late 1800s. Second, his description of the religious ideas and images of Sumeria, Greece, Mexico, India, and Asia is superficial. Finally, his argument is logically invalid due to a categorical fallacy in his thinking.

Cultural Diffusion

Back in 1927, in a book of short essays titled *Culture: The Diffusion Controversy,* Bronislaw Malinowski and Alexander Goldenweiser, two well-known anthropologists-ethnologists, repudiated "a purely mechanical view of diffusion"[8] like that of Frobenius. In their essays, both men said that although cultures often borrow ideas from other cultures, they also invent their own. In addition, they often transform and adapt the ideas they do borrow.

"Diffusion and invention are always mixed and always inseparable," said Malinowski.[9] Thus, it is not always easy to tell the difference between what was borrowed, what was invented, and what was changed. In fact, sometimes we have to just give up and admit our ignorance about the matter, said Goldenweiser.

Malinowski and especially Goldenweiser changed the way most anthropologists think about the idea of cultural diffusion, but there are still some scholars who apparently hold on to the discredited "pure" diffusion theory developed by Frobenius. In his book *The*

Flight of the Wild Gander, Campbell cites some of these scholars.[10] In that book, Campbell also mentions Malinowski in a derogatory manner and criticizes the "myopia" of the "culturalist movement"[11] in anthropology, in which Malinowski played a role. Campbell complains that the scholars in this movement fail to consider the psychological character of human societies, and he argues for "a science of myth" based on the theories of psychologists Sigmund Freud and Carl Jung.[12]

Although I am by no means an expert on the cultural diffusion controversy, it seems to me that Malinowski and Goldenweiser didn't deny that diffusion takes place, they merely tried to refine the theory. So it's not a question of pitting Malinowski and Goldenweiser against Frobenius. It's a question of examining the theory of diffusion fully and looking at the factual evidence to see if we can support the theory, deny it, or change it. The problem is that Campbell's discussion of the controversy is so brief and one-sided that, unless you are an expert, it's impossible to judge the validity of his position. It certainly seems, however, that Campbell's idea of diffusion is shallow when compared to that of Malinowski and Goldenweiser.

Like Malinowski and Goldenweiser, Melville Jacobs and Bernhard J. Stern in their classic text *General Anthropology* state that cultures often change the things they borrow from other places. They urge caution in using the process of diffusion and criticize certain diffusion scholars. Unlike Malinowski and Goldenweiser, however, Jacobs and Stern say that diffusion has been more influential in the history of human society than the process of invention. They also take Malinowski's own school of cultural anthropology, called "functionalism," to task for ignoring the historical aspect that the cultural diffusion scholars and other anthropologists bring to light. By ignoring this aspect, the functionalists fail to touch upon "the dynamic processes of change."[13] They also fail to distinguish between essential features and nonessential features of a cultural system. Thus, the idea of cultural and historical diffusion still plays an important role in cultural anthropology, although it should no longer be viewed in the naive manner of the anthropologists who were active in the late 1800s and early 1900s.

What then should we make of Campbell's favorable, almost wor-shipful, attitude toward these early anthropologists and their fol-lowers? Well, at the very least, Campbell is simplistic and inaccu-rate because he presents a superficial, outdated view of cultural diffusion. At the most, however, Campbell is deceptive or ignorant because he distorts certain facts and ignores others. But even Camp-bell's alternative theory to the "culturalist" and functional schools— a science of myth based on psychology—has problems with it.

Anthropologist E. E. Evans-Pritchard criticizes both psycholog-ical theories of primitive religion like Freud's and sociological the-ories like Émile Durkheim's, whom Campbell lumps together with Malinowski in his attack on the "culturalist movement."

In discussing the "emotionalist interpretations of religion" like Freud's, Evans-Pritchard says, "It seems to me that very little evi-dence is brought forth in support of these conclusions, not even by those who not only offer them but have also had the opportunity of testing them in field research."[14] For example, some scholars talk about feelings of awe when discussing religious behavior in primi-tive societies or ancient cultures, but other scholars talk about expe-riencing a special thrill. "Either way," says Evans-Pritchard, "how does one know whether a person experiences awe or thrill or what-ever it may be? How does one recognize it, and how does one mea-sure it?"[15] Some of the scholars themselves admit that similar emo-tions can be felt in other, nonreligious kinds of behavior, adds Evans-Pritchard. How can we even determine what emotions a par-ticular person is feeling when he engages in a religious behavior anyway?

In addition, says Evans-Pritchard, many religious rituals are "rou-tine," so it's not quite accurate to say that religious rituals are designed to relieve emotional tension. "The expression of emotion may be obligatory, an essential part of the rite itself," he adds. Fur-thermore, it is more likely that the rituals produce the emotions rather than the emotions produce the rituals. Finally, Evans-Pritchard notes that religious rituals and beliefs are part of the soci-ety into which people are born. They are thus not completely iden-tical to the "individual subjective states" of the children and neurotics Freud claimed to have found. He concludes, therefore, that psychological theories do not fully explain religious behavior, its origin, function, and structure.[16]

In the same manner, Evans-Pritchard attacks sociological theories of primitive religion like Émile Durkheim's and A. R. Radcliffe-Brown's. He criticizes them for their lack of evidence and their failure to fully explain the role, function, and character of religion in society.

At the end of his book, Evans-Pritchard argues in favor of anthropological studies that "account for religious facts in terms of the totality of the culture and society in which they are found. . . . They must be seen as a relation of parts to one another within a coherent system, each part making sense only in relation to the others, and the system itself making sense only in relation to other institutional systems, as part of a wider set of relations."[17] As one example of this kind of anthropology of religion, he cites Victor W. Turner's study of the Ndembu people in Africa.

Evans-Pritchard's suggestion seems logical to me. By accepting a simplistic and problematic method of cultural diffusion and by focusing only on the psychology of myth and religion—to the exclusion of broader perspectives—Campbell creates inaccurate, superficial descriptions and interpretations of ancient religions. This problem is particularly evident in Campbell's discussion of ancient temples and sacred mountains in *The Masks of God.*

Ancient Religious Connections

In this important passage, Campbell not only makes a historical link between the religious cultures of Sumeria, ancient Greece, India, Asia, and ancient Mexico, he also gives an interpretation of these cultures that is not merely sociological but also pantheistic. I have no objection to the first half of his interpretation, the idea that all these religious ideas and images are an attempt to bring all the parts of society "into an orderly relationship to each other." However, I do object to the pantheistic part of Campbell's interpretation.

To begin with, Campbell ignores the fact that both Sumeria and Greece had highly developed *polytheistic* religions, not pantheistic ones. The people in these ancient civilizations believed in more than one god, even if they sometimes worshiped only one of the gods. Campbell also ignores the polytheistic elements in Aztec society, and even in Hinduism and Buddhism, which both add a vast array of gods, demons, and demi-gods to their underlying pantheism and mysticism. These facts have been well documented by many scholars.[18]

Campbell is correct to believe there is a connection between Sumeria and ancient Greece that has its roots in the Mycenaean period of the Greek peninsula, from 1400 to 1200 B.C., but he makes too much out of it. Historian Moses I. Finley in *The Ancient Greeks* states that the ancient Mycenaean culture was indeed related to the Mesopotamia descendants of the Sumerian society, but he also says that ancient Greece still had economic, political, and cultural differences with the Mycenaean civilization.

"There were continuities, of course," says Finley, "but they were fragments worked into a new, unrecognizable context."[19] Although Greek myths derive from this cultural and historical background, adds Finley, they retain very little of the true Mycenaean period, "and even that is usually distorted."[20]

Finley's comments here are very strong. They call into question Campbell's thesis about these ancient civilizations.

Even if we accept Campbell's idea about a connection between these different cultures, however, we don't have to accept his presupposition that all the main religions in these cultures are fundamentally pantheistic. For example, the belief that man is a part of some universal order in the universe does not necessarily lead to a belief in pantheism. Christians believe that man is a part of God's divine order of creation, but this doesn't mean creation is itself inherently divine, or that man can become one with the "all-suffusing, all informing principle or energy" of the divine order. Neither does it mean that man can become one with God or one with nature. The same thing is true for the polytheistic societies Campbell cites.

Although he doesn't emphasize cultural diffusion as Campbell does, historian of religion Mircea Eliade, in *The Sacred and the Profane: The Nature of Religion,* also discusses religious ideas and images of temples, mountains, and cities occurring around the world. Temples are sacred places, asserts Eliade, where people can communicate with heaven, God, gods, or even divine principles. Mountains can also be sacred places, says Eliade. They "express the connection between heaven and earth." Therefore, they are "believed to be at the center of the world." To be near this center is to be at a place that is close to heaven. "Temples are replicas of the cosmic mountain," adds Eliade, "and hence constitute the preeminent 'link' between earth and heaven." Eliade also observes that founding a city is like creating a sacred place with a sacred set of laws, rules, and guidelines for human relationships.[21]

All of these ideas and images express "the desire to live in a pure and holy cosmos, as it was in the beginning, when it came fresh from the Creator's hands," declares Eliade. "Religious man can live only in a sacred world, because it is only in such a world that he participates in being, that he has a real existence."[22]

Here we can see the essential difference between Eliade's interpretation and that of Campbell. Unlike Campbell, Eliade doesn't try to make the cosmos into a god of some kind. He only uses words like *pure, holy,* or *sacred;* he doesn't say that the whole cosmos and everything in it become part of "a higher, all-suffusing, all-informing principle or energy." Thus, Eliade avoids saying that every religion is a pantheistic religion where everything is God.

Campbell's Logical Fallacy

Finally, there is a logical fallacy in Campbell's interpretation. Campbell commits a "categorical fallacy." In other words, he switches categories in the middle of his argument, without alerting his readers. How does he do this?

First, Campbell begins his argument in *The Masks of God* by talking about ancient history and society and by making a sociological interpretation of certain social facts he finds in ancient civilizations. For instance, he first talks about how religious ideas are used to bring all the parts of society "into an orderly relationship to each other." Then, however, Campbell adds a second, metaphysical interpretation to the sociological interpretation, as if the second interpretation simply flows from the first. He says that ultimately "the microcosm of the individual is brought into relation to the macrocosm of the all." Although he has given us *some* evidence (the similarities between certain religious images and certain social structures) for the first interpretation, he has given us no evidence whatsoever for the second interpretation. It comes absolutely right out of the blue, with no real facts to support it!

This whole line of argument about ancient sacred temples and sacred mountains from Campbell is bad anthropology, bad psychology, bad history, and fuzzy-minded thinking. It can easily be rejected as false.

Pantheism in the Bible and in Early Christianity?

Campbell often takes religious stories and forces them to fit his pantheistic worldview. He even does this with the Bible.

For example, in *The Power of Myth* he compares the serpent in the Garden of Eden narrative of Genesis to "immortal energy and consciousness engaged in the field of time, constantly throwing off death and being born again."[23] This pantheistic idea recalls Campbell's other quotes about energy, consciousness, and nature. As such, it plays a big role in Campbell's description of the dying god myth in the first three volumes of *The Masks of God.* (Chapter 10 refutes Campbell's use of the dying god myth to attack the historical reliability of the Bible.)

"Immortal energy and consciousness" may be what serpents represent in Campbell's theology, but the actual biblical text makes no such comparison. According to Hebrew scholar Walter C. Kaiser, "Satan's form and shape are no more implied by his appellation serpent than by the name dragon" in Revelation 12:9.[24] Thus, the word *serpent* in Genesis 3:1 is a metaphor God uses, speaking through Moses, to show the miserable condition into which Satan fell when he tempted Adam and Eve. It also demonstrates the ultimate defeat he will suffer by the "seed of the woman" described in Genesis 3:15, says Kaiser.

In *Myths to Live By,* Campbell uses another metaphor to twist the meaning of the Bible. In that book, he compares human consciousness to the light in a lightbulb. He contends that a Buddhist is someone who identifies with consciousness and who realizes "that his value derives from his power to radiate consciousness—as the value of a lightbulb derives from its power to radiate light. What is important about a lightbulb is not the filament or the glass but the light which these bulbs are to render; and what is important about each of us is not the body and its nerves but the consciousness that shines through them. And when one lives for that, instead of for protection of the bulb, one is in Buddha consciousness."[25]

Campbell's lightbulb example is illogical. The light that shines through a lightbulb is not identical to the consciousness that shines through human beings. To be conscious is to be self-aware. The light in a group of lightbulbs has no self-awareness. It falls into the category of "non-thinking things," whereas human consciousness falls into the category of "thinking things." Thus, Campbell's argument rests on a categorical fallacy. Campbell makes a false comparison between two completely separate categories.

Immediately after his lightbulb illustration, Campbell asserts the Bible teaches that God and man are not identical but that Buddhism and other Eastern religions teach that they are. This is true enough, but then Campbell claims that Jesus Christ was crucified for blasphemy because he said in John 10:30 that "I and the Father are one." Here, Campbell implies that Jesus was really a pantheist who taught ideas similar to the teachings of Buddha and other Eastern mystics.

Campbell's use of John 10:30 is totally irresponsible. This verse does not teach that Jesus advocated pantheism, or that men can become God. To see what the verse is really teaching, let's look at its immediate context.

The passage begins with John 10:22, which tells us the time of year and the place: winter, the Jewish holiday Hanukkah, in Jerusalem. Jesus is walking in the temple area, and the Jews there gather around him. They ask, "How long will you keep us in suspense? If you are the Christ [the Messiah], tell us plainly."

"I did tell you, but you did not believe," Jesus replies. "The miracles I do in my Father's name speak for me, but you do not believe because you are not my sheep. My sheep listen to my voice; I know them, and they follow me. I give them eternal life, and they shall never perish; no one can snatch them out of my hand. My Father, who has given them to me, is greater than all; no one can snatch them out of my Father's hand. I and the Father are one" (John 10:24–30).

At these words, the Jews accuse Jesus of blasphemy "because you, a mere man, claim to be God" (v. 33), but Jesus recalls Psalm 82:6–7, where God addresses some evil rulers in Israel and says, "I said, 'You are "gods"; you are all sons of the Most High.' But you will die like mere men; you will fall like every other ruler."

"If he called them 'gods,'" says Jesus, "to whom the word of God came—and the Scripture cannot be broken—what about the one whom the Father set apart as his very own and sent into the world? Why then do you accuse me of blasphemy because I said, 'I am God's Son'? Do not believe me unless I do what my Father does. But if I do it, even though you do not believe me, believe the miracles, that you may know and understand that the Father is in me, and I in the Father" (John 10:34–38).

These verses recall the first chapter of John where the author writes, "the Word was God," "through him all things were made," and "the Word became flesh and made his dwelling among us. We have seen his glory, the glory of the One and Only, who came from the Father, full of grace and truth" (John 1:1, 3, 14). These verses lend biblical support to the Christian doctrine of the Trinity. This doctrine says that within the essence of the one and only true God, the Creator of everything, there are three distinct persons.

Before Jesus declares "I and the Father are one," he claims that he gives his believers "eternal life" and that no one can "snatch" his believers out of his hand. He also states that the Father is greater than anything and no one can "snatch" them out of the Father's hand. It is at this point that Jesus says, "I and the Father are one." The implication is that he and the Father are one in power and, if the Father is greater and more powerful than anything, then Jesus also is greater and more powerful than anything. Thus, both the first person of the divine Trinity and the second person of the divine Trinity are all-powerful. In other words, they have all the power it is possible to have because they are the ultimate source of all power. Jesus repeats the same idea later in the passage when he asks the Jews in the temple to believe the miracles that he does because "the Father is in me, and I in the Father" (John 10:38). Jesus can perform miracles because he shares with the Father the divine power of the Triune God.[26]

This passage does not teach that men can become God, as Campbell implies. It teaches that Jesus Christ is God and, as such, he shares the essence of the one true God with the first person of the Trinity called the Father.

In *The Power of Myth,* Campbell also makes false comparisons between Christianity and other religious ideas. As in the examples cited above, he tries to put a pantheistic spin on everything.

The errors occur on pages 39 and 57 where he claims that all myths tell people to identify with the "Buddha consciousness" or "Christ consciousness" inside them. "We are all manifestations of Buddha consciousness, or Christ consciousness, only we don't know it," says Campbell, and we all must "wake up to the Christ or Buddha consciousness within us."[27]

To support his theory, Campbell again uses the quote from Jesus, "I and the Father are one." He also uses a quote from the Gospel of Thomas: "He who drinks from my mouth will become as I am, and I shall be he."

The Gospel of Thomas is a non-Christian text written between A.D. 100 and 140 that contains some of the accepted sayings attributed to Jesus by New Testament documents but that also contains other quotes not in the New Testament. These other quotes tend to be pantheistic in nature or expressed in terms of gnosticism. Gnosticism was a philosophical movement in the second century A.D. that claimed special knowledge of spiritual mysteries. Campbell claims that gnostic texts like the Gospel of Thomas were written "well within the period of the shaping of the [New Testament] Gospels, all four of which continued to be touched and retouched until the canon finally was fixed in Rome, toward the opening, only, of the fourth century A.D."[28]

This claim is not true, and I will refute it in chapter 11. Even if it were true, however, it would not prove that the gnostic view of Jesus Christ's teachings is more accurate than the orthodox Christian view, or that the gnostic view of Christ is similar to the New Testament view. It doesn't seem right, therefore, for Campbell to compare John 10:30 with some pantheistic quote from the Gospel of Thomas, a gnostic text with no historical connection to St. John's Gospel.

It also doesn't seem right the way Campbell mistreats Acts 1:9–10, which describes how Jesus rose bodily into the sky, a cloud hiding him from the apostles. Two angels tell the apostles, "This same Jesus, who has been taken from you into heaven, will come back in the same way you have seen him go into heaven" (v. 11).

"We know," Campbell proclaims, "that Jesus could not have ascended to heaven because there is no physical heaven anywhere in the universe. Even ascending at the speed of light, Jesus would still be in the galaxy. Astronomy and physics have simply eliminated that as a literal, physical possibility. But if you read 'Jesus ascended to heaven' in terms of its metaphoric connotation, you see that he has gone inward—not into outer space but into inward space, to the place from which all being comes, into the consciousness that is the source of all things, the kingdom of heaven within."[29]

This is a pantheistic explanation of this passage from the New Testament. It is also a dreadfully ignorant one.

The first chapter of Acts does not imply that Jesus ascended into outer space or that heaven is a physical place located somewhere in the galaxy. The passage says that Jesus "was taken up before their very eyes, and a cloud hid him from their sight." According to Dr. Richard N. Longenecker, professor of New Testament, "The cloud is undoubtedly meant to symbolize the shekinah, the visible manifestation of the divine presence and glory. Such a cloud hovered above the tabernacle" with Moses and the Jews in the wilderness (Exod. 40:34).[30] Jesus disappeared into this cloud and, from there, he went into heaven, exactly as the angels told the waiting apostles.

In Christian theology, heaven is not a physical place that exists somewhere in the material universe. Heaven is a special spiritual dimension from which God rules the universe. Jesus Christ went into this special dimension, where he directs the missionary work of his church. This missionary work is designed to spread the kingdom of God throughout the world until Jesus Christ returns.

Campbell's explanation of this passage is a silly, inaccurate interpretation. His comment about astronomy and physics is completely out of place.

Elsewhere in *The Power of Myth,* Campbell compares Jesus Christ's death and resurrection with pagan stories about a dying and resurrected vegetation god and with pagan stories about an earth goddess who gives birth to a savior god who supposedly dies and is resurrected. In chapter 10 I debunk such comparisons. For now, I simply wish to relate the most important points that Campbell makes about this comparison. Notice how Campbell casts everything in a pantheistic, mystical light.

In looking at many pagan myths and religious rituals, says Campbell, "I begin to see this incredible pattern of death giving rise to birth, and birth giving rise to death. Every generation has to die in order that the next generation can come."[31]

One of the vivid examples he uses is a New Guinea ritual where six teenage boys and one teenage girl are allowed to indulge in a sexual orgy. When the last boy is with the girl, a group of logs drops on the couple and they are killed. Then their bodies are roasted and eaten by the whole group.

According to Campbell, this ghastly ritual "is the repetition of the original act of the killing of a god followed by the coming of food from the dead savior." Incredibly, Campbell then compares this ritual to the Christian ritual of eating a piece of unleavened bread and drinking some red wine in order to symbolize or re-create the death of Jesus Christ's body and the shedding of his blood for the sins of the world. As Campbell puts it, "Christ is crucified, and from his body the food of the spirit comes." Jesus Christ "is the fruit of eternal life," adds Campbell, and to eat Jesus is to return to the original paradise of the Garden of Eden, "where you know that I and the Father are one."[32]

Ultimately, says Campbell, such rituals help us to get in touch with the divine pattern of nature where life and new birth spring from death: "You have to balance between death and life—they are two aspects of the same thing, which is being, becoming."[33]

A similar thing happens in many pagan myths about the earth goddess, Campbell claims. These myths teach compassion for all living things, he says, because all living things are divine. Campbell compares these pagan goddesses to Mary, the mother of Jesus: "The Catholic tradition is a coming together of the patriarchal, monotheistic idea of the Messiah as one who is to unite the spiritual and temporal powers, and the Hellenistic classical idea of the Savior as the dead and resurrected son of the Great Goddess by a virgin birth."[34]

What is the message in all these images, according to Campbell? That we must give "death to the animal nature and birth to the spiritual"[35] and that "the Goddess is within as well as without. Your body is of her body."[36]

The implication to all this, of course, is that within the story of Jesus Christ, there is a hidden type of pantheism which has been repressed by the Christian community. The only evidence Campbell cites for this hidden pantheism in the New Testament, however, is John 10:30, and, as we saw earlier, Campbell has taken this verse completely out of its original context and twisted it to fit his own worldview. This is more than just inaccurate and logically invalid. It is also dishonest.

Summary and Conclusion

There is little or no evidence to prove Campbell's theory of widespread pantheism and cultural diffusion in the history of religion. Campbell's interpretations of the history and anthropology of religion are one-sided. Other scholars with better credentials and more credibility have developed more reasonable interpretations using more reliable factual evidence.

As for Campbell's ability as an interpreter of the Bible, he displays little or no knowledge of the original Hebrew and Greek text and he lacks any coherent, consistent, and intelligent method of interpretation. There have been hundreds of more competent and more orthodox scholars throughout history.

Campbell's arguments in these areas are illogical at several key points. He fails to support his arguments with the facts. Instead of making his theories fit the facts, he forces the facts to fit his theories.

6

Campbell's Morality

ltimately, the problem with Campbell's worldview stems from the values he promotes. There is good evidence to show that his values are unduly biased, illogical, and based on bad arguments. They have negative consequences and do not fit the facts.

A Dramatic Interlude

One day, while he was traveling to Jerusalem with his disciples, Jesus was challenged by an expert in the Law of Moses from the Old Testament.

"Teacher," the expert asked, "what must I do to inherit eternal life?"

"What is written in the Law?" Jesus replied. "How do you read it?"

The expert answered, "'Love the Lord your God with all your heart and with all your soul and with all your strength and with all your mind'; and, 'Love your neighbor as yourself.'"

"You have answered correctly," said Jesus. "Do this and you will live."

The man was not completely satisfied with this answer. He wanted to free himself from his own guilt, so he asked Jesus, "And who is my neighbor?"

In reply Jesus told him the following story:

"A man was going down from Jerusalem to Jericho, when he fell into the hands of robbers. They stripped him of his clothes, beat him and went away, leaving him half dead. A priest happened to be going down the same road, and when he saw the man, he passed by on the other side. So too, a Levite, when he came to the place and saw him, passed by on the other side. But a Samaritan, as he traveled, came where the man was; and when he saw him, he took pity on him. He went to him and bandaged his wounds, pouring on oil and wine. Then he put the man on his own donkey, took him to an inn and took care of him. The next day he took out two silver coins and gave them to the innkeeper. 'Look after him,' he said, 'and when I return, I will reimburse you for any extra expense you may have.'

"Which of these three do you think was a neighbor to the man who fell into the hands of robbers?" Jesus asked.

The expert in the Law replied, "The one who had mercy on him."

"Go and do likewise," Jesus told him.[1]

Jesus' story gives us an important lesson in moral values. As such, it reflects the deep moral teachings found in the Bible. It also presents a striking contrast to the facile statements about morality in Bill Moyers's TV interview with Joseph Campbell.

This chapter looks at Campbell's morality, especially his ideas about loving one's neighbor, making judgments about others, and putting the sanctity of human life over that of plants and animals. It then examines his moral relativism, especially as it relates to the culture war of the last thirty years over the use of western values and logic.

Loving One's Neighbor

In the last chapter, we saw how Campbell distorts the words of Jesus Christ in John 10:30. We noted how Campbell gives a pantheistic interpretation of this verse, which in fact teaches that Jesus

Christ shares the divine essence of the one true God with the first person of the Trinity, the Father.

Even worse than this, however, is the way in which Campbell uses pantheism to distort the ethical and moral teachings in the Bible. At one point in *The Power of Myth*, Campbell tells interviewer Bill Moyers, "Ethics is a way of teaching you how to live as though you were one with the other."

"Love thy neighbor as thyself because thy neighbor is thyself," Moyers interjects and Campbell agrees.[2]

Instead of simply saying "love your neighbor as yourself," which is what the Old and the New Testaments proclaim,[3] Campbell's system of morality states that you must "love thy neighbor as thyself *because thy neighbor is thyself.*" We are all divine, says Campbell, and only when we recognize this can we truly begin to love our neighbors. Once again, this time with a little help from Bill Moyers, Campbell takes a Bible verse and twists it to fit his own worldview—mystical pantheism.

Campbell's worldview contradicts the book from which Moyers misquotes. The God who says, "Love your neighbor as yourself" in the Old Testament is the same God who says, "You shall have no other gods before me" (Exod. 20:3). The Jesus Christ who says, "Love your neighbor as yourself," is the same Jesus Christ who quotes from Deuteronomy 6:4, "Hear, O Israel, the Lord our God, the Lord is one" (Mark 12:29).

But the Joseph Campbell who agrees with Bill Moyers that you should "love thy neighbor as thyself because thy neighbor is thyself" is the same Joseph Campbell who believes in radical moral relativism. He is the same Joseph Campbell who declares, "What was proper fifty years ago is not proper today. The virtues of the past are the vices of today. And many of . . . the vices of the past are the necessities of today. . . . The old-time religion belongs to another age, another people, another set of human values, another universe."[4] He is also the same Joseph Campbell who says, "That old man up there has been blown away. You've got to find the Force inside you."[5]

These quotes from *The Power of Myth* show how vague and erratic Campbell's system of morality is. Despite the reference to loving your neighbor, it's hard to say specifically what moral demands his system makes, if any.

Campbell's moral system is inconsistent. Although Campbell sometimes uses the words of Jesus Christ and the Bible to make a moral point, he spends a lot more of his time attacking the world-view of the Bible shared by all Christian believers. This immediately prompts me to ask at least two questions: At what point is Christian morality a good thing and at what point is it a bad thing? Do we simply obey those biblical laws we like, but ignore the ones we don't like? I don't believe we have that right, although Campbell and Moyers may call me "intolerant" and "dogmatic." Campbell is being contradictory when he admires the biblical notion of loving your neighbor but then says, "The old-time religion belongs to another age, another people, another set of human values, another universe."

At one point in *The Power of Myth,* Campbell claims that "the main teaching" of Jesus is "love your enemies" (Matt. 5:44). But how do we love our enemies? "I'll tell you how to do that," says Campbell. "Do not pluck the mote from your enemy's eyes, but pluck the beam from your own."[6]

This quote from Campbell implies that *any* moral judgments we make are wrong. Campbell's statement is a paraphrase of a comment by Jesus in Matthew 7:1–5. Here is the full saying by Jesus:

> Do not judge, or you too will be judged. For in the same way you judge others, you will be judged, and with the measure you use, it will be measured to you.
>
> Why do you look at the speck of sawdust in your brother's eye and pay no attention to the plank in your own eye? How can you say to your brother, "Let me take the speck out of your eye," when all the time there is a plank in your own eye? You hypocrite, first take the plank out of your own eye, and then you will see clearly to remove the speck from your brother's eye.

Campbell's statements concerning Matthew 5:44 and 7:1–5 are incorrect for several reasons. To begin with, the "main teaching" of Jesus is not "love your enemies." Expressing love toward one's enemies is just one of many moral demands Jesus Christ makes of his followers. The main teaching of Jesus is that all people are sinners; therefore, all people need to repent of their sins and believe in Jesus as their personal, divine Savior.

"The kingdom of God is near," says Jesus in Mark 1:15. "Repent and believe the good news!"

What is the good news or gospel? The apostle Paul defines the gospel in 1 Corinthians 15:1–8:

> Now, brothers, I want to remind you of the gospel I preached to you, which you received and on which you have taken your stand. By this gospel you are saved, if you hold firmly to the word I preached to you. Otherwise, you have believed in vain. For what I received I passed on to you as of first importance: that Christ died for our sins according to the Scriptures, that he was buried, that he was raised on the third day according to the Scriptures, and that he appeared to Peter, and then to the Twelve. After that, he appeared to more than five hundred of the brothers at the same time, most of whom are still living, though some have fallen asleep. Then he appeared to James, then to all the apostles, and last of all he appeared to me also, as to one abnormally born.

To believe the gospel is to believe that Jesus Christ died for your sins, that he was buried, but that he was physically resurrected on the third day and subsequently appeared in person to many people, most of whom were still living when Paul wrote this letter, probably around A.D. 55.

Before he died, Jesus claimed to be the unique Son of God who fully shares the divine nature of God with two other unique persons, whom he called the Father and the Holy Spirit. He claimed to be sent by the Father "to give his life as a ransom for many" (Matt. 20:28). As he told Nicodemus, a member of the Jewish ruling council in Jerusalem, everyone who believes in him, Jesus, may have eternal life (John 3:14). When some people asked him one time in John 6:28, "What must we do to do the works God requires?" Jesus replied, "The work of God is this: to believe in the one he has sent." Later on, Jesus said to some religious leaders in Jerusalem, "If you do not believe that I am the one I claim to be, you will indeed die in your sins" (John 8:24). Finally, after his resurrection, Jesus told his apostles, "All authority in heaven and on earth has been given to me. Therefore go and make disciples of all nations, baptizing them in the name of the Father and of the Son and of the Holy Spirit, and teaching them to obey everything I have commanded you" (Matt. 28:19).

Even Joseph Campbell, who dismisses the authenticity of Scripture at other points in his work, admits in *The Power of Myth* that "the sayings of Jesus [recorded in the Bible] are probably pretty close to the originals."[7] Why, then, doesn't he also quote these verses I have just cited? Perhaps he doesn't quote them because they contradict his own personal worldview, mystical pantheism. I believe that this is indeed the case.

By connecting Matthew 5:44 with Matthew 7:1–5, Campbell does a grave injustice to the biblical text. When Jesus says "Love your enemies and pray for those who persecute you" in Matthew 5:44, he does not say that we should love the evil things our enemies may do or even overlook them. Christians in fact have a *moral duty* to expose the evil deeds people do. We also must repent of the evil deeds we ourselves do. We are not to subjectively judge evil as do Bill Moyers and Joseph Campbell. We must judge evil according to the *objective moral standards* God has revealed in the Bible.

Christians also have an obligation to give all people God's solution to the problem of evil and the bondage of sin—Jesus Christ's gospel message of salvation. The best way to show love for our enemies is to kindly point out to them their sin, to pray for their repentance, and to make sure that they hear and know the gospel of Jesus Christ.

When Jesus says in Matthew 7:1–5, "Do not judge, or you too will be judged," he does not mean that we should *never* make moral judgments. He is telling us to be careful how we judge other people. He is telling us to judge ourselves with the same kind of judgment we apply to others. This can be proved if you look at the last verse, "First take the plank out of your own eye, and *then you will see clearly to remove the speck from your brother's eye.*" In other words, we should not judge other people until we judge ourselves, and we should not judge other people more harshly than we judge ourselves.

"Jews and Gentiles alike are all under sin," says the apostle Paul in Romans 3:9–10. "As it is written: 'There is no one righteous, not even one.'" Paul's quotation of Scripture here is a paraphrase of Psalm 53:3, "There is no one who does good, not even one," and

Ecclesiastes 7:20, "There is not a righteous man on earth who does what is right and never sins."

If this is truly the case, then Jesus Christ's word of caution about how we judge people becomes even more clear. We must be careful how we make moral judgments of other people because we too are morally guilty of sin.

Although Campbell apparently likes the idea of "love your neighbor as yourself," he gives his readers little or no guidelines on how to put such a moral law into action. Jesus illustrates the command of "love your neighbor" with the story of the Good Samaritan, which opened this chapter. The last exchange of dialogue between Jesus and the expert in the Law of Moses gives us a good clue for interpreting the story: We show love for our neighbor whenever we show mercy to the suffering, needy people that we meet on the road of life.

God's demand for love and mercy does not contradict his demand for justice against sin, cruelty, and evil. The New Testament writers praise love, joy, peace, kindness, mercy, patience, faithfulness, and self-control, but they also condemn murder, adultery, evil thoughts, sexual immorality, stealing, malice, pride, hypocrisy, outbursts of uncontrollable anger, blasphemy, envy, idolatry, lust, sorcery, drunkenness, selfishness, and heresy. God requires us to be loving and merciful, but he also requires us to make a stand against evil, including the evil that lurks within our own hearts.

Joseph Campbell's moral system doesn't quite jell. It's a quivering mass of simplistic statements, trite slogans, and emotional arguments. He tries to borrow a few things from Christian morality, but he perverts that morality in order to serve his own dehumanized worldview. If you are going to borrow the moral command "love your neighbor as yourself" from the Bible, why not borrow other biblical injunctions as well? If you are going to accept Jesus Christ's law of love and forgiveness, then why not accept his salvation message of redemption and physical resurrection?

God Bless the Children, Not the Beasts

One of the most foolish and damaging ideas in Campbell's theology is his comparison of human life with animal life and plant life.

In his theology, animals and plants are conscious in some way and are part of a divine planet. Campbell's view of morality fails to make a distinction between the value of human life and that of animal and plant life. It leads to a pantheistic system of morality where sea turtle eggs and trees are as valuable as the lives of individual human beings. In Campbell's system of morality, saving the spotted owl or helping a beached whale are as important or even more important than saving an unborn child from abortion.

Campbell's pantheism causes him to personify nature, and even the earth itself, making it a divine, conscious organism from which everything, including man, evolves. At the same time, Campbell's pantheism causes him to deify mankind and make people divine.

These two notions could lead to some strange dilemmas. If I am god and so is that tree over there, why should I be allowed to cut down the tree to build my house? There are lots of hungry people in this world. Maybe they would prefer to murder me and use my body for food but keep the tree alive so they can admire its beauty down through the years.

"We are the fruits of an intelligent earth," says Campbell.[8] To him, paradise exists in the here-and-now, and mankind already lives in a wonderful, magnificent garden called Earth. The key to enjoying the bliss in this world garden is to become one with the god within you and the god within everything and everyone around you.

This "ecology myth" fascinated Campbell. He often mentioned it as the one myth that modern society should embrace wholeheartedly. We can see echoes of this kind of pantheistic thinking in the Gaia myth that permeates some New Age, neo-pagan, and environmental activist groups, and even some scientists. This myth treats "Mother Earth" as a single organism that may even be conscious in some way and that gives energy to all life.

Douglas R. Groothuis discusses the pantheistic ideas and political agenda of these groups in his book *Unmasking the New Age*. Many of the people in these groups "blame Christianity for the present ecological crisis," he says. "They believe that a God distinct and separate from nature can do little to ensure the sacred quality of nature. Nothing less than the oneness of all things—god, man and nature—can insure a whole and balanced view of the natural environment" according to these ecology pantheists. They reject any view, therefore, that turns nature into a purely physical object without an inherent spiritual character. "In this instance," says Groothuis, "Mother Earth replaces Father God."[9]

Such pantheistic ideas have become increasingly accepted in today's society, as Joseph Campbell's popularity attests. Although political unity among New Age, neo-pagan, and environmental groups "is not so much organizational as it is ideological,"[10] many of the groups often exchange ideas and hold conventions and conferences together. One of their utopian dreams is to establish a one-world government and a new economic order that will spread peace, prosperity, and pantheism across the galaxy, much like the *Star Trek* mythos of the late Gene Roddenberry.[11]

In criticizing the worldview of these groups, it would not be right to say that everything they stand for is wrong. There is, however, a lot of evidence from political experts, economists, and scientists refuting many of their sociopolitical ideas. For instance, many of their attacks on capitalism as a viable economic system are factually incorrect and not well thought out, and their concern about world environmental disaster is overstated and needs more scientific proof. More important, though, their use of pantheism to support their agenda is intellectually unsound and morally dubious. Here is a quote from Campbell that puts this pantheistic agenda into perspective:

> We are the earth, we are the consciousness of the earth. These are the eyes of the earth. And this is the voice of the earth. . . . The only myth that is going to be worth thinking about in the immediate future is one that is talking about the planet, not the city, not these people, but the planet, and everybody on it.[12]

With this statement as a backdrop, it is perhaps easy to see why Campbell is so concerned about ecology and why he criticizes western civilization's religious, economic, and political heritage and institutions.

You don't have to be a pantheist to see value in human life, or even to see value in nature or plants and animals. Contrary to what Campbell teaches on page 32 of *The Power of Myth,* the Bible does not tell us to condemn nature, nor does it tell us to take all the joy out of our present life. The Bible teaches respect and human responsibility for God's creation. It shows us how to put the love and joy of God into a fallen world full of evil and sinful people. We show love for our neighbors, not because they are divine or because they are good people, but we show love for them because every human being has been created by God in his own *image* or *likeness.* As such, every human being is really our brother or sister and deserves our love. The best way to show our love is to preach repentance and forgiveness of sins through the gospel of Jesus Christ.

We must reclaim "Mother Earth" for Father God, the Creator of everything.

Campbell's Moral Relativism

Campbell's books contain many words of compassion for other human beings, but they also contain words of hatred for people who disagree with him, especially orthodox Christians and orthodox Jews. He bitterly attacks them for being dogmatic, but he himself is often guilty of the same thing. Campbell hates dogma, but he is always very dogmatic about his hatred.

Despite his statements about morality and his moralistic complaints about religious Jews and Christians, Campbell's pantheism eventually leads to total moral relativism. This is most clear in the following comment by Campbell: "Everything arises in mutual relation to everything else, so you can't blame anybody for anything."[13]

This is one of the most immoral statements in all of Campbell's books on myth. If you can't blame anybody for anything, then you can't blame Adolph Hitler for murdering six million Jews, you can't blame Stalin for starving millions of Soviet people to death, you can't blame Jack the Ripper for slaughtering women, and you can't even blame misguided zealots for burning innocent people at the stake in the name of Christianity.

This statement by Campbell is itself evil, because you can, *and you should,* blame the people who commit these kinds of horrible crimes. Otherwise, what right do we have to stop people from doing such evil acts? What right do we have to punish them for their crimes?

In essence, moral relativism says there are no moral absolutes—no absolute, objective moral standards for behavior. Moral relativism is false because it contradicts itself. At the same time it claims there are no moral absolutes, it makes an absolute statement about morality.

According to Christian philosopher Stuart Hackett in *The Reconstruction of the Christian Revelation Claim,* radical moral relativists usually give two arguments to support their belief. First, they note that moral beliefs differ widely from society to society, group to group, and person to person. Therefore, they argue, objective and absolute moral truth does not exist, and "the truth status of moral beliefs is wholly relative to the variable opinions and preferences" of the particular person or people who hold them.[14] Second, they claim that since moral beliefs are the result of nonrational psychological factors, it is logically impossible to determine objective, absolute moral truth.

Hackett says both these reasons are illogical and false because they confuse moral truth with moral belief. Beliefs about morality vary, Hackett agrees, but moral truths never vary. Moral beliefs and moral truths do not share "the same logical status" or "the same logical fate. . . . Beliefs can logically be false, while truths cannot logically be false."[15]

Hackett also notes that the second claim is itself, by its own standards, a subjective belief about morality. Therefore, it "destroys the objectivity of its own truth-claim."[16] If there is no objective, logical way to determine absolute moral truth, then there is no way to even determine the truth of moral relativism. Consequently, moral relativism becomes just another theory about morality with no more compelling believability than any other theory.

Campbell's belief in moral relativism is both morally flawed and logically invalid. It undermines the moral foundation of western civilization. Without any belief in absolute moral standards, our society would crumble and human life would lose its inherent moral value. In fact, there is good evidence to show that American society may already be crumbling and that human life in many people's eyes has indeed lost much of its inherent moral value.

Since the 1960s, one of the most popular phrases in American culture has been the phrase, "Do your own thing." This hedonistic type of moral relativism has led inevitably to a breakdown in ethical values across the country. The fast rising murder rate in many of our cities attests to this fact. American cities seem to be self-destructing. Human life is considered almost worthless in many areas.

Why have we reached this horrible state? Because people like Joseph Campbell and Bill Moyers have rejected almost all the moral traditions that helped make the United States one of the greatest and most benevolent nations on the face of the earth.

Historian Paul Johnson in his brilliant work *Modern Times: The World from the Twenties to the Eighties* describes the "moral anarchy"[17] resulting from the twentieth century's adoption of moral relativism. He blames both the rise of Nazi Germany and the rise of brutal communist dictatorships on the increase in moral relativism. Without absolute and objective moral standards, individual moral responsibility—the idea that each one of us is morally accountable for our own behavior—is eroded and all sense of moral duty disappears. Fascism and Marxism are secular political theories that filled the gap left when people no longer adhered to strict moral standards based on the Bible. In a few short years, both political systems murdered more people than all the so-called religious wars throughout the whole of human history. Only when these bankrupt systems were opposed and defeated by the United States, with its Protestant Christian heritage, did the evil begin to stop.

By rejecting our heritage of strict Christian morality and trying to replace it with some vague, illogical system of pantheism and radical moral relativism, Campbell not only demonstrates his intellectual failure but also his lack of moral vision and historical knowledge. Absolute, objective, and eternal moral truths or laws do indeed exist. Our society cannot function without them. For example, it is always morally wrong to torture a baby and it is always wrong to rape a woman. There is no way morally or logically to justify such horrible crimes. Even so, there will always be someone who objects to the idea of any moral absolutes.

Remember our friend Bill the skeptic in chapter 1? He has a sister Susan who is just as skeptical as Bill. Imagine that you, a believer in moral absolutes, are talking with her now.

"There are no moral absolutes," says Susan. "Just because *you* can find no way morally or logically to justify torturing a baby doesn't mean no one else can. The Nazis felt perfectly justified when they murdered Jewish babies."

"You're still confusing moral belief with moral truth," you reply. "Evil people may try justifying murder, but that doesn't make murder right and stopping murder wrong. I can believe that elephants are pink, but that belief doesn't make them pink."

"Maybe so," agrees Susan, "but when you talk about moral absolutes, you imply that there aren't any gray areas. You also imply that there will never come a time when absolute moral values conflict. For example, what would you do if a woman comes running up to you and says, 'Please hide me! There's a man trying to rape me. He's following me now.' Would you tell the rapist where you hid the woman?"

"Of course not."

"But wouldn't that be telling a lie? And wouldn't that be violating one of your precious little moral absolutes?"

"Yes and no. In the example you're giving me, there are two moral absolutes in conflict—never tell a lie and don't rape women. The law against lying is a lesser law than the one prohibiting rape. It's okay to lie to a rapist in order to protect another human being. Just because I believe in moral absolutes doesn't mean that all moral absolutes are equal in rank. And it doesn't mean there aren't gray areas. Criminal law is filled with many kinds of borderline cases.

"Absolute moral standards exist. They are undeniable. To deny that such standards exist is itself an attempt to set up an absolute moral standard—the standard of radical moral relativism."

"OK, Mr. Philosopher," Susan retorts. "You got me. Moral absolutes do exist. But the highest moral absolute is radical moral relativism."

Summary and Conclusion

In this chapter, I have shown how Campbell uses pantheism to distort the ethical and moral teachings of Jesus in the New Testament. I have also shown the moral bankruptcy of his views about ecology, which are part of his pantheistic worldview. Finally, I have proven that Campbell's radical moral relativism is logically invalid and morally unstable. People can still choose to be irrational and believe that moral relativism is true, but they cannot practice such a philosophy consistently.

7

The Traditional Values of Western Civilization

C hristian morality and the sanctity of human life over animal and plant life aren't the only things in western culture Campbell rejects. Campbell attacks western culture as a whole, using broad generalities to do it. At one point in *The Power of Myth,* for instance, Campbell declares, "The power impulse is the fundamental impulse in European history. And it got into our religious tradition."[1] Campbell never fully explains, however, what he means by "power impulse." The closest he comes to explaining it, perhaps, is his frequent criticism of the Europeans' bad treatment of the Native American peoples throughout the centuries. Although there is a lot of truth in such criticism, Campbell makes it sound as if European culture is mostly horrible and Native American cultures are all sweet and pure. He also indicts the Europeans for mistreating nature and praises the Native Americans who he says have great respect for nature. Here, Campbell blames Christianity, which he says "has really castrated nature. And the European mind, the European life, has been, as it were, emasculated."[2]

Rational Thinking

Campbell's ideas about truth, logic, reason, nature, morality, history, and western culture are by no means unusual. In fact, society is now engaged in a great culture war over these very issues. We saw some of this war taking shape in the 1992 U.S. elections. We also could see it in much of the controversy surrounding the five-hundred-year celebration of Christopher Columbus's first voyage to the New World. In 1988, some student protesters at Stanford University in Northern California could be heard chanting, "Hey, hey, ho, ho, western culture's got to go." Their protests prompted a change in the western culture curriculum to a multicultural approach.

Campbell himself rejects the value western civilization places on rational thinking. To Campbell, logic and reason cannot be used to find truth because there is no truth to be found (except, contradictorily, the "truths" he believes).

In recent years, many intellectuals have decided that the classical system of logic adopted by western civilization is no longer valid. Like Campbell, they believe that truth is relative, not absolute or transcendent. Some have even claimed that the classical system of logic is inherently racist and sexist because it rejects other kinds of thought and experience which, it is claimed, are prevalent in non-white, minority cultures, and among women.

This is exactly the position of Howard University professor Jane Flax, a feminist who rejects traditional western beliefs about truth, logic, knowledge, personality, and language. Like many of the other intellectuals critical of western culture, Flax would like to replace these beliefs with a radical feminist, multicultural socialism flavored with a heavy dose of Marxism. Apparently, to some people, there is at least one dead white European male, Karl Marx, who is more equal than others.

Flax's kind of radical left-wing political thought has permeated many of our largest and most important universities, including Harvard, Stanford, Yale, Northwestern, and many state-run colleges.

The trend toward intellectual and moral relativism has been increasing since the late 1970s, but it began at least as far back as the late 1960s, if not earlier. Recently, many people on both the right and the left have been debating how strong this trend really is and how dangerous it really is. Personally, I believe it *is* strong and dangerous, but I also believe that people on both the left *and* the right have sometimes overstated their respective cases.[3] It does not matter, however, how strong this trend is or even how dangerous it might be. What really matters is what is the truth about western civilization? What are the facts? What do they show?

The argument that the values of classical western logic are too narrow and even racist and sexist is a ridiculous one. Those of us who adopt the western method of logic do not claim that it is good simply because we ourselves believe in it. And we don't think it is true because it was developed primarily by white European males. Certainly not! We believe in this system of classical logic because 1) it has stood the test of time; 2) it is useful in helping us to separate what is true from what is false; and 3) everyone uses it whenever they think, speak, and write, even those who deny it. Remember what chapter 1 said—you have to use the Law of Noncontradiction in order to deny the Law of Noncontradiction.

To call the laws of logic sexist and racist because they were discovered and developed by white European males is itself racist and sexist. To call the laws of logic sexist and racist because some white European males used them to discriminate against non-white people and women is irrational. It is an emotional argument. People can use the laws of logic improperly. They can also use them to promote evil and prevent goodness. This does not mean, however, that the laws of logic are themselves improper and evil.

No. The laws of logic are true. Western civilization merely discovered the laws of logic; it did not invent them out of thin air.

Transcendent Moral Order

Traditionally, western civilization not only proclaims that the laws of logic are absolute and transcendent, it also declares that there exists a transcendent moral order. This moral order has given us specific values, traditions, rules, and guidelines. These values, traditions, rules, and guidelines equip us with good principles for both our public and our private life. Among these principles are the sanctity of human life and heterosexual marriage, the need to punish evil, and the value of offering forgiveness to those who renounce the evil they have done and who try to make restitution for such evil. Every person has an individual moral responsibility to obey these basic principles, whether or not they themselves are religious.

Historically, capitalist democracies like the United States and Great Britain and monotheistic religions like Judaism and Christianity, especially Protestant Christianity, have been the purveyors and guardians of these principles. They have had an extremely beneficial influence on western civilization and human history in general.

As Dr. John Warwick Montgomery points out in *Where Is History Going?,* without "the linear, goal-oriented Christian view of history," it is doubtful if the western notion of progress in human affairs would have been so strong. "It is in the realm of the West's biblical faith," says Montgomery, "that the explanation of our civilization's amazing vitality and urge to 'rise' ought chiefly to be sought."[4]

At this point, people on the left might object, "Yes, western civilization has shown a great ability to grow, but this growth has caused more bad things than good." When asked to prove such an assertion, they usually cite events like the Crusades, the Spanish Inquisition, mistreatment of Native Americans by Europeans, four hundred years of black slavery, denial of rights for minority groups and women, western colonialism and imperialism, and exploitation of the working class by rich capitalists.

Although these events have a degree of historical truth, their occurrence does not undermine the validity of western logic. We should look at the historical evidence and see what the history of western civilization and Christianity actually shows. Only then will we have the tools to judge western culture and evaluate Campbell's criticisms.

Roots

Western civilization has historical roots extending all the way back into ancient times. It has roots in the Middle East, in ancient Sumeria, Mesopotamia, Egypt, ancient Greece, ancient Rome, and ancient Israel.

The first evidence of any writing we have is from ancient Sumeria. The beginnings of science and medicine apparently originate from Egypt. Math and philosophy began in Greece. The Jews and the Romans gave us law. Along with math and philosophy, the Greeks gave the ancient western world a common language. Along with law, the Roman Empire gave the ancient world a common country. Into this cultural jumble stepped the Bible. Preserved by Jews and Christians, it spread the ideology of ethical monotheism.[5]

The first Christians promoted "great social change in certain areas," says historian Earle E. Cairns. "The early Jerusalem church insisted on the spiritual equality of the sexes and gave much consideration to the women of the church. . . . The creation of a group of men to take care of the needy was another remarkable social phenomenon that occurred in the early years of the church."[6] Both of these concerns have played an important role throughout the two-thousand-year history of Christianity.

When the Roman Empire fell, Christianity became the major social, political, and religious force in that part of the world. Eventually, Christianity extended its influence as far west as Great Britain and as far east as Russia.

"In all probability," says historian of religion Mircea Eliade, "neither before nor afterward has any historical society experienced the equivalent of [the] equality, of the charity and brotherly love that were the life of the Christian communities of the first four centuries."[7] These communities helped preserve the ancient culture described above. They also served as a civilizing force in spite of the chaos and cruelty that followed the destruction of the Roman Empire.

For example, the Byzantine Christians copied many classical manuscripts written by the ancient Greeks and others. Christian monks in Ireland also knew Greek and copied important manuscripts. Several alphabet systems, such as the Cyrillic alphabet, were developed by Christian scholars. In addition, Christians helped civilize the extremely cruel Vikings, who enjoyed tossing babies into the air and sticking them on their spears.[8] They also helped civilize the many Teutonic, Slav, and Mongol people who migrated into Europe between A.D. 375 and 1066:

> The greatness of the civilization that western Europe was to develop was not so much due to the irruption of fresh, vigorous barbarians into the empire as it was to the mass conversions of these barbarians of northwest Europe to Christianity.[9]

Because of their influence, Christians were able to transmit many elements of Greco-Roman culture to these pagans.

Unfortunately, however, the increase in power for the Christians did not end all the abuses of power and violence inflicted by human beings against their brothers and sisters. In fact, this increased power eventually led to the Crusades and the Spanish Inquisition in the second millennium. It also led to many abuses of power within the office of the Roman Catholic pope or papacy. Even so, despite the secularization and militarization of the church's power, the church often tried to limit the horrors of warfare in the Middle Ages. Churches, cemeteries, monasteries, and convents were set up as sanctuaries and even hospitals.

"One should always remember," says Cairns, "that although the Crusaders had economic or political interests, the primary motive of the Crusades was religious."[10] The Crusades were aimed mostly at the Muslims who controlled the Holy Land, but with the First Crusade from 1095 to 1099, the Jews also became a target. Previously, the Jews had mostly suffered persecution in the eastern sections of Christianity. Thousands of Jews were murdered under the new wave of anti-Semitism during the Crusades, but thousands of Jews were also protected by more sympathetic Christians, including Roman Catholic officials.[11]

Thus, despite the Crusades, the medieval church made many positive contributions from A.D. 590 to 1305:

> It gave Greco-Roman culture and the Christian religion to the Germans who took over the Roman Empire. It provided the only real culture and scholarship, which kept learning alive through the work of such scholars as Bede, Alcuin, Einhard, and others. The moral tone of society was improved by the mitigation of the evils of slavery, the elevation of the position of women, and the softening of the horrors

of feudal war. The Roman church sponsored what relief and charitable work was done in the Middle Ages. It provided an intellectual
synthesis for life in the theological system that the Scholastics developed and it impressed on men their solidarity as members of the
church. . . .[12]

In addition, by beginning to develop a systematic theology, which
subjects all areas of life to Jesus Christ, the church gave western
culture a complex but dynamic worldview that spurred people on
to higher levels of productivity and progress.

Reformation

In the fourteenth century, papal power began to decline due to
corruption and immorality within the hierarchy of the church and
due to the rise of powerful nation-states, especially in France and
England. "King and middle class cooperated" in these nation-states,
says Cairns. "The king with his national army gave security so that
the middle class could carry on business safely; and the middle class
in return gave money so that the king could run the state."[13]

One hundred years earlier, in 1215, England's King John signed
the Magna Carta. This little document was mainly a "statement of
the barons' feudal rights in relation to their overlord," but it also
contained "clauses favorable to the church, cities, merchants, the
Welsh, and even the king of the Scots."[14] It eliminated some harsh
taxes and established a due process of law. The English Parliament
was strengthened by this agreement and the Magna Carta became
the historical foundation of democratic capitalism in England and
later in the United States.

At about this time, rudimentary forms of capitalism had begun
to appear, although the idea of capitalism and a cash and credit
economy did not really take root until the Renaissance and the
Protestant Reformation, around 1500. Eventually, the banking
expertise of medieval cities in northern Italy passed to German
bankers, then to bankers in Holland and England. International
trade and the need to finance armies were a large part of this
process. For many different reasons, Jews played a major role in

this process, although their influence has been exaggerated and demonized by anti-Semites like Karl Marx and Adolf Hitler.[15]

Throughout its nearly four-hundred-year history (1480–1834), the Spanish Inquisition executed approximately 32,000 people, burned nearly 18,000 in effigy, and gave lesser punishments to 290,000 other people.[16] Most of these people were Jews who had claimed to be converted Christians after they were pressured to do so. Although this record is terrible enough, it is important to point out that Stalin killed about ten million people in the terror-famine of 1930–33 and had one million people executed in 1937–38. By comparison, Adolf Hitler murdered six million Jews in four short years. If you reject Christianity because of the Spanish Inquisition, surely you must reject Marxism based on the history of Stalin, the Khmer Rouge in Cambodia, and Mao Tse-Tung in China.

By the 1500s, the plea for reform in the western church could no longer be stopped. Too many religious, political, economic, cultural, and intellectual changes had occurred. All of these factors led to the Protestant Reformation and the Roman Catholic Counter-Reformation.

The three greatest figures in the Protestant Reformation were Martin Luther of Germany and Huldreich Zwingli and John Calvin of Switzerland. In addition to his theological contributions, Luther called for universal elementary education and an increase in the power of the lay Christian within Christianity. Zwingli accepted most of Luther's reforms but was less strict than Luther and even more democratic. Calvin also encouraged education. He established the Academy, a university in Geneva, Switzerland. This later served as a spur to Calvinists in America who founded several colleges. Like Luther, Calvin wrote extensively on theology and his writings have had great influence. The church government he set up in Geneva became a model for other Protestant churches. Although "Calvin used the state to inflict . . . severe penalties" on rebellious people,

> Calvin also influenced the growth of democracy because he accepted the representative principle in government of the church and the state. He believed that both the church and the state were created by God for the good of men and that they should work together amicably in the furthering of Christianity.[17]

In general, the Protestant Reformation led to a revival of religious individualism and the translation of the Bible into languages other than Latin and Greek. This in turn led to an increasing interest in literacy and education, including the establishment of elementary, secondary, and university schools. "The Reformation also stimulated the rise of empirical science," says Cairns. Christian scientists used the idea of God's moral law to help develop the idea of a material universe run by physical laws. This idea still stands strong today. In addition, "insistence upon the spiritual equality of men led to an insistence upon their political equality [and] promoted the rise of democracy in both the church and the state." Finally, although the Protestant Reformation did not begin the rise of capitalism, it "stimulated capitalism" because it discouraged opposition to lending money at interest rates and encouraged thriftiness, saving money, and hard work.[18]

The Roman Catholic Counter-Reformation revitalized that church, increasing its missionary and education work. It also led to positive structural and moral reforms and a better diversity throughout this church. Unfortunately, both it and the Protestant Reformation also led to more violent conflict among Christians, including open warfare.

New World

In the sixteenth and seventeenth centuries, Christianity helped spur the Age of Discovery. Christopher Columbus's first voyage to the New World was financed by two Jews, one of whom converted to Christianity. North America was settled mostly by Protestants fleeing persecution or by Protestants trying to spread the new Christian Reformation to the new land.

Much has been written about the terrible treatment of Native Americans by Europeans. Sympathy for the plight of Native Americans has often led to a naive view of their culture, however. Many people don't like to acknowledge the fact that Native Americans could be, and often were, just as brutal as and even more brutal than the Europeans. The full truth has seldom been told.

Although thousands of Native Americans were killed by Europeans, the Native Americans did their fair share of killing as well.

Also, although the Spanish and Portuguese enslaved millions in Latin America, most Native Americans throughout the New World died simply because of the diseases the Europeans brought with them. To blame the Europeans for these diseases would be ridiculous.

For seven hundred years, the Spanish had fought wars with the Islamic Moors who conquered Spain in 711. It was hard for the Spanish to turn off their re-conquest mentality. After the Moors were finally expelled from Granada, Spain, in 1492, the Spaniards were urged to turn their attention to the Americas and not to Europe or the Middle East. When they got to the New World, they found many tribes, like the Aztecs in Mexico, already occupying the land. They began to conquer the New World just as they had conquered Spain.

The Aztecs were fierce warriors who "prized the warlike virtues and worshiped cruel war gods."[19] They sacrificed thousands of other tribespeople to these war gods. Their religious places in Mexico City were filled with the gruesome evidence of this cruelty, a shocking and repulsive sight to the Spaniards who first entered the city. Consequently, when the Spaniards retreated from Mexico City, their leader, Cortés, enlisted the aid of the other tribes, many of whom were only too happy to slaughter Aztecs. In the Spaniards' final assault on Mexico City, over 90 percent of the attacking force was composed of Native Americans, not Europeans.

When the Spanish came to the New World, the Mayan civilization in Central America had already suffered "centuries of civil war."[20] At the same time, the Incas in Peru had a strict socialist society where the common people were treated almost like slaves by the ruling class.

When Christopher Columbus first landed in the Caribbean, he found two warring tribes, the Caribs and the Arawaks. The Caribs were fierce warriors like the Aztecs. They had a habit of capturing Arawak women and making them concubines. Consequently, the Arawaks enlisted the aid of the Europeans in their fight against the Caribs.

Tribal warfare was also a common occurrence among Native Americans in North America, including the famous Plains Indians who fought the U.S. government in the late 1800s.[21] It isn't necessarily true that Native Americans were really interested in protecting the natural environment around them. According to author Robert Royal, they "often exhausted the resources of a certain area, then moved on." He adds: "The Algonquins, Iroquois, and other groups . . . tortured and sacrificed to war gods captives from other tribes to maintain 'harmony'" with nature.[22] Royal says the Indians regularly killed and tortured other Indians before the Europeans came. Critics of western civilization often view European expansion in a negative light, says Royal, while at the same time they praise the Incas for building roads to increase their empire or praise other tribes for taking part in extensive trading networks.

Finally, Native Americans do not have a spotless record when it comes to the mistreatment of women. In many tribes, there was a strict system of sex roles where difficult domestic tasks were reserved for women while men assumed the more prestigious hunter/warrior role. Royal notes that the Pawnee made a yearly sacrifice of a young maiden.

Thus, the idea that the white settlers were mostly evil but Native Americans were mostly good and pure is a gross simplification. There were cruel and evil men among both groups. There were also many brave and good men on both sides. Even so, the incredibly negative impact of the Europeans on the lives of Native Americans, and on the people of Africa who became slaves in the New World, cannot be denied. In reality, the Bible condemns the kinds of evil that the white settlers often did.

We must remember, however, that the moral heritage and democratic values of the Protestant Reformation played a significant role in founding the first two capitalistic republics in the modern world, Great Britain and the United States. Their systems of government were a definite improvement over the empires of the ancient world and the feudal societies and powerful monarchies of the Middle Ages.

Over the centuries, democratic capitalism has fueled a tremendous growth of economic prosperity and technological progress. In general, it has advanced and protected political, economic, and religious freedom. Contrary to what many socialists claim, it has also created wealth, not spread poverty. For example, the western nations who use this system continue to produce agricultural surpluses. They have given billions of dollars in aid to poor nations to help them fight famine and improve their economy. In this century alone, democratic capitalism has saved millions of lives by halting Adolf Hitler and imperialist Japan's march of terror and by containing imperial communism's reign of terror in the old Soviet Union, Red China, Cambodia, and Castro's Cuba. Because of it, and the legacy it owes to Protestant Christianity, millions of people today enjoy the most economic, political, and religious freedom known by any group of people in all of human history.

Of course, we can all point to great evils done under this system, but let's not forget the following two truths: "All have sinned and fall short of the glory of God" (Rom. 3:23), and "Power tends to corrupt; absolute power corrupts absolutely" (Lord Acton).

Lord Acton, of course, was speaking of human power, not the power of God, who is the ultimate source of all goodness.

Whether or not you believe God exists, however, the fact remains that "balance of powers," one of the key concepts of the U.S. Constitution, is based on these two similar truths about human nature.[23] Even the idea of putting antitrust laws and other legal limits on big business is based on them.

Evil is ubiquitous—it can spread where you least expect it. Before we start pointing a finger at other people about their sins, we should first take a look in the mirror. As Jesus said, "First take the plank out of your own eye, and then you will see clearly to remove the speck from your brother's eye."

It is true that in the past, and even today, people have used the Bible to justify evil. Good things can be abused. There was a time, not so very long ago, that the United States Supreme Court, in the early 1800s, used the Constitution to justify slavery, or, at the very least, to let it continue. And it was only a very short time ago that a man named Charles Manson used the "Love Generation" of the sixties and a rock song by the Beatles called "Helter Skelter" to spread his own peculiar brand of hate, murder, and mayhem.

What shall we conclude then? That we should toss out the whole of western tradition and culture because most of it was created and spread by a bunch of "dead white European males" who sometimes used it to commit terrible sins? God forbid!

Any human system of government, any human lifestyle, any human culture is subject to the sinful nature that lurks in the heart of every human being. If we ignore this fact or try to sweep it under the rug, we will do so at our own peril. That's why it is important to remember the eternal moral truths taught by Moses, Jesus Christ, and their followers.

Closing Thoughts on Morality

The issue surrounding Joseph Campbell and his work is not only a matter of truth. It's also a question of values. Values are extremely important. They impact our government, our cities, our schools, our places of worship, our families, our homes, and our quality of life. Before we start changing value systems, we'd better carefully consider what we are doing. Unfortunately, in many ways, the camel's nose, head, humps, and legs already seem to have snuck in under our tent. America stopped the Nazis in Europe and the Communists in the Soviet Union, but it can't seem to stop the destruction of the family in the suburbs or in the inner city, and the gang-related violence in its streets. It seems reasonable to ask ourselves if, rather than eliminating the Ten Commandments from the walls of our public schools, as the autocratic Supreme Court decided, we should put them back up.

In his books and recorded lectures and interviews, Campbell attacks western values and traditions and praises eastern ones. He makes Native American culture in North, Central, and South America sound pure and lovely. He criticizes traditional Christian morality while at the same time using the words of Jesus to promote his own pantheistic, mystical interpretation of the Bible. As we have seen, however, the laws of logic, the historical record, and the actual biblical text prove him wrong.

In reality, western civilization has brought the world democracy, freedom, constitutional government, the laws of logic, the rule of law, scientific progress, technological wonders, modern medicine, and a set of moral guidelines rooted in the Bible. Western countries like Great Britain and the United States have not always followed these values and principles, but they have spread them more fully than any other culture in history.

Throughout the centuries, Christianity has brought relief to the sufferers of war, natural disaster, and famine. Without Christianity, there would probably be no organization like the Red Cross. Christians have helped start thousands of hospitals and hundreds of soup kitchens and orphanages. Christian missionaries have brought education, medicine, and agriculture to many areas on the fringes of civilization. As historian Kenneth Scott Latourette points out, "Christianity has been the means of reducing more languages to writing than have all other factors combined. It has created more schools, more theories of education, and more systems than any other force."[24]

Contrary to popular belief, Christianity has helped improve the status of women throughout the world. It has spread the twin ideals of marriage and traditional family life. Both of these have, in general, encouraged altruism and love. They have helped to protect women and children from the evil that comes when men are allowed and even encouraged to stay unmarried and sexually promiscuous.

Our inner cities are being torn apart today because the sexual revolution, coupled with the socialist welfare state, has resulted in a tremendous rise in the number of single mothers who must raise young men without fathers. These young men join gangs for the male fellowship, but these gangs sell drugs, steal, murder, and help produce more single mothers on welfare. This is what happens when a modern society loses its moral direction. This is what happens when the biblical roots of western civilization are almost completely destroyed by self-righteous intellectuals like Joseph Campbell.

In contrast to this, Christianity has inspired people to fight suffering, spread religious and political freedom around the world, heal the sick, stop corruption, speak out against hypocrisy, and reform prisons. Christians helped put an end to slavery in the United States. African American Christians started the Civil Rights Movement under the leadership of Martin Luther King and ended forced segregation in the United States. Other Christians supported President Ronald Reagan's fight against the "Evil Empire" of the former Soviet Union, which ranks with Adolf Hitler's Nazi Germany as the most immoral government in human history. Many Christians continue to oppose tyranny in other countries.

Jesus Christ's ministry of three short years "has done more to regenerate and soften mankind than all the disquisitions of philosophers and all the exhortations of moralists."[25] The good Christians have done far outweighs the bad.

As we saw at the end of chapter 4, Christianity teaches that God is a person who exists outside the space and time of the material universe but who can act within that universe. Viewed as such, God is separate from his creation. He is also the divine foundation of all the rational categories that Campbell tries to eliminate. As Jesus Christ says in John 4:24, "God is spirit; and those who worship Him must worship in spirit and truth" (NASB).

The Bible says that God has established an "objective moral order."[26] He not only establishes the moral order; his personal nature is also the ultimate source and expression of the moral order. This moral order gives all people an inherent moral worth but also demands from them certain duties, responsibilities, and obligations, in both their relationships with God and their relationships with other human beings. The Bible commands us to avoid idolatry, murder, thievery, deceit, lust, sex outside of heterosexual marriage, envy, strife, boasting, malice, sorcery, outbursts of uncontrollable anger, drunkenness, selfish ambition, pride, heresy, adultery, blasphemy, and foolishness (see Gal. 5:19–21 and Mark 7:20–23 in the New Testament). Micah 6:8 in the Old Testament commands us "to act justly and love mercy and to walk humbly with your God." We are supposed to treat other people the way we would like to be treated. We are commanded to love God with all our heart and mind and soul and strength, and to love our neighbor as ourself.

If this transcendent and objective moral order, rooted in a transcendent and eternal God, does not exist, then man truly is adrift in a dark and stormy sea of moral chaos where power is the only thing that matters. To quote a character from Woody Allen's film *Crimes and Misdemeanors*, "If God doesn't exist, then life is a cesspool."

In such a dark, chaotic world, Joseph Campbell's own beliefs about morality are themselves meaningless.

8

Origins

n the first chapter of *Myths to Live By,* Campbell describes a conversation he overheard between a mother and her son. The two people were discussing the evolution of man. The mother wanted to talk about Adam and Eve, according to Campbell, but the son wanted to talk about evolution science.

"Those are only theories," said the mother.

"Yes I know," replied the son, "but they have been factualized: They found the bones."[1]

Campbell sides with the son's viewpoint. Throughout his whole first chapter, he tries to show how science has completely refuted the Bible. For instance, he claims the Bible teaches that the earth is flat and science has, of course, proved that the earth is round. Science has also dated "the earliest appearance of manlike creatures on this earth a million years earlier than the biblical date for God's creation of the world," says Campbell.[2]

Campbell is only partly right. Science has indeed disproved the theory of a flat earth, but nowhere does the Bible teach this theory. In fact Job 26:7 in the Old Testament says God "suspends the earth over nothing," and Isaiah 40:22 in the Old Testament says God "sits enthroned above the circle of the earth."

Campbell is probably thinking about Bible verses like Isaiah 11:12, which says that God "will assemble the scattered people of Judah from the four quarters of the earth," or Revelation 7:1, which says, "After this I saw four angels standing at the four corners of the earth." In both of these cases, the Bible is not teaching geography or astronomy. It is making prophetic utterances about the future, using figurative language. As a person who is constantly talking about figurative language and metaphor, Joseph Campbell's approach to biblical interpretation on page two of *Myths to Live By* makes no sense.

Also, although some scientists have dated the bones of some supposed human "ancestors" millions of years in the past, the first truly "manlike" creature, *Homo sapiens,* doesn't really appear in the fossil record until approximately 250,000 years ago at the most. In fact, some scientists writing today believe that the first truly human creature doesn't appear until 15,000 to 40,000 years ago.

Scientific methods for dating and interpreting the fossil record are not as conclusive and reliable as Campbell leads his readers to believe. To apply the word *manlike* to these fossils that Campbell mentions is itself a vague, unscientific approach. A creature can conceivably be both manlike and apelike at the same time, yet that doesn't necessarily make him an "ancestor" to either apes or men. Significantly, Campbell doesn't use the word *apelike* in his book, perhaps because that would undermine his argument in support of the theory of human evolution.

Later in *Myths to Live By* Campbell says the Bible teaches that 1656 years elapsed between Adam and Noah.[3] This statement and others by Campbell indicate he believes the Bible teaches that the earth was created around 4000 B.C.

Campbell's view of what the Bible teaches is not only narrow-minded, it's dead wrong. According to Dr. Hugh Ross in *The Fingerprint of God,* the church as a whole never taught a 4000 B.C. date for the creation of the earth. Such a date wasn't taught by any Christians until Irish Archbishop James Ussher (1581–1656) taught it in the seventeenth century.[4] In reality, the Bible gives us no date for God's creation of the world. In fact, some of the best and most conservative Christian scholars working today believe that the Bible doesn't even teach a recent creation of the earth. They believe that the Bible allows for an earth that is even four billion years old, the date that modern science usually gives for the creation of our planet. They also contend that it is silly for people to take the first book of the Bible, Genesis, and use it to compute the actual length of time from Adam to Noah.

By asserting such an artificially narrow time frame for the Bible's record from Adam to Noah, Campbell sets up a straw man he can easily knock down. He erects a weak, imaginary interpretation of the Bible and makes it sound as if this is what the Bible really teaches. Campbell's interpretation is so narrow that the Bible itself is made to appear ridiculous, especially in light of all the "scientific" evidence about the apparent age of the earth. Such a "straw man" argument is a flagrant logical fallacy. Such a fallacy doesn't prove Campbell's point; it shows the weakness of his argument.

Throughout his work, Campbell tries to use science and history to show that the Bible is false, but his explanations of science and history are superficial and filled with informal logical fallacies. Not only does he present illogical straw man arguments, he also makes inappropriate appeals to scientific authorities. For instance, to simply say "they found the bones" is not a proper appeal to scientific evidence. It is an emotional, unsupported argument designed to rattle one's opponent and to cut off debate.

Campbell commits other logical fallacies when he talks about the origin of man.

In defending evolution, Campbell seems to be saying, "Science claims to reveal truth. Science says that man gradually evolved from the animals. Therefore, evolution must be true." This argument is a fallacy because it is a circular argument. It tries to prove evolution by appealing to science, but it never gives us reasons to believe that science always reveals the truth. Why should we believe evolution is true simply because science says it is true? "They found the bones" is the kind of argument that doesn't make sense, especially coming from a man who says that there is no such thing as ultimate truth.

Campbell is also guilty of "special pleading." He ignores the philosophical, scientific, and historical evidence against the various positions he takes, and he seldom, if ever, discusses the best evidence and arguments that the best orthodox Christian scholars present whenever they talk about the Bible or about science and the philosophy of science.

The next two chapters refute Campbell's ideas about science and the Bible by examining what both Christian and non-Christian scholars say about these subjects. These chapters use science, history, philosophy, theology, and the science of interpretation (hermeneutics) to show that Campbell is incorrect about the origin of man and the Bible. They also examine scientific theories of human evolution and nonreligious theories about the history of religion. My ultimate goal here is to give an explanation of the origin of man in the light of current evidence. Contrary to what Campbell says, my research indicates that the Bible is true and doesn't contradict what science knows.

A Philosophical Interlude

In chapter 1, I indicated that philosophy is a better candidate for rational thinking than science. To support this position, I quoted philosopher Larry Laudan, who believes we should stop trying to justify or validate any activity just because it claims to be scientific. Instead, says Laudan, we should simply ask ourselves what is *reliable* knowledge and what is *unreliable* knowledge: "Our focus should be squarely on the empirical and conceptual credentials for claims about the world. The 'scientific' status of those claims is altogether irrelevant."[5]

Throughout this book, therefore, I have used logical arguments and factual evidence to support my case against Joseph Campbell. My approach is a philosophical one, but it also relies on research from other areas of knowledge such as history, anthropology, archeology, comparative religion, psychology, political science, and theology. Like the natural sciences, all of these other areas have a philosophical dimension that cannot be ignored. These areas also often overlap each other.

In fact, there is really no clear line of division between science and these other fields of knowledge, or between science and non-science:

> Science is not an airtight compartment isolated from philosophy, theology, and other disciplines. It interacts with other fields of study in complicated ways. Only someone out of touch with the history of science could believe otherwise.[6]

Thus there is a "continuity"[7] between science and philosophy and between science and these other fields. For example, although there are some areas of science that have nothing to do with psychology and vice versa, other areas do overlap. When quantum mechanics, for instance, starts talking about the relationship between the scientific observer and the experiment he is conducting, it touches on issues concerning psychology as well as philosophy.

Every time a scientist sits down to determine a proper method for an experiment, he becomes involved, if only slightly, in philosophical issues about physical reality and human knowledge. The existence of something called science and something called non-science is itself a philosophical question, as well as a historical one. Scientists cannot use the scientific method, which is primarily empirical, to test the rational truth of the scientific method. The scientific method must be rationally justified and confirmed by philosophy, by the systematic study of the intellectual foundations of all knowledge.

Actually, however, if you look at the idea of the scientific method, you will find there is no one thing that can be called the scientific method. What we really find, as I noted in chapter 1, are *many different methods* used in *many different ways* in *widely different situations*—not only scientists but also historians, psychologists, anthropologists, archeologists, political scientists, and even theologians can all use similar methods in many different ways. A theologian who tries to discover what the Bible says about the doctrine of creation is using, at the very least, a crude form of the scientific method called inductivism.[8] Science, by its very nature, raises questions about the nature of reality and the nature of being, about the nature and limits of human knowledge, and about the nature, validity, and measure of values and value judgments.

Scientists often imagine themselves as detached, objective observers of physical phenomena, but their work is filled with many abstract concepts, philosophical assumptions, and intellectual presuppositions. For example, science "assumes that the laws of logic are true, that numbers exist, that language has meaning, that some terms refer to things in the world, [and] that truth exists and involves some sort of correspondence between theories and the world."9 Science also makes assumptions about morality (scientists must be honest), knowledge (theories should be kept as simple as possible but also must be sufficiently broad and deep), and methodology (scientists should show disinterested skepticism). It uses theoretical terms like *electron, DNA,* and *natural selection* to describe physical phenomena, but such terms depend on a conceptual and theoretical framework in order to generate meaning. The word *meaning* is itself an abstract, nonmaterial concept with philosophical implications.

Although most of what science does seems beneficial to society, much of it is still fraught with an anti-Christian, materialistic bias. Unlike many people, I believe it is okay to have a bias in favor of one viewpoint and against other viewpoints, so long as you openly acknowledge your bias. Just because you have a bias doesn't mean you aren't speaking truthfully. The problem is too many self-proclaimed scientists are unwilling or unable to admit their bias, especially if they spend a lot of time in the public eye. These scientists often confuse their personal philosophic, religious, and political beliefs with scientific truth. For example, there are several important popular scientists, such as Carl Sagan and the late Isaac Asimov, who write "science books" for mass audiences. They mix the scientific information in their books with philosophical, religious, or political viewpoints coming from their atheistic, pantheistic, or socialistic worldviews. When doing this, however, they seldom alert their audiences to their bias. In many ways, Joseph Campbell's work is a part of this dangerous trend.

We should realize that when we look at the history of religion, the Bible, and evolution, we are operating in a philosophical arena. We should also realize that not only do the scholars we cite probably have philosophical, religious, and political biases, so probably do we. Just because we can't achieve 100 percent objectivity, however, and just because we probably are biased doesn't mean we can't know what the truth is. Moreover, just because Christian scientists and atheistic scientists use value-laden language and make value judgments doesn't mean their positions on evolution are automatically false.

Sometimes an atheist can speak truth. Sometimes a Christian can too. And sometimes science is wrong.

Truth often calls for a subjective response, a personal commitment or belief, but there are objective standards we can use to help us know what is true. These standards entail, but are not limited to, logical arguments and factual evidence.

What the Bible Really Teaches

"In the beginning God created the heavens and the earth" is the first sentence of the first chapter of Genesis, the first book of the Bible.

Chapter one of Genesis not only says that God created the universe and the earth, it also says God separated the light in the universe from the darkness and formed the atmosphere on the earth. God then separated the land on the earth from the water and commanded the land to produce vegetation, including plants, trees, and fruit. At this point, God let the sun and the moon appear in the sky "to separate the day from the night, and let them serve as signs to mark seasons and days and years." He also created fish in the water, birds to fly in the sky, livestock, "creatures that move along the ground," and wild animals. Finally, God said, "Let us make man in our image, in our likeness, and let them rule over the fish of the sea and the birds of the air, over the livestock, over all the earth, and over all the creatures that move along the ground." God created both male and female. He blessed them and told them, "Be fruitful and increase in number; fill the earth and subdue it." Here, the creation passage comes to a partial conclusion: "God saw all that he had made, and it was very good. And the evening took place, and the morning took place, a sixth day."

Much has been written about this passage, and about the account of Adam and Eve in the following two chapters of Genesis. Many people focus on the six days mentioned in the text, which seem to contradict what modern science claims about the creation of the earth and the universe and about evolution. Some people, like Campbell, dismiss the Bible without looking at all the evidence. They claim that science proves the biblical story of creation is false. Other people attack modern science and say that the true scientific facts prove that evolution is false and the Bible is true. Still other people claim that the six days of creation are purely figurative and that Adam and Eve were not historical individuals. They believe God used some kind of evolutionary mechanism to create life in the universe and to develop human beings who think and speak.

Many of this last kind of people, who are known as "theistic evolutionists," "conceive of Homo sapiens as gradually developing from subhuman hominids and then finally developing a consciousness of God—at which moment, whenever it was, the ape-man became 'Adam.'"[10] Hebrew scholar Gleason L. Archer cites the view of Lecomte de Nouy, who suggests that, probably around 30,000 B.C. the Cro-Magnon species "became truly man by a sort of spiritual mutation that conferred on him the capacity of responsible moral choice."[11] Archer, a professor of Old Testament with a Ph.D. from Harvard, says such views cannot be reconciled with the biblical text, which presents Adam and Eve as historical people who had "personal emotions and responses."[12] To prove this point, Archer cites chapters two and three of Genesis in the Old Testament and 1 Timothy 2:13–14 in the New Testament: "For Adam was formed first, then Eve. And Adam was not the one deceived; it was the woman who was deceived and became a sinner." Thus, Archer contends that both the text of the Old Testament and the text of the New Testament indicate that God did not use an evolutionary mechanism to create the first truly human man and woman.

The next chapter examines in detail evidence for and against theories of human evolution. At that point, we will decide whether Archer is right that God did not use evolution to create people. For now, however, we must ask how we should interpret the six days of creation in chapter one of Genesis. By doing this we will be in a better position to critique Campbell's view of the origin of man and the Bible.

There are at least ten major ways to interpret the description of the six days of creation in Genesis 1:

1. God created the earth in six consecutive 24-hour days.
2. The six days are six consecutive 24-hour days, but there is a huge, indefinite time gap between Genesis 1:1 and Genesis 1:2, which can be translated "the earth *became* formless and empty" instead of "the earth *was* formless and empty."

3. The six days represent six chronological geologic ages.
4. The six days are a literary device that represent six creation stages of indefinite length.
5. The six days are a literary device that represent six intermittent 24-hour days occurring simultaneously with six overlapping periods of divine creation. These creative periods are still going on. The seventh day of rest in Genesis 2:2, 3 will not occur until God creates the new heavens and new earth (Rev. 21:1–8).
6. The six days are a literary device, an "artistic arrangement . . . to bring out certain themes and provide a theology of the sabbath."[13] They are not intended to be interpreted literally.
7. The six days are a literary and prophetic device whereby God reveals the story of creation in six "pictorial"[14] days.
8. The story of creation in Genesis 1, as well as the Garden of Eden story in chapters 2 and 3, is a symbolic and fictional story revealed to man by God. As such, it presents us with some spiritual and moral truths, but that is all it does.
9. The story of creation in Genesis is a fairy tale invented by human beings. Like the rest of the Bible, it doesn't teach us any ultimate truth whatsoever.
10. The six days of creation have some other meaning undiscovered by us and known only to God.

If you study the biblical text and read what other scholars have said about it, I believe you will conclude with me that, of all these different interpretations, numbers four, five, and six make the most sense. Likewise, numbers two, three, eight, and nine can be rejected because they don't fit the text. What is the evidence for this conclusion?

According to Archer in *Encyclopedia of Bible Difficulties,* in the original Hebrew text of Genesis 1, all of the references to the first five days of creation lack a definite article. Instead of saying "the first day," the actual text reads, "And the evening took place and the morning took place, day one." The other passages read "a second day," "a third day," and so on. Archer contends that the lack of a definite article indicates that the six days are a literary device designed by the author to represent six indefinite stages of creation. They are not designed to be interpreted as six literal 24-hour days.

Old Testament scholar Ronald F. Youngblood, in *The Book of Genesis: An Introductory Commentary,* and Hebrew scholar Walter C. Kaiser Jr., in *Toward an Old Testament Theology,* both agree with Archer's view of the word "day" in the Hebrew text of Genesis 1. They believe it's not necessary to view the six days of creation as six literal and consecutive 24-hour days.

"The omission of the definite article *(the)* from all but the sixth day," says Youngblood, "allows for the possibility of random or literary order."[15] Youngblood also says Christian theology traditionally teaches that God's seventh day of rest "is still in effect and will continue forever" (see Heb. 4:1–11).[16] Therefore, he concludes, the six days of creation "are literary and timeless, not literal and timebound."[17] Adds Kaiser:

> The sixth creative period of time must have lasted more than twenty-four hours, for Adam grew lonely for a companion (Gen. 2:20). Surely this took more than an afternoon's idle thought! Moreover, he busied himself with the task of naming the animals as his loneliness continued to build. Finally, God created a woman, and it was still that sixth "day."[18]

Archer himself cites this peculiar sixth "day" in his own book and points out that Genesis 2:2 and 3, which describe the seventh day, do not mention evening and morning, unlike the first six days.

Robert C. Newman, who holds a Ph.D. in astrophysics from Cornell University and a theological degree from Faith Theological Seminary, also believes that the six days are a literary device. He suggests, however, "that the 'days' of Genesis 1 are twenty-four hour days, sequential but not consecutive, and that the creative activity largely occurs between days rather than on them."[19] In other words, "each Genesis day introduces a new creative period."[20] Thus, we can think of the six 24-hour days as being intermittent, i.e., that there are regular or irregular breaks in their continuity. Newman says that the six days occur chronologically and simultaneously with six overlapping creative periods, but that the days do not immediately follow one after the other.

Newman provides a list of the six creative periods: 1) formation of the earth; 2) formation of the atmosphere and the ocean;

3) formation of dry land and vegetation on the land; 4) oxygenation and clearing of the atmosphere so that the sun and moon are clearly visible; 5) creation of air and sea animals; and 6) creation of land animals and man.[21] According to Newman, the six periods "are still going on" and will "end together at the seventh day (still future) when God will have completed his creation."[22] Newman concludes:

> God highlights these seven days, among the many actually occurring during creation, in order to set up an ordinance by which man is to commemorate creation. The six days of work remind him that he was created by God, and the seventh day of rest looks forward to God's rest, when redeemed man will rejoice with all creation in the new heavens and new earth (Rom. 8:18–25; Heb. 4:1–11).[23]

Unlike Newman, Archer, Kaiser, and Youngblood, Christian theologian Henri Blocher, in *In the Beginning: The Opening Chapters of Genesis,* says that the seven days in Genesis 1 and 2 provide *only* a literary framework. "The author's intention is not to supply us with a chronology of origins," says Blocher.[24] Nor is it meant to really coincide with the actual sequence of events when God created the heavens and the earth. Instead, the author merely

> wishes to bring out certain themes and provide a theology of the sabbath. The text is composed as the author meditates on the finished work, so that we may understand how the creation is related to God and what is its significance for mankind.[25]

Ultimately, says Blocher, the seven days in the text are designed to show us that entering God's "rest" and having a proper relationship with him are more important than work. After all, as Jesus told Satan in the desert, "Man does not live on bread alone, but on every word that comes from the mouth of God" (Matt. 4:4).

Whichever of these three interpretations you pick, it is clear from the text itself that Genesis 1:1–2:3 is written in a literary style.[26] We are not supposed to interpret the six days literally. Thus, God could have started creating and forming the universe billions of years ago. To quote Archer again:

The purpose of Genesis 1 is not to tell how fast God performed His work of creation (though, of course, some of His acts, such as the creation of light on the first day, must have been instantaneous). Rather, its true purpose was to reveal that the Lord God who had revealed Himself to the Hebrew race and entered into personal covenant relationship with them was indeed the only true God, the Creator of all things that are. This stood in direct opposition to the religious notions of the heathen around them, who assumed the emergence of a pantheon of gods in successive stages out of preexistent matter of unknown origin, actuated by forces for which there was no accounting.[27]

Christian theologian James Oliver Buswell Jr., who agrees with Archer and Kaiser that the word *day* in Genesis 1 is used in a figurative way, says the text is written in a style conducive to memorization. Moses wrote Genesis "for the spiritual instruction of the Hebrew people," Buswell declares. "The first and most important thing for these men to learn is that God is the Creator and ruler of all things, and that He is the one who has the authority to give them the promised land to which they are journeying."[28] This is the main purpose of the text, he adds.

As you can see, there are many well-qualified, orthodox Christian scholars who believe it is wrong to take the first part of Genesis and apply specific historical dates to God's work of creation. Their evidence for this perspective is both compelling and convincing. The Bible does not seem to teach that the earth was created in 4000 B.C. or that Adam and Eve were created only six thousand years ago. The biblical text allows for the four-billion-year-old or older earth postulated by modern science. The author of Genesis uses the six days of creation as a literary device. The author is not trying to say God created the universe and everything in it in six 24-hour consecutive days without interruption.

Gaps in the Genealogies?

If you continue reading Genesis, you will find that chapters five, ten, and eleven contain long lists of the generations of human beings who lived between Adam and the first Hebrew patriarch, Abram or Abraham. In the past, some Christian scholars have misinterpreted these lists and used them to support the 4000 B.C. date for the creation of the earth. Other Christian scholars, however, who were equally as conservative and orthodox in their theology, disagreed with them.

In *A Systematic Theology of the Christian Religion,* Buswell cites nineteenth century theologian B. B. Warfield who, along with other scholars, believed that these lists were never meant to be an exhaustive record of all the generations from Adam to Abraham. For example, when Genesis 5:6 says, "When Seth had lived 105 years, he became the father of Enosh," the Hebrew word for father in that passage can mean "ancestor." Also, when Genesis 10:2 lists the six "sons of Japheth," the word "sons" can be translated "descendants," "successors," or "nations."[29] Thus, there are probably gaps in these genealogies, perhaps huge ones.

Buswell agrees with Warfield, who believed Adam may have been created as long ago as 20,000 years ago or even 200,000 years ago. As we will see later, such a range is well within the parameters of scientific dating for the earliest *Homo sapiens sapiens,* or modern man.

Archer, in *A Survey of Old Testament Introduction,* the revised edition, agrees that there are gaps in these genealogies, but he rejects the idea that Adam may have been created as long ago as 200,000 years ago or even 20,000 years ago. Instead, he contends that there are "possibly five or six thousand years between Adam and Abraham,"[30] who probably lived between 2200 and 2000 B.C. "However the statistics of Genesis 5 may be handled," says Archer, "they can hardly end up with a date for Adam much before 10,000 B.C." Consequently, Archer believes that all the bones of "men," which scientists date between 10,000 B.C. and 200,000 B.C., "must have been advanced apes or anthropoids possessed of considerable intelligence and resourcefulness—but who completely died off before Adam and Eve were created."[31]

Archer supports his position by pointing out that when God created Adam and Eve, he created them in his own "image" and "likeness" (Gen. 1:26–27) and gave them "something of His own Spirit" (Gen. 2:7).[32] This image and Spirit are not physical things. They are immaterial entities that gave Adam and Eve the ability to communicate and have fellowship with God, to make moral choices, to think rational thoughts, and to be self-aware. As Hebrew scholar Walter C. Kaiser Jr. puts it, "God is the prototype of which man and woman are merely copies, replicas . . . and facsimiles."[33]

Therefore, says Archer, Adam and Eve, as well as their descendants, are completely different creatures from those that scientists claim lived before 10,000 B.C. "There may have been advanced and intelligent hominids who lived and died before Adam," says Archer, "but they were not created in the image of God."[34] There is no evidence, adds Archer, that these creatures had "a true human soul."[35] Therefore, there is no contradiction between what the Bible says about Adam and his descendants and what science says about hominids and other similar creatures who lived before 10,000 B.C.

Although Archer makes some excellent points, Buswell's and Warfield's idea that Adam may have been created 20,000 or even 200,000 years ago seems more reasonable. In order to prove this point, let's translate Genesis 11:10–11 the way it should probably be translated: "Two years after the flood, when Shem was one hundred years old, he became the ancestor of Arphaxad. And after he became the ancestor of Arphaxad, Shem lived five hundred years and had other male and female descendants." Translated in this way, the text seems to allow for much wider time gaps than those in which Archer believes.

Nor is this biblical text necessarily teaching us that Shem himself lived to be five hundred years old. Instead, we can view Shem and the other people mentioned in the genealogy list of chapter eleven as being "representative of whole family units."[36] Thus, each of the family units extended for several hundred years, but the individuals themselves did not.

The Bible doesn't tell us how to compute the length of time between Shem and Arphaxad and the rest of the descendants of Adam and Noah. It is just trying to give us some of the historical highlights of the most important people, families, and nations from Adam to Noah and Noah to Abraham. It is not necessary to limit our biblical interpretations of these passages to Archer's narrow time frame, and certainly not to Campbell's view of these biblical passages.

As we will see in the next chapter, Archer is right when he says that many of the humanoid bones that scientists date before 10,000 B.C., especially those before 200,000 B.C., probably have no connection whatsoever to the human communities that appear in history after 10,000 B.C. He exaggerates, however, the differences between some of those manlike creatures who lived before 10,000 B.C. such as the Neanderthal "race" (who lived approximately 150,000 or 85,000 B.C. to 35,000 B.C.) or the Cro-Magnon "race" (who lived approximately 35,000 B.C. to 10,000 B.C.), and those who lived after 10,000 B.C.

Although the dates for these early races are approximate and although there are some valid criticisms we can make of the dating techniques scientists use, the evidence of the biblical text and the evidence from modern science allow for the creation of spirit-filled men as early as 200,000 B.C. and as late as 35,000 B.C. when Cro-Magnon "man" probably appears on the scene. If the earth is truly four billion years old, as most scientists today believe and the biblical text seems to allow, then the difference between Archer's 10,000 B.C. date for the first true man and woman and the dates for Neanderthal "man" and Cro-Magnon "man" is so small as to be inconsequential.

The Bible teaches that God is the Almighty Creator who created the universe out of nothing. He created the earth and everything in it, including the spirit-man called Adam, who was the latest and highest being of God's creation. The Bible does not teach, however, a creation week of seven consecutive 24-hour days. Nor does it indicate that only a short time period occurred between God's creation of Adam and the birth of Abraham. It is wrong, therefore, to apply specific historical dates to the information given in the first eleven chapters of Genesis, but this is exactly what Joseph Campbell does.

Campbell's worldview forces him to take a faulty and unduly biased interpretation of the Bible. He uses this interpretation to make harsh accusations against the Bible and against those who cherish it. If anyone is being intolerant, judgmental, arrogant, and dogmatic, it is he.

Exchanging the Truth of God for a Lie

Before we tackle the topic of human evolution and the historical development of religion in the next chapter, one more biblical question needs to be answered. What does the Bible really teach about the origin and history of religion?

First, the Bible says that sometime in the distant past the first man and the first woman had a personal relationship with the one true God, who created the whole universe and everything in it (Gen. 1–2). Eventually, however, they disobeyed God and fell into sin and immorality (Gen. 3). Although God punished them, he still offered them and their descendants a chance to remain in fellowship with him. He also set up moral and ethical laws for them to follow.

Some people continued to practice this original "ethical monotheism." Most people, however, did not, even though, as the apostle Paul said in a letter sent to the Christian church in Rome, "God's invisible qualities—his eternal power and divine nature—have been clearly seen" throughout the physical world (Rom. 1:20).

According to the apostle Paul in this letter, many of these non-believers fell into idolatry.

> They became fools and exchanged the glory of the immortal God for images made to look like mortal man and birds and animals and reptiles. Therefore God gave them over in the sinful desires of their hearts to sexual impurity for the degrading of their bodies with one another. They exchanged the truth of God for a lie, and worshiped and served created things rather than the Creator—who is forever praised.
>
> Romans 1:22–25

Because these people exchanged the truth of God for a lie, says Paul, God delivered them over to gross immorality and to a "depraved" mind:

> They have become filled with every kind of wickedness, evil, greed and depravity. They are full of envy, murder, strife, deceit and malice. They are gossips, slanderers, God-haters, insolent, arrogant and boastful; they invent ways of doing evil; they disobey their parents; they are senseless, faithless, heartless, ruthless. Although they know God's righteous decree that those who do such things deserve death, they not only continue to do these very things but also approve of those who practice them.
>
> Romans 1:29–32

Therefore, if what the Bible says is true, when looking at the history of man, we should find some form of ethical monotheism existing side by side with other kinds of religions and with all kinds of evil. We should find these things to be true both in the distant past and in the present. This is exactly what the second half of my next chapter explores.

Summary and Conclusion

Joseph Campbell uses science to support his religious worldview of mystical pantheism. He quotes scientists like physicist Erwin Schrödinger[37] who believe that all living things are part of some all-encompassing, impersonal being or essence. At the same time, he uses science to undermine belief in the Bible. In doing so, however, he advocates a narrow interpretation of the biblical text which doesn't hold up.

As we have seen, the Bible actually gives us very little indication of how old the universe is, how old the earth is, or how many years really transpired between the creation of Adam and the birth of Abraham, the first Hebrew patriarch. Thus, the only real conflict between modern science and the Bible is the scientific theory of human evolution, which says that human beings and apes are descended from a common ancestor. Campbell accepts this theory completely, but many, if not most, orthodox Christian scholars do not. Therefore, the next chapter examines this issue and looks at the history of human religion, which Campbell claims has also undergone a kind of evolution.

As usual, finding out the truth about these topics is not a question of how many scholars we can cite, but what evidence they give for their position. How reliable is their evidence? Does it adequately satisfy the tests for truth in chapter 1?

9

Evolution and the Great High God

he fossil findings of modern science have captured the public imagination. Our popular culture is filled with fantastic images of dinosaurs, cavemen, and other strange creatures, most now extinct.

If we listed the appearances of these pop culture icons, we would probably have to start with Jules Verne's *Journey to the Center of the Earth* or *The Lost World* by Sir Arthur Conan Doyle, the creator of Sherlock Holmes. After that could come *King Kong* and the comic strip cavemen "Alley Oop" and "BC." Add *One Million BC*, a 1940 film starring Victor Mature, and its 1966 remake *One Million Years BC*, starring Raquel Welch. And there's also *Caveman*, the comedy film with ex-Beatle Ringo Starr. More recently, we have author Michael Crichton's novel *Jurassic Park* and the film version by Steven Spielberg, where scientists are able to create live dinosaurs in a test tube, and the TV show *Dinosaurs* with live action puppets. Then, of course, there's always *The Flintstones*.

This small list shows the storytelling power evolution science evokes. Even scientists aren't immune to this power.

For example, pro-evolution writer Roger Lewin in *Bones of Contention* cites Dr. Misia Landau's observation that most paleontologists and anthropologists like to invent stories about the bones and fossils they uncover. The idea, for instance, that some apes were more curious and restless than other apes and it was those apes who are the ancestors of modern man is a fanciful story that many Darwinists have artificially imposed on the fossil record. We have to be careful, therefore, when we deal with scientific data like the fossil record, not to invent or believe some fable that sounds plausible but really has little or no basis in fact.

Evolution is the great secular myth of the twentieth century. It tells a story many people find compelling. But are there any good reasons to accept this story as nonfiction? Is there adequate evidence to support it? Is Joseph Campbell's belief in evolution correct? Is the theory of evolution a proven scientific fact? Have scientists actually "found the bones" to prove evolution is true?

A growing number of scientific experts and other educated people are answering no to all these questions. They claim that both the laws of logic and the empirical or factual evidence show that the theory of evolution is an elaborate fairy tale spun by partisan scientists, a sad case of wishful thinking. They allege that many evolution scientists engage in subjective, speculative thinking unsupported by factual evidence and that the scientists sometimes even distort the facts to fit their theories.

The first part of this chapter examines some of the best arguments against scientific evolution. Next, we launch into a discussion about the origin of human life. Finally, we discuss what historical research reveals about the early development of human religion. The goal of this chapter is to show the inherent inadequacies of evolutionary theory and to affirm consistency between the biblical data and what we know about human origins.

Evolution: Science Fact or Science Fiction?

Evolution is the theory that animals, birds, reptiles, fish, plants, human beings, and other living creatures on earth originated from common ancestors through a purely natural process or causal agent over a long period of time. This process involves an elaborate series of random variations or mutations, coupled with a mechanism of "natural selection," which helps preserve only those mutations and changes that contribute to the organism's survival. According to this theory, today's apes, monkeys, and humans are descendants of common ancestors who lived millions of years ago. These common ancestors are themselves descendants of other common ancestors in the distant past. All of these creatures have undergone gradual, or sometimes sudden, genetic and physical changes and mutations.

Scientists who believe evolution is true generally cite three kinds of evidence to support their position:

1. The biological classification of all living species, including man;
2. The "similarity of form and function at both the microscopic and macroscopic level" within and among these species;[1] and
3. The fossil record.

Michael Denton in *Evolution: A Theory in Crisis* and Phillip E. Johnson in *Darwin on Trial* refute all three kinds of evidence in their books. Denton is a medical doctor and biologist, a non-Christian; and Johnson is a law professor at the University of California at Berkeley, where he specializes in the logic of arguments and the reliability of evidence. Although Johnson is a Christian, his book does not support the literal six-day interpretation of Genesis 1, nor does it offer a Christian interpretation of the scientific evidence. This book examines the evidence for and against evolution from a logical and empirical viewpoint.

Both Denton and Johnson comprehensively evaluate the scientific research for and against evolution. After discussing the evidence, they each conclude that neither the fossil record, nor the biological classification of species, nor the form and function at the microscopic and macroscopic level within and among species supports the theory that species evolve from common ancestors through a purely natural process of random mutation and natural selection. The power of their arguments is staggering—they quote extensively from scientists who are pro-evolution and they brilliantly point out the logical fallacies and lack of empirical confirmation on the part of evolutionists.

Denton and Johnson make several important points. Denton meticulously examines the evidence for the biological classification of all living species. He shows how the empirical evidence indicates: 1) sharp discontinuities between species; 2) biological "isolation"[2] of various species; 3) a pattern that is not sequential; 4) species containing special traits that never change within the members of those species; and 5) an order of nature exhibiting a regular hierarchy that doesn't allow for a random evolutionary process. Thus, the actual evidence reveals profound and insurmountable divisions within the biological classification of species. These divisions can be proven empirically. They undermine the theory that random genetic mutations can help a species change or evolve into a different species. Therefore, says Denton, different species cannot have common ancestors.

Evidence from microbiology (at the microscopic level) also supports this pattern of discontinuity, isolation, division, and hierarchy. According to Denton and Johnson, if one looks at the cells and molecules that support life, not only does one find extremely complex wholes with incredibly delicate parts, one also finds clear-cut divisions and no intermediate or transitional forms. Comparative molecular studies show that the molecules clearly exhibit "a highly ordered, non-overlapping system composed of groups within groups, of classes which are inclusive or exclusive of other classes."[3]

At the microgenetic or microscopic gene level, adds Denton, you need DNA, RNA, and chains of amino acids forming complex proteins. A random mutation in one area would destroy this complex mechanism, and the organism would probably not survive. Johnson notes that even evolution scientists disagree over whether micromutations or macromutations are necessary for evolution to occur. Thus, the molecular evidence at the microscopic level has actually created more problems for the theory of evolution. Neither chance mutations nor natural selection can explain this evidence. They cannot explain the "ordered pattern of diversity"[4] in nature.

Finally, empirical evidence shows that there are large, systematic or nonrandom "gaps" in the fossil record. These gaps are unexplainable by gradual evolutionary theory. When scientists look at the fossil record, they find that living organisms always appear fully formed and always retain the same basic characteristics. In other words, there are really no transitional or intermediate fossils. The fossil record thus contains no objective confirmation of evolution!

"Bird and bat wings appear in the fossil record already developed," says Johnson.[5] No scientists have ever confirmed the gradual evolution of wings and eyes from the fossil record, nor even the sudden evolution of such complex structures or organs in the fossil record. Evidence from the fossil record also discloses that organisms, after they appear in the record, display basically no significant physical changes throughout their history.

Denton mentions several classic examples of alleged transitional or intermediate species, such as the lungfish and the archaeopteryx—a primitive bird from the Jurassic geological period—but notes that these species contain important organ systems that are not transitional or intermediate. The archaeopteryx, for instance, possesses a central nervous system typical of all birds. The lungfish has no transitional organ systems at all, adds Denton. He also mentions several alleged examples of evolution by some species, such as the horse, but explains that these examples are few and exhibit only minor changes. Therefore, they represent examples of only gradual microevolution *within* species and not gradual macroevolution *between* species. These examples lack evidence of the kind of major transitional links required within the fossil record to prove the theory of gradual macroevolution.

In reality, the evidence in the fossil record against gradual evolution is so clear-cut that some scientists, such as Stephen Jay Gould, have proposed a new theory whereby sudden changes in remote areas are coupled with minor gradual changes to produce new species. This new evolution theory is called "punctuated equilibrium." Using this theory, Gould and other evolution scientists try to explain away the gaps in the fossil record. In effect, the evolution scientists say evolution is either so slow and gradual you don't notice it or so swift, sudden, and remote you can't see it.

This new theory merely manipulates the interpretation of the empirical evidence. It is fallacious to argue one's case on the *absence* of evidence, as do Gould and his colleagues. Denton in fact says that Charles Darwin, the father of modern evolution, believed that such a theory of sudden macroevolution would point to divine creation or special creation, not to the kind of natural evolutionary process he assumed.

The evolutionary concepts of common ancestors, chance mutations, "natural" selection, and transitional links remain only theoretical entities. These theoretical entities are "conspicuously absent from the fossil record even after long and determined searching."[6]

Despite what Joseph Campbell claims, the actual scientific evidence raises substantial doubt about the truth of evolution. Neither the biological classification of living species, nor the microscopic and macroscopic levels of form and function, nor even the fossil record supports the theory of organic evolution.

Compared to other scientific claims, evolution is one of the least substantiated and most speculative in the history of science. It doesn't fit the empirical evidence. It is also logically inconsistent. Although it says mankind evolved at least partly by nonrational chance, it also asserts that rational scientists can use rational methods to describe how this random evolution takes place. This seems to be a logical contradiction. If human thought and knowledge is a product of blind chance, then human thought and knowledge cannot be trusted to be non-blind and predictive. If our rational, personal minds are all or even partly the result of random, non-purposeful chance, how is it possible that we can use our minds to separate fact from fiction? How can we ever perceive error and how do we account for it? If evolution is true, why is science, which depends on predictability and logical order, a reliable way to obtain knowledge?

Evolution thus undermines the rational justification for the reliability of science. If evolution were really true, then we would be unable to truly use science to understand and comprehend the material universe, because science itself would be part of the same random phenomenon. Darwin and his followers tell a fantastic story, but their story has never satisfied basic tests for truth.

Adam—Just a Monkey's Uncle?

There are many pro-evolution sources that discuss the fossil record with regard to monkeys, apes, and men. In my research for this book, I examined books, articles from *Science News* and *Sci-*

entific American, and the 1989 editions of *The New Encyclopaedia Britannica Micropaedia* and *Macropaedia.* Many of the books
and articles on evolution disagree with one another when it comes
to dating the fossils. This fundamental confusion throws doubt on
the entire slime-to-man theory.

In chapter 2 of *Myths to Live By,* taken from a lecture Campbell
delivered in 1966, Campbell claims scientists have discovered "distinctly humanoid jaws and skulls" dated to "about 1,800,000 years
ago."[7] On the next page, he declares: "Our first tangible evidences
of mythological thinking are from the period of Neanderthal Man,
which endured from ca. 250,000 to ca. 50,000 B.C. . . . ."[8]

Both of these statements are false.

The bones of *Homo habilis* that Dr. L. S. B. Leakey discovered
in Olduvai Gorge in East Africa are indeed dated to about 1.8 million years ago, but they are not "distinctly humanoid." In fact, a 1989
textbook on geology and evolution, *Historical Geology: Evolution
of the Earth and Life through Time,* says that *Homo habilis* is
now considered extremely apelike, not distinctly humanoid.[9] In making such distinctions, evolution scientists look at skull bones, brain
capacity, eyebrow ridges, teeth, and the physical ability to walk
erect.

The first distinctly human fossils are those of *Homo sapiens.* Scientists believe this species is the first fully erect humanoid and the
first to have the kind of brain capacity to match modern humans or
Homo sapiens sapiens. The most reliable date scientists now give
for the appearance of *Homo sapiens* is about 200,000 years ago.
Before *Homo sapiens,* there was a creature called *Homo erectus,*
who lived about 1.6 million years ago to 300,000 years ago.

The teeth of *Homo erectus* are more manlike than apelike, but
there are other unique features of *Homo erectus* that neither apes
nor humans share, such as thick skull bones and eyebrow ridges.
According to the 1989 edition of *The New Encyclopaedia Britannica Macropaedia,* the evidence of evolution from *Homo erectus*
to *Homo sapiens* is still uncertain. There is no overlap in the fossil
record between these two species, and, in fact, there are no examples of any link between their skull size and shape or between the
"cultural achievements"[10] of the two groups of creatures. Even the
geology/evolution textbook just cited admits, "The evolution of mod-

ern humans from *H. erectus* is not completely clear from the fossil record."[11]

This same textbook dates Neanderthal Man, who is now considered to be just another race of *Homo sapiens*, from about 150,000 years ago to 32,000 years ago, or about 148,000 B.C. to 30,000 B.C. This is over 100,000 years later than the earliest date for Neanderthals given by Campbell. *The New Encyclopaedia Britannica Micropaedia* is even more conservative. Although it says scientists apparently have found some fossil forerunners of Neanderthal Man as old as 100,000 to 150,000 years, Neanderthals probably did not appear until about 75,000 to 100,000 years ago, or about 73,000 B.C. to 98,000 B.C. The "most numerous and complete skeletal remains"[12] of Neanderthals date from about 85,000 to about 35,000 years ago, or between 83,000 B.C. and 33,000 B.C. during the Last Glacial Stage in Europe.

It is perhaps possible that these dates for Neanderthal Man have been vastly inflated by secular scientists. It is also possible, however, that the flood described in Genesis, whether local, as some Christian scholars believe, or worldwide, as others believe, occurred sometime before the Neanderthal period. The post-flood period of the Neanderthals was a period of ice ages, and the flood may have been a catalyst for such a climate change. The facial structure of Neanderthal Man is very similar to that of the Eskimo, whose facial bones have been modified due to the tough diet and weather endured in the frozen north. Neanderthal Man is known to have lived mostly in cold climates. Instead of being a separate species of humanoid, he could have been, and probably was, simply of another race, even though some secular scientists believe Neanderthal Man was a species unrelated to modern human beings.

If we accept either possibility, however, the *Britannica Macropaedia* says, contrary to Campbell, "little can be confidently inferred about Neanderthal beliefs and rituals."[13] Physiologist Jared Diamond says similar things in *The Third Chimpanzee: The Evolution and Future of the Human Animal.* "Neanderthals were the first people to leave undisputed evidence of fire's regular use," notes Diamond. "Neanderthals may also have been the first people who regularly buried their dead, but that's disputed, and whether it would imply religion is a matter of *pure speculation*" (my emphasis).[14]

Diamond believes Neanderthals probably died out because they couldn't compete with the superior Cro-Magnon Man, who lived approximately 35,000 to 10,000 years ago, or about 33,000 B.C. to 8,000 B.C. Diamond also claims Cro-Magnons were "anatomically fully modern,"[15] but Neanderthals were not. The other secular sources cited above, however, don't say Cro-Magnons were "fully modern," although they do mention the tremendous cultural changes that apparently occurred when Cro-Magnons supposedly replaced Neanderthals.

The Cro-Magnons in Europe are famous for their cave paintings and other prehistoric art. In volume one of *The Masks of God,* first published in 1959, Campbell states that female statues created by Cro-Magnons are examples of an early belief in mother goddesses, but anthropologist Sarunas Milisauskas calls such interpretations "only speculations."[16] Campbell also discusses one of the most famous of all cave paintings, called "the Sorcerer of Trois Frères," a striking figure that looks part human and part animal. Campbell gives the painting his typical mystical, pantheistic interpretation (he says the painting symbolizes the union of man with God),[17] but historian of religion Mircea Eliade says this kind of art may simply mean these Cro-Magnons worshiped a "Lord of Wild Beasts," or Lord of Creation, who helped them have success in hunting animals.[18] Such a divine figure has more in common with the God of Genesis than with the impersonal, pantheistic god of *The Power of Myth.* If this is true, it would knock a huge hole in Campbell's theories about primitive art, religion, ritual, and mythology. It would also lend support to the apostle Paul's comment in the first chapter of Romans that human beings have always known about the monotheistic and ethical God of the Bible.

In reality, says Christian scientist Hugh Ross, "evidence for religious relics and altars dates back only 8,000 to 24,000 years" or 6,000 B.C. to 22,000 B.C.[19] C. Simon, writing in *Science News,* backs this up. He says the oldest known religious shrine dates to only about 14,000 years ago (12,000 B.C.). "Evidence of religious ritual" in cave paintings, decorated objects, and burials older than this date "has been difficult to justify," adds Simon.[20]

This last bit of information not only refutes Campbell's statements in *The Masks of God* and *Myths to Live By,* it also presents dates

closer to those of Christian scholar Gleason Archer, who believes
that all the "manlike" creatures who lived before 10,000 B.C. lacked
"a true human soul."[21] Therefore, argues Archer, they would also
lack any kind of religion. In *The Power of Myth*, Campbell himself
admits that "until you have writing, you don't know what people
were thinking."[22]

This comment reveals the intellectual inconsistency Campbell
brings to his writings. If we can't really know what people were thinking before writing was invented, about 4000 B.C., then why does
Campbell make all those bold statements in his earlier works about
the religious thinking of men who lived before 4000 B.C.? Why does
he spend all those pages in *The Masks of God* writing about caveman paintings and religion? Why does he talk about "mythological
thinking" in the Neanderthal period? Could it be that Campbell
doesn't know what he's talking about? Perhaps Campbell's fables
satisfy a spiritually starving public eagerly seeking anything that
smacks of religion, especially if it is not orthodox Christianity, regardless of its logical contradictions and historical errors.

Christopher B. Stringer in "The Emergence of Modern Humans"
(*Scientific American*, December 1990) mentions some theories
which, if true, refute Campbell's ideas about the history of early man
and support our interpretation of the Bible's account in the first
eleven chapters of Genesis. Stringer claims the latest evidence indicates that both Neanderthal Man and modern humans are probably
descended from a common ancestor traceable to about 200,000 years
ago. This is the earliest approximate date Christian scholar James
Oliver Buswell gives in *A Systematic Theology of the Christian
Religion* for the creation of Adam and Eve. Buswell bases his theory
on a translation of the original Hebrew text of the genealogy tables
in Genesis from Adam to Abraham, the first Hebrew patriarch.

In 1987 and 1988, says Stringer, scientists found Neanderthal
bones in the Middle East dated about 60,000 years ago. He claims
there is evidence of early modern humans in the Middle East dated
about 40,000 years earlier. "The oldest-known records of modern
humans are found in southern Africa and Israel," he adds, "and are
dated to approximately 100,000 years ago. . . ."[23]

Stringer's dates lend support to the possibility that the Genesis
flood, whether local or worldwide, may have caused or helped cause

a colder climate that resulted in a new "race" of men, which today we call Neanderthals. The culture of these Neanderthals may have declined to a "primitive" state, and, when they tried to move back to the warmer climates in Europe and the Middle East, their culture could not compete with the descendants of the "early modern humans," which included the Cro-Magnon race and which eventually led to a more advanced culture, that of *Homo sapiens sapiens.*

Stringer's point of view is one of several cited in an article on human evolution in the March 14, 1994, issue of *Time* magazine. According to this article, there is still much debate among scientists over how to fit Neanderthal Man into the evolutionary scheme invented by Charles Darwin and others. As I noted earlier, some scientists still believe Neanderthal Man is not related to *Homo sapiens* and *Homo sapiens sapiens.* Evolution scientists are also divided over the issue of *Homo erectus* and their alleged migration from Africa.

Looking at the evidence presented in *Time,* I can see no solid evidence whatsoever to support the theory that *Homo erectus* somehow "evolved" into Neanderthal Man or into *Homo sapiens* and *Homo sapiens sapiens.* The secular scientists cited in that article continue to make philosophical assumptions unsupported by any facts. They not only assume that common characteristics between *Homo sapiens, Homo erectus,* and other species prove a common evolutionary link, they also assume that all this alleged history occurs purely by natural means. They refuse to consider the alternate possibility that these common characteristics indicate instead a common intelligent designer, God, who takes an active role in creation.

As Dr. J. P. Moreland notes in *Scaling the Secular City,* the idea of God is not just a religious concept, it is also a philosophical one. Evolution science often uses philosophical concepts like "natural" selection or "random" mutations to explain the world, so why can't we use words like *God* or *progressive creation* to explain the similarities and differences between *Homo erectus* and *Homo sapiens?* Using the words *God* and *progressive creation* is in fact a more intelligent solution than using terms like *natural selection* and *random mutation* because it provides a better explanation for the gaps in the fossil record and supplies a more reasonable foundation for why we can rely on various scientific methods and the laws of logic. Given this truth, instead of excluding the term *God* from science classrooms, our public schools should rather be excluding the words *natural selection* and *random mutation*. This is not a question of "separation of Church and State"; it's a question of truth.

Interestingly the article in *Time* admits that the dating techniques of evolution science are hardly foolproof, especially when trying to date fossils over 200,000 years old. Even if we accept the alleged dates for all these fossils, however, that still leaves us with both Christian scholar Gleason Archer's theory about the history of Adam and Eve, which goes back less than 15,000 years, and Christian scholar James Oliver Buswell's theory, which allows for a 200,000-year-old Adam and Eve. Whether we accept Archer's view, Buswell's view, or something in between, the fact remains, in spite of everything Campbell claims in his books, evolution science and its theories about *Homo habilis, Homo erectus, Homo sapiens,* the Neanderthals, Cro-Magnon Man, and *Homo sapiens sapiens* do not refute the Bible at all. In reality, the opposite is true—recent evidence from geology, paleontology, and anthropology actually strongly supports the Bible's basic view of man's origins and thus refutes Campbell's work. It also lends support to my interpretation in chapter 8 of the first eleven chapters of Genesis.

There are still some questions to be answered and more research to be done in geology, paleontology, anthropology, and even the field of biblical interpretation. None of these things, however, are liable to tip the scales of truth in Joseph Campbell's direction. Far from it. In fact, the more questions scientists and theologians answer and the more research they do, the less reliable Campbell's work becomes.

Christians have *nothing* to fear from scientists who study the fossil record of human beings. We have found the bones, and the bones don't contradict God's Word. Indeed, they are consistent with the belief that human beings *did not* evolve from animals.

The truth is, scientists often "overlook the differences and exaggerate the similarities"[24] between the fossils of *Homo sapiens* and those of *Homo habilis* and *Homo erectus.* They also often overlook the similarities and exaggerate the differences between Neanderthals, Cro-Magnons, and *Homo sapiens sapiens,* or modern man. Their theory of evolution requires not only small physical changes taking place gradually but also transitional forms and large physical changes from one species to another. The fossil record indicates neither of these things. It contains large systematic gaps that cannot be explained purely by natural means.

Natural evolution is an impersonal, nonrational mechanism; personal, rational minds cannot somehow evolve from a purely impersonal, nonrational cause. There must be a supernatural, personal cause for the creation of rational human beings with self-awareness. It stretches the bounds of credulity to believe that Mozart, Plato, Aristotle, computers, and human culture are merely the result of an impersonal, nonrational mechanism that operates even partly by random mutations that conveniently turn out to be positive.

If our personal, rational minds are all or even partly the result of chance, then there is no way of really knowing the truth of our thinking, and there is no reason to believe that our thoughts about evolution are even valid. It is just as easy for chance to destroy life as it is for chance to create life, and it would be harder for chance to sustain life once life began.

The existence of science is itself an argument against evolution. Science is a rational activity in which personal human beings engage. If the random mutation theory of evolution is true, however, then science would be rationally unreliable. Science works, therefore God exists. Evolution by design is possible, but evolution by chance is clearly not, especially if we're dealing with the alleged evolution of a personal, rational being who is self-aware, i.e., man. Only an Intelligent Designer with a personal, rational mind could create and sustain a world that includes other personal, rational minds. The Christian worldview is not opposed to science and logic; it actually provides a solid, intellectual foundation for science and logic.

The Great High God

Until about the 1920s, most anthropologists applied the idea of evolution to the origin and history of religion. Like many anthropologists working today, their worldview was mostly atheistic. They believed that the religious ideas of human beings have no objective basis or substantiation. Consequently, most anthropologists claimed that the religious culture of man "evolves" from simple forms to more complex forms. They developed theories to explain how religious ideas began and grew.

Some anthropologists, such as Sir Edward Burnett Tylor, thought religious ideas started with animism.[25] Other anthropologists believed religion began with ancestor worship. Still others believed religion started with some form of totemism,[26] or fetishism,[27] or magic and witchcraft, or with some primitive form of pantheism, nature worship, or belief in mana.[28] From these kinds of origins, man's religion next developed forms of polytheism, as well as higher levels of pantheism. Finally, they said, religious man developed ethical monotheism, which eventually gave way to the beginnings of philosophy and to science and psychology.

Joseph Campbell accepts this basic story. This theory of religious evolution plays a major role in his *Masks of God* books, the first volume of which was published in 1959. It also plays a prominent role in Campbell's *Flight of the Wild Gander*, first published in the early 1970s.

By at least the 1920s, however, anthropologists had found evidence that began to positively refute this theory of religious evolution. The evidence became so overwhelming that Melville Jacobs and Bernhard J. Stern, in the 1955 edition of their classic text *General Anthropology,* wrote:

> Present knowledge of peoples in primitive economies suggests that there is no reason why a god concept should not have been present in Paleolithic and modern food-gathering heritages at the same time that animistic beliefs were held. Where there are polytheistic beliefs there can also be, at the same time, beliefs in spirits, *mana* [authors' emphasis], and in one superior god, comparable to a monotheistic concept. *There is nothing mutually exclusive in these four concepts of the supernatural, and sufficient evidence is lacking to enumerate their probable order of development.* Furthermore, one cannot assert that a monotheistic concept tended to evolve often from an earlier stage of polytheism. *It is possible that some polytheistic beliefs are historical combinations of several monotheistic concepts from each of several peoples whose ideologies have fused.*[29]

This passage was written a good four years before the first volume of Campbell's *Masks of God* was published and yet it refutes some of Campbell's most basic premises. *Masks of God* is an outstanding case of ignoring the evidence and making the facts fit one's theory.

Most anthropologists now acknowledge that monotheistic beliefs can be found in many of the most "primitive" and isolated cultures on earth. Such beliefs can be found existing side-by-side with beliefs in magic, animism, totemism, polytheism, and pantheism. For instance, even in cultures with a strong polytheistic belief system, you will also find the idea that, once upon a time, there was an original and even benevolent "sky god" who created the world but who then forsook it and withdrew into heaven. According to Mircea Eliade, these kinds of gods often leave "their sons or their messengers or some other divinity who is subordinate to them, and who continues to be occupied with the creation in some sort, with its perfection or maintenance."[30] In many primitive religions, adds Eliade, "the Supreme Beings progressively lose their religious importance, and . . . they are replaced by other divine figures nearer to man."[31]

The research of Jacobs and Stern and Eliade chiefly matches that of Father Wilhelm Schmidt (1868–1954), the Austrian ethnologist who is probably most responsible for the abandonment of the progressive evolution theory of religion developed by Tylor and others. An abridged English edition of his book *The Origin and Growth of Religion: Facts and Theories* was first published in 1931. In that book, Schmidt extensively surveys the work of those anthropologists who believed in the theory of religious evolution. Schmidt discusses research in the 1800s actually supporting the idea that many primitive cultures have a strong belief in only one god, a "supreme sky-god" or "primitive high god."[32] He then discusses the progressive recognition of this research in the twentieth century. Finally, he presents his own research supporting this primitive monotheism view of the history of religion and answers some of the critics of this primitive high god theory.

Schmidt contends that "the most ancient of human cultures" displays a strong belief in ethical monotheism.[33] They believe in a supreme benevolent god who created the world and who also sometimes creates other spiritual beings. Schmidt says these other beings, though superior to mortal man, seldom, if ever, approach the lofty attributes of the Supreme Being.

"The Supreme Being of the primitive culture," writes Schmidt, "is not nearly so indissolubly connected with the sky as he is in the later cultures, especially that of the pastoral nomads. Among most peoples it is said that he used formerly to live on earth with men, whom he taught all manner of good and instructed in their social and moral laws."[34] For examples Schmidt cites the primitive high gods of the Southern Andamanese, the Southeast Australians, the North Central Californians, Native Americans of the Northwest, and many Native American Algonkin tribes. Schmidt also mentions a belief among some North American primitive cultures that the Supreme Being came down to earth from the sky, but he reports that most of the primitive cultures he studies believe that the Supreme Being "left the earth, generally because of some sin of mankind, and went up to heaven, where he now lives."[35]

Although the Supreme Being in these primitive cultures often "cannot be perceived by the senses," an emphasis is frequently placed on his transcendent personality.[36] This personality has certain qualities or attributes, adds Schmidt. The Supreme Being is, among other things, eternal, all-knowing, all-powerful, good, creative, and morally righteous.

As "the creator and source of morality," the Supreme Being imparts a moral code for all men to live by, Schmidt reports.[37] Those who obey the moral code will be rewarded in the afterlife, but those who disobey and do evil will be punished:

> The lot of the wicked is often described expressly as one of painful punishment, by fire and heat, as among the Ajongo Negrillos and the Southern Wiradyuri; but it may also be by cold, or by wanderings without rest. In other cases it consists simply in exclusion from the happiness of the good, or in an empty shadow-life.[38]

Even Schmidt's critics admit that many of the most primitive cultures contain monotheistic elements, but they don't believe their monotheism is as highly developed as Schmidt assumes. Nor do they agree with his belief that primitive monotheism was the first religious belief. One such critic cited by anthropologist Charles J. Adams

in *The New Encyclopaedia Britannica Macropaedia* and by Sir
Edward Evans-Pritchard in *Theories of Primitive Religion* is historian of religion Rafael Pettazoni (1883–1959).[39] Neither of these
sources, however, mentions Father Schmidt's telling criticisms of
Pettazoni. Considering the wealth of material Schmidt presents in
The Origin and Growth of Religion and elsewhere, their discussions of his work are extremely superficial.

Adams even misrepresents Schmidt's work. He claims Schmidt
makes "a very long jump from the premise that primitive tribes have
high gods to the conclusion that the earliest men were monotheistic."[40] This is a false characterization of Schmidt's work. Schmidt
does not simply claim that primitive tribes have high gods. He claims
that "the most ancient" of these tribes have a strong belief in high
gods who make high moral demands on their followers. In other
words, Schmidt claims the earliest tribes have a belief in ethical
monotheism. Adams's criticism of Schmidt's theory is based on an
inaccurate description of Schmidt's work.

Although Pettazoni admits many primitive cultures have sky gods,
he does not believe this is true monotheism, which he claims is actually a negation or denial of polytheism and, as such, must not historically precede polytheism but succeed it. Pettazoni calls these sky
gods merely a dim personification or embodiment of the physical sky.

In his own work, Schmidt rejects Pettazoni's critique. "The out-
lines of the Supreme Being become dim only among later peoples,"
says Schmidt. Furthermore, "a being who lives in the sky, who stands
behind the celestial phenomena, who must 'centralize' in himself the
various manifestations [of thunder, rain, etc.], is not a personification of the sky at all."[41] No other expert links the primitive high gods
solely to a personification of the physical sky, notes Schmidt.[42] Pettazoni lumps all the high gods together, he adds, and proposes no
objective, scientific methods to determine which cultures are more
ancient than others. Schmidt also claims that Pettazoni fails to study
Schmidt's work seriously and often relies on incorrect translations
of Schmidt's German.[43] Finally, Schmidt states that Pettazoni's definition of monotheism, which always links monotheism to a denial of
an earlier polytheism, does not match the usage of the term in German, French, or English, where the usage does not depend on any

reference to earlier beliefs in polytheism. Nor does it match the way anthropologists use the term to describe religious beliefs.

Ernest Brandewie, who translates some of Father Schmidt's writings in *Wilhelm Schmidt and the Origin of the Idea of God,* says that Pettazoni seems to define Schmidt's primitive ethical monotheism out of existence. He calls Pettazoni's definition an "arbitrary" straw man argument.[44] Even so, Brandewie criticizes Schmidt's firm belief that ethical monotheism was the earliest religious idea, although he praises Schmidt's basic method and his general use of sources. "Schmidt certainly showed that religion is important to people, a lesson all the more useful to recall the more secular the modern world becomes," says Brandewie. "And Schmidt showed that religion is not just left-over legend among the groups he studied . . . but was closely connected with ethical life. . . ."[45]

Whether or not we accept all of Schmidt's work, it is disappointing that neither the *Encyclopaedia Britannica* nor Evans-Pritchard mentions Schmidt's criticism of Pettazoni. Recognition of Schmidt's criticism would have been more in keeping with Jacobs and Stern's *General Anthropology* which lends support to Schmidt's rejection of Pettazoni's idea that monotheism always is a denial of earlier forms of polytheism. "One cannot assert that a monotheistic concept tended to evolve often from an earlier stage of polytheism," they declare.[46]

Christians do not have to show that the first religious belief was some form of ethical monotheism in order to defend biblical monotheism. All that is necessary is to show that monotheistic beliefs go back in history as far as any other known religion. This is exactly what Schmidt proves. Even Evans-Pritchard notes that most anthropologists have abandoned all evolutionary schemes for the historical development of religion. He says they have also found monotheistic beliefs existing side-by-side with other religious beliefs.[47]

Evans-Pritchard gave the lectures on which his book was based in 1962. Jacobs and Stern published the second edition of their book in 1955. Joseph Campbell's work, published mostly between 1959 and 1987, must therefore be considered hopelessly out of date.

Christian scholar Arthur C. Custance, in volume four of *The Doorway Papers,* agrees with Campbell when he says, "Until you have writing, you don't know what people were thinking." Custance thinks it is more reasonable to start with what we know and proceed to the unknown rather than start with the unknown and apply it to what we do know. Thus, says Custance, we shouldn't speculate about what religious ideas prehistoric people held until we see what the earliest writings of human beings show.

Custance, who affirms Father Schmidt's work of the 1920s and 1930s, says that the earliest examples of human writing from Sumeria, Egypt, China, India, and even Italy and Greece show a widespread acceptance of ethical monotheism. As human culture progresses, says Custance, this original monotheism often sinks into a gross polytheism where people take the attributes of the one true god and distribute them among an increasing proliferation of gods and demi-gods. Later writings from these ancient cultures reveal an amazing collection of thousands of gods and spirits, but earlier writings show a drastically smaller number of such beings. Moreover, contained within these earlier writings is a belief in a Supreme Being who rules benevolently from heaven.

Custance's argument is persuasive because of the evidence he presents to support it. Unfortunately, he relies too much on hard-to-confirm research predating Wilhelm Schmidt's work.

The same reference used by Custance for the early Chinese name for the one true god, Shang Ti, is mentioned in volume one of Eliade's *A History of Religious Ideas* and in Don Richardson's *Eternity in Their Hearts*. Richardson's book contains a favorable critique of Father Schmidt's work. It also contains further evidence of primitive ethical monotheism supporting Schmidt's theory and supporting Custance's view. Thus, if you add the evidence from Custance to that of Eliade, who admits that the primitive high gods "progressively lose" their original religious importance, and to that of Jacobs and Stern, Richardson, and Brandewie, then the bulk of the evidence strongly favors Father Schmidt's theory of the origin of religion.

Charles Joseph Adams's and Evans-Pritchard's handling of the primitive high gods theory is superficial when compared to Schmidt's own writings, especially if you read Schmidt's persuasive, detailed criticism of the research of those scholars who oppose the primitive monotheism theory. Ironically, Joseph Campbell himself discusses Father Schmidt's work in the first volume of *The Masks of God*[48] but fails to mention Schmidt's theory about primitive ethical monotheism.

It is not necessary to prove that ethical monotheism was the first and oldest religious belief. All that is needed to affirm the biblical view is to show that ethical monotheism is at least as old as any other religious idea. This is exactly what the evidence shows. And that's all we need in order to refute Campbell's ideas about the origin and evolution of religious thought and mythology. It's also all we need to affirm St. Paul's view in chapter 1 of Romans that all men have known about the one true God. We can verify the basic history of human religion as given in the first eleven chapters of Genesis.

The Bible is right. Ethical monotheism is not a later development in the history of man. It did not develop from any other religious idea. If anything, the reverse is true. From the very beginning, man has known about the one true God, the Lord of creation.

Summary and Conclusion

In the last two chapters, the evidence has refuted Joseph Campbell's views concerning science, evolution, the origin and development of religion, and the alleged discrepancy between modern science and the Bible. Science, history, archeology, and anthropology don't contradict the Bible's view of man, the apparent date of his origin, or the development of his religious ideas. Despite what Campbell states, the Bible does not teach that the earth is only a few thousand years old. If you use proper methods of interpretation, you cannot apply specific historical dates to the lives of human beings who lived from Adam to Abraham. The biblical text allows for the possibility of an earth that is four billion years old or more.[49] The text allows us to believe that the first true man, or *Homo sapiens,* was created 150,000, 200,000, or even 250,000 years ago, *and* to believe that this first man was named Adam.

Just because *Homo sapiens* seems to share some important characteristics with today's great apes and chimpanzees and with yesterday's "hominid" animals doesn't mean it shares a "common ancestor" with them. My two house cats have two distinctly different personalities and sometimes even appear quite "human," but that doesn't mean that cats and human beings "evolved" from similar organic life forms. In fact, it may simply mean that an all-powerful Creator, or God, used similar designs to create both humans and animals.

"Raw energy cannot (by itself) bring order out of chaos."[50] Complex life forms need a blueprint, such as DNA, and a means of converting energy, such as the digestive system. The amount of information for this kind of blueprint precludes the involvement of a purely natural random process. Only a God like the one found in Genesis and Romans can explain the creation of such a complex, rational organism as mankind.

Although he eschews all attempts to achieve rational, objective truth when it comes to religion and morality, Campbell uncritically accepts the truth claims and metaphysical worldview of modern science. This leads him to adopt an outdated view of the historical development of religion. As we have seen, this view does not fit the facts. Indeed, the facts actually seem to support what the Bible says about the early religious beliefs of human beings.

Chapter 14 of Genesis describes a unique encounter between Abraham, the first Hebrew patriarch, and a man named Melchizedek, King of Salem, later called Jerusalem. Melchizedek was "priest of God Most High," says the text, and he blesses Abraham in the name of that God.

Here we have an example, Melchizedek, of someone in an ancient, probably pagan, society who worships the same God that the early Hebrews worshiped. This passage in Genesis thus lends credence to the research on the primitive high god idea presented in this chapter.

In conclusion, therefore, not only have we disproved Joseph Campbell's view of the Bible and science and of the Bible and evolution, we have also refuted his statements about the religious beliefs of Neanderthal Man and his basic view about the origin and evolution of religion. In the case of Father Wilhelm Schmidt's work on primitive ethical monotheism, we have shown that Campbell doesn't even acknowledge the solid research of a famous scholar in his own field whose work doesn't fit Campbell's own extremely biased theological perspective.

Campbell's inadequate research and illogical argumentation may look and sound impressive on a PBS sound stage, but the facts and a critical examination of his writings reveal his ideas are fundamentally flawed.

10

The Great Bible Debate

he books of the Bible are not simply essays on spiritual and moral matters; they claim to record historical truth. Deuteronomy 31:24–26 tells us Moses wrote the Book of the Law in the Old Testament, which includes the Ten Commandments. The Bible says this Law was given to Moses directly by God.

The Greek physician Luke, a close friend of the apostle Paul, writes in the New Testament, "I myself have carefully investigated everything from the beginning" (Luke 1:3). Hebrews 2:3–4 says Jesus Christ's message of salvation "was confirmed to us by those who heard him. God also testified to it by signs, wonders and various miracles, and gifts of the Holy Spirit distributed according to his will." In 1 Corinthians 15:1–7, the apostle Paul speaks about the resurrection of Jesus Christ and about Christ's appearances to Peter, the twelve apostles, to James (the brother of Jesus), to Paul, and to over five hundred other witnesses.

Like other people hostile to orthodox Christianity,[1] Joseph Campbell rejects these passages that defend the historical truth of the Bible. Not only does he deny the historical reliability of the Bible, he also tries to change the meaning of the Christian message. In order to refute his objections quickly and precisely, I have broken down his arguments into five themes:

1. Criticism of the Old Testament
2. Criticism of the virgin birth of Jesus Christ
3. Criticism of Jesus Christ's sacrifice on the cross
4. Campbell's use of pagan mystery cults
5. Campbell's use of gnostic gospel

None of Campbell's arguments are new, and all of them have been refuted by other, well-qualified scholars.

This chapter examines the arguments on both sides of these five issues and replies to a particular comment made by Campbell in his book *Flight of the Wild Gander* about 2 Peter 1:16–18. Campbell's comment is an excellent example not only of his hostility toward orthodox Christians, but also his lack of knowledge about biblical scholarship. By focusing on such examples, we can demolish Campbell's view of the Bible and give readers a better handle on the historical accuracy of God's Word.

The Five Books of Moses

In *Myths to Live By, The Masks of God: Occidental Mythology,* and elsewhere, Joseph Campbell attacks the historicity of the Old Testament, especially the first five books of the Bible, which were probably written, except for certain minor passages,[2] by the Jewish religious prophet and leader Moses. At one point, Campbell writes that the Hebrew texts of the Old Testament

> were not composed by "God" or even by anyone named Moses, but are of various dates and authors, all much later than was formerly supposed. The first five books of the Old Testament (Torah) were assembled only after the period of Ezra (fourth century B.C.), and the documents of which it was fashioned date all the way from the ninth century B.C. (the so-called J and E texts) to the second or so (the P, or "priestly" writings).[3]

Campbell goes on to write that there are two accounts of the great flood and two accounts of creation in Genesis, the first book of the Bible attributed to Moses.

While it may be true that many secular and some Christian scholars agree with Campbell's assessment, many other scholars over many decades have presented ample evidence against such criticisms. In *The Five Books of Moses,* first published in 1943, over twenty-one years before Campbell published *Occidental Mythology,* Oswald T. Allis, who taught for nineteen years in the Department of Semitic Philology at Princeton Theological Seminary, defends the Mosaic authorship of the first five books of the Old Testament. In his book, Allis also refutes the J, E, and P theory assumed by Campbell. This theory is called the "Development" or "Graf-Wellhausen Hypothesis," named after K. H. Graf (1865) and J. Wellhausen (1878), who developed the theory over a century ago. More recently Allis's research was affirmed by Gleason Archer, who refutes the J, E, and P theory in *A Survey of Old Testament Introduction.*

Archer complains that the scholars who continue to support this theory have an "antisupernaturalist bias"[4] against the Bible. Their worldview doesn't allow for the possibility of a personal God who can intervene in history; therefore they must give a natural explanation for every miraculous event and all the God-inspired language in the Bible. This attitude also compels them to ignore the strong monotheistic language of the text, says Archer. Because they believe in the evolutionary theory of religion, refuted in the last chapter, they take passages of the Old Testament and read into them evidence of an early form of animism or a crude form of polytheism. They claim Jewish writers after Moses took the stories in the first five books and applied a monotheistic layer to them.

The scholars who support the Graf-Wellhausen theory and other similar theories also favor evidence from ancient non-Jewish texts against the Bible. When there is an apparent discrepancy between the Bible and an ancient text from non-Jewish cultures, writes Archer, these scholars prefer the evidence from the non-Jewish text. Such a preference represents a gross bias against the biblical text. Scholars like Campbell should not reject the historical veracity of the Bible simply because it presents a religious viewpoint they dislike; nor should they automatically accept the historical reliability of the non-Jewish source simply because it contradicts the Bible's viewpoint. Christians owe a debt of gratitude to archeologists like William F. Albright, says Archer, who have confirmed much of the historical background to the biblical text.[5]

Two things scholars like Campbell cite to try to prove that more than one person wrote the first five books of the Bible, says Archer, are the use of different names for God in the text and the use of repetition and duplication in the text. Archer correctly notes that such literary devices have been used by individual authors throughout history, from ancient times to the present. He also notes that non-biblical Hebrew literature often uses repetition and duplication within a text by one author.

The biblical account of the Exodus in the Old Testament contains many details, says Archer, which indicate an actual participant witnessed the events. For example, "the author of Genesis and Exodus shows a thorough acquaintance with Egypt, as one would expect of a participant in the Exodus."[6] The author uses Egyptian names; a large number of Egyptian words, as compared to the number used in the rest of the Bible; genuine Egyptian titles of the period; knowledge of the culture in that part of the ancient world; familiarity with the geography, plants, and animals of Egypt and the Sinai peninsula where the Hebrews wandered in the wilderness; and "a large number of idioms and turns of speech which are characteristically Egyptian in origin, even though translated into Hebrew."[7] Furthermore, the author displays no such special knowledge of the Promised Land of Canaan, which is exactly what one would expect if the first five books of the Bible were written by Moses, who died before the Hebrews entered the Promised Land.

Finally, Archer contends that Moses had the qualifications to write the first five books. Not only was he educated in the Egyptian court, which meant he could write, but he would have had access to the oral traditions of the Middle East as well as of the Hebrew people descended from Abraham. Archer concludes,

> There is a most remarkable unity of arrangement which underlies the entire Pentateuch [first five books] and links it together into a progressive whole, even though successive stages in revelation (during Moses' writing career of four decades) result in a certain amount of overlapping and restatement . . . it is quite unreasonable to sup-

pose that a leader of Moses' background and education was too illiterate to commit a single word to writing.[8]

As for Campbell's contention that there are really two accounts of creation and two accounts of the great flood in Genesis, such arguments have been clearly refuted by Archer in *Encyclopedia of Bible Difficulties,* by Oswald T. Allis in *The Five Books of Moses,* by John W. Haley in *Alleged Discrepancies of the Bible,* by Josh McDowell and Don Stewart in *Answers to Tough Questions Skeptics Ask about the Christian Faith,* and by other scholars in other books. An examination of these books or any conservative, orthodox Christian commentary on Genesis, such as Ronald F. Youngblood's *The Book of Genesis: An Introductory Commentary,* provides persuasive evidence for the unity of the Pentateuch.

The Virgin Birth of Jesus Christ

In *The Power of Myth* Campbell says, "The virgin birth comes into Christianity by way of the Greek tradition."[9] He mentions the Greek stories of Leda and Persephone. He then mentions India and the Hindu religious tradition and explains that the virgin birth theme "is the birth of spiritual man out of the animal man." This "spiritual man" is really a god, according to Campbell, and that god is really you, not Jesus:

> So you're thinking about Jesus with all the sentiments relevant to how he suffered—out there. But that suffering is what ought to be going on in you. Have you been spiritually reborn? Have you died to your animal nature and come to life as a human incarnation of compassion?[10]

Campbell develops similar ideas in *The Masks of God: Occidental Mythology,* where he compares the virgin birth of Jesus Christ to the Greek story of Danae and the Zoroastrian story of Saoshyant, the savior-god.

Campbell's arguments here are also nothing new. They have been easily refuted in the past, and the refutations have stood the test of time. His comparisons of Jesus Christ's virgin birth with these pagan stories are false, and his interpretation of the meaning of Christ's virgin birth has nothing to do with the biblical text.

J. Gresham Machen (1881–1937), the premier conservative defender of the virgin birth, taught New Testament at Princeton Theological Seminary for twenty-three years and founded Westminster Theological Seminary in 1929. According to Machen in his classic book *The Virgin Birth of Christ,* first published in 1930 (a second edition was published in 1932), none of these pagan stories are really virgin births. Either the god or gods have sex with human beings or the human father participates in some kind of sexual union with the mother. The birth of Jesus Christ, described in the New Testament, is completely different—no sexual union is implied in those texts referring to the virgin birth.

In the Greek story of Leda, Leda is visited by the god Zeus in the form of a swan and gives birth to an egg from which came Helen of Troy, Clytemnestra, Castor, and Polydeuces. Since Leda's husband also makes love to her shortly after Zeus, the exact paternity of these quadruplets is open to question. Regardless, both encounters are sexual.

In the story of Persephone, Zeus rapes his sister Demeter, and Persephone is born. Later on in this story, Demeter lures Zeus to a cave where she has hidden their daughter Persephone. The god visits his daughter in the form of a snake and has intercourse with her. Persephone gives birth to the god of bread and wine, Dionysus. Eventually, the god of the underworld, Hades, kidnaps Persephone and makes her his wife. Demeter the mother mourns for her daughter and lays a curse on the land, which becomes desolate. Persephone finally is allowed to spend eight months of the year with her mother, but four months in the underworld, which is why the earth remains barren during the winter.

In the Greek story of Danae, Zeus visits Danae in the form of a golden shower and achieves sexual union with her. Danae gives birth to the Greek hero Perseus, the slayer of Medusa and an ancestor of the powerful Hercules.

In the Zoroastrian story of Saoshyant, the god Zoroaster's sexual seed is miraculously preserved in Lake Kasaoya. A virgin bathes in the lake, is impregnated by the seed, and later gives birth to Saoshyant, the savior-god.

Contrary to what Campbell says, none of these stories are virgin birth stories. They aren't even remotely comparable to the virgin birth of Jesus Christ.

Machen points out in his book that critics of the virgin birth of Christ have never been able to explain the origin of this Christian belief. In fact, they can't even agree among themselves on any one theory for its origin. All of their references to pagan religions have proven erroneous.

The virgin birth of Jesus Christ is a unique event with no parallel in religious literature; it is predicted in Isaiah 7:14 in the Old Testament, which is quoted in Matthew 1:23.

> Therefore the Lord himself will give you a sign: The virgin will be with child and will give birth to a son, and will call him Immanuel.
>
> Isaiah 7:14

This verse, from one of the greatest Hebrew prophets, has an important parallel in Isaiah 9:6–7:

> For to us a child is born,
>   to us a son is given,
>   and the government will be on his shoulders.
> And he will be called
>   Wonderful Counselor, Mighty God,
>   Everlasting Father, Prince of Peace.
> Of the increase of his government
>   there will be no end.
> He will reign on David's throne
>   and over his kingdom,
> establishing it and holding it
>   with justice and righteousness
>   from that time on and forever.
> The zeal of the Lord Almighty
>   will accomplish this.

The virgin birth of Jesus Christ is not a pantheistic story about the birth of divine, spiritual man out of the animal man. It is the historical story of the transcendent, eternal, personal Creator-God made flesh.

In the beginning was the Word, and the Word was with God, and the
Word was God. He was with God in the beginning. Through him all
things were made; without him nothing was made that has been made.
... The Word became flesh and made his dwelling among us. We have
seen his glory, the glory of the One and Only, who came from the
Father, full of grace and truth.

John 1:1–3, 14

The pagan stories of Leda, Persephone, Danae, and Saoshyant
pale in comparison with the virgin birth of Christ, the Word made
flesh.

The Dying and Rising God

Related to Campbell's view of the virgin birth of Christ is his comparison of Christ's death on the cross and later resurrection with
pagan stories or myths of the dying and rising god. Campbell uses
these stories to attack the historicity of the New Testament.

In volumes one and three of *The Masks of God,* Campbell compares Jesus Christ's sacrifice on the cross with the Greek story of
Dionysus, who was born from a union between the Greek god Zeus
and his daughter Persephone.[11] In that story, the jealous wife of
Zeus, Hera, sends two of the Titans, the old Greek gods supplanted
by Zeus, to kill Dionysus. The Titans kill Dionysus and eat everything but his heart. Zeus discovers this and slays the two Titans.
The goddess Athene then presents the uneaten heart to Zeus, who
brings Dionysus back to life.

Elsewhere in *The Masks of God* books, Campbell compares Jesus
and Dionysus to ancient Egyptian stories, Central and South American stories, and stories of vegetation gods in primitive jungle vil-
lages and in agricultural societies.[12] In making these comparisons,
Campbell constantly objects to the orthodox Christian approach to
the death, burial, and resurrection of Jesus Christ. The Christian
view is that these events are history and fulfilled prophecy. Campbell says all these stories should instead "be read as poetry, as art,
as a vehicle not of empirical information but of experience." When
we do this, says Campbell, we realize that "the living God" is not
separate and apart from us, but "within all and of no definition."[13]

In *The Power of Myth* Campbell picks up this same theme. He compares Jesus Christ's death and resurrection with pagan stories and sacrificial rituals in primitive "planting cultures." He claims that the rituals are "the repetition of the original act of the killing of a god followed by the coming of food from the dead savior."[14] He compares the rituals to the Christian act of the Lord's Supper or holy communion, where bread and wine are eaten and drunk as a special sign and commemoration of Jesus Christ's sacrifice on the cross. He attaches a particular meaning to it:

> Christ is crucified, and from his body the food of the spirit comes. . . . Jesus is the fruit of eternal life, which was on the second forbidden tree in the Garden of Eden. . . . The Garden is the place of unity, of nonduality of male and female, good and evil, God and human beings. You eat the duality [the fruit of the tree of the knowledge, or experience, of good and evil], and you are on the way out [of the Garden]. The tree of coming back to the Garden is the tree of immortal life, where you know that I and the Father are one.[15]

Campbell sees all religions and myths in terms of his mystical and pantheistic worldview. His worldview is pantheistic because he believes that the whole universe and everything in it are part of a divine, but impersonal, force or consciousness, or god. His worldview is mystical because he believes that one of our goals as human beings should be to "become one" with this underlying force or consciousness.

Campbell implies that within the sacrificial death and resurrection of Jesus Christ is a hidden meaning of mystical pantheism that allegedly has been repressed by the Christian community. Campbell twists the events in Jesus Christ's life and the events in the Garden of Eden account in the Old Testament into a pantheistic, mystical mix. In doing this, he distorts the biblical texts that describe these events.

For example, the Bible never says the Garden of Eden is "the place of unity, of nonduality of male and female, good and evil, God and human beings." If you look at the Genesis text itself, you will find that man is made in God's "image" or "likeness." He and God are not "one" in the sense that Campbell means it. Also, there is no indication in the text that good and evil are two aspects of the same

thing, as Campbell implies. The text actually indicates that goodness is action in obedience to God's moral commands and evil is
action in rebellion to God's moral commands. Campbell's idea about
good and evil is a pantheistic notion foreign to the biblical text.
Finally, there are actually two people in the Garden, one male and
one female. Although Genesis 2:24 says, "A man will leave his father
and mother and be united to his wife, and they will become one
flesh," the passage refers to the sexual union representing their
pledge to each other in marriage. It would be wrong to read some
form of pantheism into this verse.

Likewise, the words "I and the Father are one" from John 10:30
are words Jesus applies to his eternal relationship with the Father,
the first divine person of the Holy Trinity. There is no logical or textual reason to apply these words to the relationship between human
beings and the Father.

Campbell treats the biblical text like a wax nose that he can shape
and form according to his personal whims. He ignores the grammatical, philosophical, and historical context of the biblical text, as
well as the immediate and larger contexts of the text. He also ignores
the special figures, genres, and literary categories established by
the writers of the biblical text. And when he compares the pagan
stories of the so-called dying and rising god with the death and resurrection of Jesus Christ, he ignores the insurmountable differences
between them.

Campbell's view of all these pagan stories of the dying and rising
god not only is unbiblical, it is completely false. Joseph Campbell was
influenced in his view of these stories by W. Robertson Smith, a professor of Arabic at Cambridge; by psychologist Sigmund Freud; and
by anthropologist Sir James Frazer, author of *The Golden Bough.*

Smith believed that the ancient societies in the Middle East were
organized by clans with special sacred relationships to certain gods
and certain totem animals connected to the gods and to the clans.
In periodic rituals, these clans allegedly killed the totem animals
and ate them in sacred feasts. The clan and its god communed by
eating the animal together. However,

> since god, clansmen, and totem were all of one blood, the clansmen
> were partaking in a sacred communion not only with their god but

also of their god, each member of the clan incorporating sacramentally a particle of the divine life into his own individual life.[16]

"The evidence for this theory . . . is negligible," writes Sir Edward Evans-Pritchard in *Theories of Primitive Religion* (1965). The only possible instance of such rituals is among Australian aborigines, he asserts, "and the significance of that instance, even if its veracity be accepted, is dubious and disputed."[17] Many primitive cultures don't even have bloody sacrifices, he adds, and among most of those that do, the sacrifice is not considered a communion. There is also no evidence to support psychologist Sigmund Freud's similar theory about the father-god who is murdered by his sons and eaten, says Evans-Pritchard.[18]

The myth of the dying and rising god also plays an important role in Sir James Frazer's highly influential book, *The Golden Bough,* but the assertions in this book have also been refuted. "The Frazerian construct of a general 'Oriental' vegetation god who periodically dies and rises from the dead has been discredited by more recent scholarship," writes Walter Burkert, a professor of classical philology and scholar of ancient Greece.[19] In rejecting the myth of the dying and rising god, Burkert mentions the stories of the Egyptian god Osiris; the nature goddess Cybele and her resurrected lover, Attis; the Greek god Dionysus; and the Persian god of light, Mithra, who enjoyed a cult status in Rome after the first century. In his own books, Campbell mentions all these stories as examples of the dying and rising god, but Burkert dismisses them as such.

Both Evans-Pritchard and Burkert are well-respected scholars in the secular world. Their research matches that of Christian scholars J. Gresham Machen in *The Origin of Paul's Religion* (1925) and Ronald H. Nash, chairman of the department of philosophy and religion at Western Kentucky University, in *Christianity and the Hellenistic World* (1984).

Both Machen and Nash discuss the stories of Osiris, Cybele and Attis, Dionysus, and Mithra in great detail. They deny there is any thematic connection between these stories and the story of Jesus Christ. In discussing Osiris and Attis, Machen writes:

The "resurrection" of these gods is very different from what is meant by that word in Christian belief. The myth of Attis, for example, contains no mention of a resurrection; though apparently the cult, in which mourning is followed by gladness, did presuppose some such action. In the myth of Osiris also, there is nothing that could be called resurrection; after his passion [or suffering] the god becomes ruler, not over the living, but over the dead.[20]

Nash agrees with Machen[21] and adds that there is no evidence of any resurrection associated with the Persian god Mithra. "Mithraism had no concept of the death and resurrection of its god and no place for any concept of rebirth," says Nash. "If rebirth appears at all in the cult, it was a late addition," after Christianity began.[22] To support his claim, Nash points out the dates of a Mithras wall painting— late second century A.D.—and of an inscription—A.D. 391. If anything, Mithraism was probably influenced by Christianity.

Some scholars claim to have found another alleged comparison between Christianity and the ancient mystery cult surrounding the Greek god Dionysus. In their secret worship of Dionysus, this cult allegedly had a frenzied religious ritual where they tore a sacred bull into pieces and ate its raw flesh. Apparently, the bull may have symbolized the god himself. Consequently, some scholars have compared this ritual to the Christian practice of the Lord's Supper, where Christians ingest unleavened bread and wine, the flesh and blood of Christ.

Burkert says even if we could prove such rituals existed, "they did not amount to 'eating the god.'"[23] Instead, he suggests they were an enactment of an ancient hunting ritual that symbolized the cycle of life and death in nature.

Both Machen and Nash point out that the religious ritual associated with Dionysus died out long before the birth of Christ. Thus, there is no historical connection between the two rituals, even if we assumed that the spiritual concepts behind both rituals were exactly the same, which they aren't. It is hard to see why the early Christians would have adopted "a savage stage of religion which even paganism had abandoned," says Machen.[24]

There simply is no comparison between any of the alleged pagan notions of eating the god and the Lord's Supper. In addition to the dating problems, says Nash, we also know very little about the sacred meals of the pagans. This suggests to Nash that these sacred meals weren't very important. If you really want to find out the source for the Lord's Supper, adds Nash, it makes more sense to look for it in the Jewish passover feast rather than any alleged pagan sources. It should also be noted that, unlike the pagan rituals, the Lord's Supper was instituted by Jesus Christ while he was still alive. The disciples ate his flesh and drank his blood while Jesus, a flesh-and-blood, living human being, sat with them. Nash concludes:

> The death of Jesus differs from the deaths of the pagan gods in at least six ways. (1) None of the so-called savior-gods died for someone else. The notion of the Son of God dying in place of his creatures is unique to Christianity. (2) Only Jesus died for sin. It is never claimed that any of the pagan deities died for sin. . . . (3) Jesus died once and for all (Heb. 7:27; 9:25–28; 10:10–14). In contrast, the mystery gods were vegetation deities whose repeated death and resurrection depict the annual cycle of nature. (4) Jesus' death was an actual event in history. The death of the god described in the pagan cults is a mythical drama with no historical ties. . . . (5) Unlike the mystery gods, Jesus died voluntarily. . . . (6) And finally, Jesus' death was not a defeat but a triumph. Even as Jesus was experiencing the pain and humiliation of the cross, He was the victor. The New Testament's mood of exaltation contrasts sharply with that of the [pagan] religions, whose followers wept and mourned for the terrible fate that overtook their gods.[25]

Campbell's Use of Pagan Mystery Cults

Related to his criticism of Jesus Christ's sacrificial death on the cross is Campbell's use of pagan mystery cults, which flourished in the ancient Greco-Roman world. Campbell claims that Christianity's story of Jesus Christ is borrowed from the same "archaic"[26] religious background as these cults. Although he admits that Christianity is different because Christians believe that Christ's story is not just spiritual truth but also historical truth, he obviously prefers the "archaic," nonhistorical, religious tradition, which to him is more suitable to the worldview of mystical pantheism.

In 1958, one year before Campbell started publishing his fanciful theories in the *Masks of God* volumes, Mircea Eliade published in *Patterns of Initiation* a series of lectures he had given at the University of Chicago in the fall of 1956. In one of those lectures, Eliade said recent research did not support the theories that the origin of Christianity was influenced by pagan mystery cults. "There is no reason to suppose that primitive Christianity was influenced by the Hellenistic mysteries," said Eliade.[27] In fact, the reverse may actually be true:

> The renaissance of the mysteries in the first centuries of our era may well be related to the rise and spread of Christianity. . . . certain mysteries may well have reinterpreted their ancient rites in the light of the new religious values contributed by Christianity.[28]

Eliade added that it was only much later, when Christianity had to compete with the renaissance of the mystery cults, that Christians began to borrow from the religious symbols of these cults. They did this in order to help them explain their religion to others (not to modify it), thereby hoping to win new converts.

Campbell has turned history inside out. He takes out old theories, dusts them off, and tries to pass them off as new. He does this despite all the evidence accumulated over the decades against them.

Even before Eliade published his 1956 lectures, Christian scholar J. Gresham Machen refuted the pagan mystery cult theories in 1925 in *The Origin of Paul's Religion.* Here is a summary of a few of Machen's points.

In the first place, as Eliade later said, most of the mystery cults developed after Christianity. Only in the case of the cult of Dionysus can we point to a mystery cult that made a significant impact before Christianity, but this cult died out long before Jesus Christ and the Christian apostles, who came from a Jewish background, were born.

Second, Machen wrote that the mystery cults and the religions from which they grew "were tolerant of other faiths; the religion of Paul [the Christian apostle], like the ancient religion of Israel, demanded an absolutely exclusive devotion. . . . Amid the prevailing syncretism of the Greco-Roman world, the religion of Paul, with the religion of Israel, stands absolutely alone."[29]

Machen also showed that one can't compare any of Paul's Christian doctrines with beliefs of the mystery cults. He proved these cults were not the source of the Christian doctrine of the Spirit; the Hebrew Old Testament was the true source. Furthermore, unlike Christianity, the pagan mystery cults had no strong consciousness of sin. Neither did they influence the Christian doctrines concerning baptism and the Lord's Supper.

Getting baptized or partaking of the Lord's Supper does not grant redemption and salvation in Christianity. "Salvation according to Paul was dependent solely upon faith," wrote Machen, "the simple acceptance of the offer contained in the message of the Cross."[30] It was also "based upon a supernatural act of God—the resurrection of Jesus Christ," Machen added.[31]

"Christ died for our sins," says Paul in 1 Corinthians 15:3, and "he was raised on the third day according to the Scriptures" (v. 4). Therefore, "if you confess with your mouth, 'Jesus is Lord,' and believe in your heart that God raised him from the dead, you will be saved" (Rom. 10:9).[32]

Walter Burkert also confirms the general thrust of Eliade's and Machen's research in *Ancient Mystery Cults,* as does Ronald H. Nash in *Christianity and the Hellenistic World.* Burkert sees "hardly any evidence for baptism in pagan mysteries." He mentions the New Testament writings of Paul and the third chapter of the Gospel of John where Jesus talks about being "born again" or "born from above." Although the mystery cults speak about the cycle of life and death, Burkert says there is nothing within them "as explicit and resounding" as the passages from Paul and John regarding "dying with Christ and spiritual rebirth." Burkert firmly concludes: "There is as yet no philosophical-historical proof that such passages are directly derived from pagan mysteries."[33]

Burkert also points out that the mystery cults never created strong religious communities as did Judaism or Christianity.

The Jews had refused total integration into ancient society, and with Christianity there appeared an alternative society in the full sense of potentially independent, self-sufficient, and self-producing communities. Here we find from the beginning a concern for the poor, economic cooperation quite uncommon in pagan religion, and the inclusion of the family as the basic unit of piety in the religious system. To educate the children in the fear of God suddenly became the supreme duty of parents, as the Apostolic Fathers already taught. And since the believers were at the same time encouraged to multiply, with a new morality ousting all the well-established forms of population control such as the exposure of children, homosexuality, and prostitution, the [church] became a self-reproducing type of community that could not be stopped.[34]

These words from Burkert scream off the page, clearly demonstrating the great gap separating historical Christianity from the pagan mystery cults of ancient Greece and Rome. Ronald H. Nash's arguments are as strong.

Like Eliade and Machen, Nash shows that most of the mystery cults developed after Christianity began, not before. He notes, however, that even if this were not the case, it wouldn't prove the mystery cults actually influenced Christianity. Nash also shows that many scholars previously borrowed terms from Christianity and falsely applied them to pagan rituals. Finally, Nash says Christianity is different from the mystery cults because it is a monotheistic religion, contains a firm body of doctrinal teachings, and claims to be historical.

There is no evidence whatsoever that Christianity borrowed anything from the religious background of the pagan mystery cults.

Campbell's Gnostic Gospel

In *The Power of Myth,* Campbell refers to *The Gospel According to Thomas,* an ancient religious text compiled about A.D. 140. This text belongs to a diverse religious movement started during the second century called gnosticism. Linguistically, gnosticism derives from the Greek word for knowledge, *gnosis,* which in a religious context can refer to secret religious knowledge.

Scholars differ over the origin of gnosticism. They also don't agree about how exactly to define it. Essentially, however, gnosticism contains a "fundamental dualism," which envisions two worlds at war, one of light and one of darkness, "two superhuman forces (the good god of light and the demons of darkness), and . . . two parts to human beings (a good soul imprisoned in an evil body)." In this metaphysical system, human beings are "sparks"[35] of the divine god of light. They must be aroused from their unconscious awareness as divine sparks by a special knowledge, or *gnosis,* so they can attain salvation and redemption from the evil material world and return to the god of light.

One gnostic story is of a gnostic redeemer sent by the god of light to waken the human souls to their divine essence. This gnostic redeemer gives the human souls "a secret knowledge" about their divinity and shows them how to return to the world of light. He then goes back to the heavenly realm "to prepare the way for his followers after their death."[36]

The original gnostics applied this story to the life of Jesus Christ. In doing so, they accepted a particular unbiblical view of Jesus called docetism. According to docetism, Jesus never really had a physical body, he only *seemed* to have one. This view directly contradicts such New Testament passages as Luke 24:38–42; John 1:14; 20:27; Colossians 2:9; and 1 John 4:2–3.

When he talks about the gnostic text of *The Gospel According to Thomas* in *The Power of Myth,* Joseph Campbell refers to these gnostic beliefs. He also compares Jesus Christ to Siddhartha Gautama (ca. 566–486 B.C.), the prophet from India called "the Buddha," or "the Enlightened One," who became the founder of the Eastern religion known as Buddhism. Says Campbell:

> We are all manifestations of Buddha consciousness, or Christ consciousness, only we don't know it. The word "Buddha" means "the one who waked up." We are all to do that—to wake up to the Christ or Buddha consciousness within us. This is blasphemy in the normal way of Christian thinking, but it is the very essence of Christian Gnosticism and of the Thomas gospel.[37]

In *The Masks of God: Occidental Mythology,* Campbell also mentions the docetic doctrine of the gnostics and attaches it to both Jesus Christ and to the teachings of some Buddhists in the first centuries A.D. To prove these connections, he quotes extensively from the so-called *Acts of John,* a false text written in the second century A.D., which contains both gnostic and docetic teachings. He also lists several passages from *The Gospel According to Thomas,* which contain quotes alleged to be from Jesus. These quotes give the impression Jesus actually taught some form of mystical pantheism, the worldview Campbell advocates in all of his writings. Finally, in the same book, Campbell admits that *The Gospel According to Thomas* belongs to the second century A.D., long after the crucifixion of Jesus Christ and long after the death of Christ's apostles. He fails to acknowledge the fact that it is also long after the composition of the books of the New Testament. He claims the New Testament Gospels—Matthew, Mark, Luke, and John—which describe the life, teachings, death, and resurrection of the historical Jesus Christ, "continued to be touched and retouched until the canon finally was fixed in Rome, toward the opening, only, of the fourth century A.D."[38]

Once again, Campbell's historical chronology is way off base. As chapter 12 shows, there is ample evidence that the four Gospels in the New Testament have not been "touched and retouched" by Christians or anyone else. Indeed, the evidence actually suggests that all of the Gospels, including the Book of John, were written before A.D. 70 and that the original text of these ancient documents has been carefully preserved. Unlike the four Gospels, *The Gospel According to Thomas* provides no historical or biographical framework for its collection of alleged sayings of Jesus Christ. Although this gnostic text contains some sayings which "closely parallel"[39] some of the sayings in Matthew and Luke, and may even represent earlier versions of these sayings, none of these sayings are among the pantheistic passages in *Thomas* cited by Campbell.

Moreover, there are no examples of any gnostic redeemer stories and hymns before A.D. 140. In fact, according to Nash in *Christianity and the Hellenistic World,* much of the textual support for the gnostic redeemer doctrine "post-dates the New Testament by several centuries."[40] By contrast, the redeemer hymns of Philippians and 1 Timothy in the New Testament can be dated to around A.D. 60 to 65. It is more reasonable to believe, therefore, that the gnostic redeemer doctrine is a second century revisionism of the historical life of Jesus Christ presented by the New Testament writers and preached by the Christian community in the first century A.D.

As I indicated earlier, the gnostic doctrine of docetism, which says Jesus only seemed to have a physical body, bears no relation to the teachings of the New Testament documents. The orthodox Christianity that these documents espouse contains a monotheistic, ethical doctrine of redemption from sin completely foreign to the Hellenistic, pagan world of gnosticism. Even Campbell indicates this is true when he says gnosticism teaches "blasphemy in the normal way of Christian thinking."

Campbell's gnostic gospel of Christ consciousness and Buddha consciousness is part of his overall goal to historically validate his own worldview of mystical pantheism. At the same time, he tries to refute the historical reliability of the worldview in the New Testament, the foundation of Christian orthodoxy. Not only does he have few facts to support these claims, he approaches the subject with an air of superiority and self-righteous hostility. Nowhere is this more evident than in a passage from his book *The Flight of the Wild Gander.*

In that book, Campbell derisively mentions New Testament scholar Rudolph Bultmann (1884–1976) who, despite his other unorthodox teachings, believed that Jesus Christ actually rose from the dead. Campbell then critically quotes 2 Peter 1:16, which says, "We did not follow cleverly invented stories when we told you about the power and coming of our Lord Jesus Christ, but we were eyewitnesses of his majesty." Campbell claims this letter was not written by the apostle Peter and says modern science has completely destroyed the cosmological and historical validity of the Bible and the church. Speaking of Bultmann and the alleged writer of 2 Peter, Campbell declares:

> One can only suggest to these stubborn gentlemen that if, instead of insisting that their own mythology is history, they would work the other way and dehistoricize their mythology, they might recover contact with the spiritual possibilities of this century and salvage . . . whatever may still be of truth to life in their religion.[41]

In this passage, Campbell conveniently picks the one book of the New Testament, 2 Peter, the authenticity of which has been questioned more than any other New Testament book (although it meets standard tests of canonicity). He neglects to mention that most of the other books of the New Testament, such as the four Gospels or the letters of the apostle Paul, have unequivocal evidence to support their authenticity. The authorship and historicity of 1 Corinthians 15:1–7, for instance, is beyond question. In it, the apostle Paul presents the gospel of Jesus Christ's sacrificial atonement for our sins and his physical resurrection. Paul says this is an eyewitness testimony, which not only he, but also Peter, James, the other apostles, and over five hundred other people experienced. Campbell also fails to mention any of the positive evidence in support of 2 Peter's authenticity. For example, in 2 Peter, the author refers to a unique incident between Peter, James, John, and Jesus related in Mark 9:2–13. If Peter did indeed write 2 Peter, then this reference would be perfectly natural.[42]

Once again, Campbell stacks the deck in his favor and against historical orthodox Christianity. In effect, he has censored reliable evidence refuting his own fanciful, subjective worldview. This distortion of the facts clearly shows Campbell's undue bias. Such a distortion is extremely dangerous because it deceives the uninformed who are inclined to accept Campbell's credentials and theories at face value.

In this age when many people seem to be overly anxious to question all authority, it seems strange indeed that so many people are so willing to accept the spurious claims of people like Joseph Campbell. A healthy skepticism can be good, even if applied to the beliefs proclaimed in this book.

Joseph Campbell's attitude toward the books of the Bible, however, is not a healthy skepticism. It is openly hostile and filled with illogical arguments, false evidence, and subjective statements.

In all my reading and studying of Campbell, I have yet to find one thing Campbell says against the Bible that can't be refuted by looking at the actual scientific, historic, and archeological evidence or by reading the text in its proper context. Despite all of his criticisms, the biblical record stands intact.

Summary and Conclusion

For over two hundred years, there has been an unprecedented attack on the historical authority of the Bible. Joseph Campbell is just one person in a long line of biblical critics. He borrows from the work of these critics but never mentions that a considerable amount of research has proven their theories wrong.

Contrary to Campbell, this chapter has proved that, in all likelihood, Moses did indeed write the first five books of the Old Testament. The J, E, and P theory Campbell supports has long been disproved by other, more reliable scholars. The virgin birth of Jesus Christ bears no relation to the pagan stories and Greek religious traditions Campbell mentions. According to other scholars, such as Sir Edward Evans-Pritchard and Walter Burkert, there is little or no evidence to support theories about an archaic dying and rising god myth that influenced the first Christians. There is little thematic connection between such a story and the teachings found in the New Testament. Also, there is persuasive evidence to show that Christianity was not influenced by pagan mystery cults or by second century gnostic teachings.

In his writings, Campbell cites all sorts of discredited theories to undermine the historical reliability of the Bible. From these theories, he develops all sorts of ideas to twist the meaning of God's word in the Bible. The fact that he does this to the Bible is not the only issue which concerns me. I would oppose Campbell if he did the same thing to any other piece of historical writing, literature, music, poetry, film, or work of art.

In the last ten chapters, Campbell's seven major themes have been refuted as has his worldview of mystical pantheism. In the next two chapters, it is only fair that I present logical arguments and factual evidence to support my own worldview—the traditional, orthodox teachings of the Christian church rooted in the historical documents of the Bible.

11

Cosmos or Theos: Does God Exist?

n the beginning . . ."

Two of the most important books of the Bible open with these words. In Genesis Moses reveals the Divine Creator, and in his book about the life of Jesus, the apostle John describes the Divine Word, or Logos, who "became flesh and made his dwelling among us" (John 1:14).

Can we trust these words anymore? Does God really exist? Did God really become man, as described in the New Testament, and bring a message of forgiveness to the human race?

In answering these questions, we must remember that all truth claims should be *logical* and they should fit the *facts*. In order to know what is true and what is false, we must look at the factual evidence before us. This evidence must not violate the basic laws of logic—it must contain no contradictions or logical absurdities. In chapter 1, I listed seven rational and empirical tests for truth, which I then applied to Joseph Campbell's seven basic themes. As I indicated at the close of the previous chapter, it is only fair that we now use these same tests to evaluate the Christian worldview, which Campbell refused to accept.

There are at least three irrefutable, logically undeniable, and factually reliable arguments for the existence of God. Theologians and philosophers often call these three arguments the *transcendental argument,* the *cosmological argument,* and the *moral argument.* Although these arguments sometimes overlap, we will consider them one by one.

The Transcendental Argument

The word *transcendental* refers to something that is ultimate in some way. According to the transcendental argument, the laws of logic have no ultimate foundation unless they are rooted in a personal God.

Some skeptics claim that Christians shouldn't even use logic and language to prove the existence of God. They argue that it is impossible to show that logic has any actual relationship to reality. In addition, they sometimes assert that language itself is merely a kind of arbitrary system of signs, which society artificially imposes on itself and its environment, according to man-made social conventions. There may be a small element of truth in the second proposition about language, but if logic and reason have no real relation to the way things truly are, then why even try to convince anyone else of your position? Why use logic and language to refute the validity of logic and language?

As I noted in chapter 1, language itself depends on logic. In logic we have the Law of Identity, or A is A; the Law of Noncontradiction, or A is not non-A; and the Law of the Excluded Middle, or A is either B or non-B. Thus, apples may be compared to apples, but apples are different from oranges. However, both apples and oranges are kinds of fruit—they aren't vegetables.

Without such logical distinctions, it is impossible to derive any meaning out of language, but if meaning is impossible, then communication between human beings is useless. So why do skeptics even try to communicate with anyone else?

When you deprive logic and language of all value, you defeat your own argument by contradicting yourself. You can't use logic and language to deny the validity of logic and language. To do so violates the Law of Noncontradiction. Even atheist Antony Flew writes in his book *Thinking Straight,* "To tolerate contradiction is to be indifferent to truth."[1] Logic and language are more than just arbitrary systems of signs and ambiguous metaphors. We can rely on the basic laws of logic and on the value of language, which is founded on logic. The problem comes when we try to apply these tools. We don't always apply them properly. The fact that we do not always apply logic and language properly, however, does not mean they are not true or can never be used adequately.

The basic laws of logic are essentially reliable and true. They also are independent and transcendent—their truth does not depend on what we think or do; it does not depend on whether we believe them or like them. Even when we reject the basic laws of logic, we are using those laws to do so.

The laws of logic are also independent and transcendent because they are universally applicable. As such, they are not dependent on the material, changing, finite universe. They are thus abstract or nonmaterial as well as unchanging, absolute, and eternal. If they were not unchanging, absolute, and eternal, they would not be transcendental or universal and they would then be inherently unreliable.

Finally, the laws of logic are personal—only persons can understand them and use them. Since we, however, are fallible, limited, and material personal beings, the laws of logic cannot originate with us. They must be rooted in an absolute, transcendent, eternal, nonmaterial, personal being or spirit who never changes and who is independent of the material world. Thus, the laws of logic "can have no absolute basis unless personality itself has an absolute basis." The "ultimate foundation" of logic "must reside in a supreme self or nowhere."[2] God is therefore the divine source of the basic laws of logic.

Conclusion: The existence of God is logically undeniable. It is *rationally* inescapable. Otherwise, the laws of logic have no absolute basis, and all human knowledge is ultimately unreliable. If you deny God's existence, then you must also deny the existence of transcendent, unchangeable, universal, eternal, absolute, nonmaterial, and personal laws of logic. This would clearly be contradictory because you inevitably would have to use such laws in the very same statement where you deny them.

The Cosmological Argument

Cosmology is a branch of philosophy examining the origin, operation, and order of the universe. The cosmological argument tries to show that a personal God is the only logical explanation for the existence of a universe such as ours.

Throughout recorded history, there have been many versions of the cosmological argument, some more sound than others. The version I will present here is more simple and direct than most of the others. It is also a logically infallible one because it is based on an undeniable fact: You either exist or you don't exist.

To say, "I don't exist," however, is not a logical statement. Why? Because you must first exist before you can deny the reality of your existence. Something that is truly nonexistent cannot affirm or deny anything. Therefore, it is self-refuting, or self-contradictory, for you to say, "I don't exist." It violates the Law of Noncontradiction:

> No one can deny his own existence without affirming it. One must exist in order to deny that he exists, which is self-defeating. But whatever is undeniable is true, and what is unaffirmable is false. Hence, it is undeniably true that I exist.[3]

Conclusion: You exist and you can know for certain that you exist. The fact that you can *know* that you exist means that you have a mind that is self-aware. Your mind is that part of you that perceives, feels, thinks, reasons, and makes decisions. Such a mind is personal; you have personality.

From this starting place, we proceed to the next important question facing us: Does the universe that we perceive with our minds exist or not? I believe it does indeed exist, for several reasons.

First, if the universe does not exist, then how do some people get the idea that it does? Second, if the universe we perceive around us is not real but is instead an illusion, as some Eastern religions and philosophers believe, then who is really having this fantasy, who is having this dream? What some people call illusion, fantasy, and dream, other people call reality. Objectively, there is no difference between the two words when they are used in this way. A difference that makes no difference is no difference at all, so it seems less confusing and more reasonable to call the universe real. Finally, if the universe does not exist, then it would be hard to rely on the reasoning of my own mind for anything, because it is through that mind that I perceive the universe around me. Thus, if the universe we perceive does not exist, we couldn't rely on anything that modern science tells us, we couldn't rely on anything that human language reveals to our minds, and we couldn't even rely on the thought processes that suggest to us that the universe is an illusion.

Conclusion: The universe does exist; it is undeniably real.

This conclusion raises two other important questions. How did the universe get here? Where does it come from? There are two possibilities. Either the universe has always existed in one form or another, which means it is eternal, or else the universe had a beginning, which means it is not eternal. To say that the universe is eternal is not logical. To begin with, the universe could not be eternal because anything which is eternal is, by definition, essentially timeless, and the universe clearly extends through time. It is possible, in fact, for the universe not to have existed at all—its existence is not inevitable. Also, since the universe itself is made up of "contingent entities, states, events, and processes"[4] that extend through time in duration, then the universe also must be contingent or limited.

Some people claim that the universe has undergone an infinite series of births, deaths, and rebirths. This idea of an infinite regression is "rationally unintelligible."[5] It does not give an adequate reason for the existence of the universe. For instance, what would happen if you tried to write an endless series of checks in order to pay off a debt? The debt would never get paid because there would be no end to the transaction and the person you owe would never receive any real value. In the same manner, an endless series of births, deaths, and rebirths of an eternal universe would never lead to an actual universe. There would always need to be an external cause with some kind of starting point (like a bank account with real money where a final check could be cashed).

If the universe is eternal, why does it exist in time? If the universe is eternal, why is every part of the universe, such as my body, not eternal? If the universe is eternal, why does it seem to be changing? If the universe is eternal, why is there error in the universe? Where do logic, reason, personality, and consciousness originate? How can we be certain that our thought processes are reasonably reliable?

Conclusion: The universe is not eternal. It had a beginning.

If this is true, then either the universe created itself or it was created by something or someone else. The universe must have already existed, however, to create anything, even itself, but if it already existed, it didn't have to be created. It would therefore have had to exist and not exist at the same time in the same place. This is clearly impossible. It violates the Law of Noncontradiction. Also, if the universe created itself, how does human personality originate and why should we rely on the human reasoning that says the universe created itself?

Some people still contend, however, that the universe just popped into existence from nothing. People who believe this theory can never cite an example of something that just pops out of nothing. Material objects like the universe just do not go about popping up here and there. This theory is also illogical because it cannot account for the existence of human beings with personal, rational minds. It doesn't adequately explain how a material universe that just pops up out of nothing could also lead to human beings who invent and use computers.

Conclusion: The universe was created by something or someone else.

Now, either this creator is impersonal or personal. If the creator is impersonal, then how does something impersonal produce something personal, like human beings who invent and use computers? Only persons can create other persons. If the creator is impersonal, how could we rely on our thought processes which are personal, not impersonal? The person who says the creator is impersonal relies on personal thought processes in order to make that claim. He therefore defeats his own argument by claiming that the creator is impersonal. As I wrote in chapter 9, only an intelligent designer, or God, with a personal, rational mind could create and sustain a world that includes other finite, personal, rational minds.

Conclusion: The universe was created by a personal someone, a personal being separate from the universe. For practical purposes, we can call this being "God."

Some people believe that the universe was created by many gods, not by just one God. If the universe was created by many gods, however, then these gods could not be eternal or non-caused. You can't have two or more ultimate, eternal, uncreated gods existing apart from the universe. One of them would always lack some essential attribute that the other possesses. You can also only have one best of anything. Why postulate two or more gods to create the universe when you really only need one?

Conclusion: The universe was created by one God.

Either the one God is absent or he is immanent, which means he is present and active in the world. If God is absent, however, how is the universe sustained? Also, why would a personal God create the universe, and human beings who can speak and write, and then disappear? How is that even possible? Such a view seems implausible at best. Why wouldn't God want to communicate with the human beings he created and take an active role in their lives, especially if he created them for an intelligent purpose?

God must therefore be immanent. He must be present and active in the world, and he must be able to communicate with people here on earth, or else he could not be the ultimate cause of this universe and of our existence. If God could create the universe out of nothing, then it is reasonable to assume that he can also communicate with human beings.

Conclusion: The one God is immanent—he is *outside* the material universe, but he can act *within* that universe. If this is true, then everything in the universe is immediately in his presence. This means God is actually omnipresent as far as this universe is concerned. Also, since God is a personal being who can act within the universe that he created out of nothing, then it must also be true that God can communicate with human beings within the universe. Furthermore, since God is a personal being, he not only has the ability of self-awareness but is also able to reveal to us things about himself and to reveal things he knows to be true. Conversely, he also has the ability to conceal these things from us. It is logically possible, therefore, for us to discover what God has revealed to us.

So far, I have shown that the existence of personal, rational minds is undeniable; that the existence of a finite, physical universe is undeniable; and that the existence of a personal, rational, immanent God who created the universe is undeniable. Our rational personalities, our physical nature, and our "essential spiritual selfhood" are grounded in the personal, rational, and "transcendental spiritual selfhood of God as Absolute Mind." In effect, I have proved the following statement: "I think, therefore God is!"[6]

There is one more thing I wish to address in this version of the cosmological argument: Either the essential nature of the one true God contains more than one person, or it does not.

My argument here does not claim that there is more than one God. It only claims that within the one essence of God, there may exist more than one person. Such a concept is completely logical. It merely states that within the nature of God there exists one "what," or one essence, and more than one "who," or more than one person. "Whatness" and "whoness" are separate rational categories. They do not contradict each other. Thus, in combining these two categories, I do not violate the Law of Noncontradiction.

There *must* be more than one person within the one essence of God; otherwise, God is not an ultimate, transcendent, personal being. To put it another way, God cannot have a personal relationship with individual persons and groups of people unless there also exists an ultimate, personal, transcendent, and eternal relationship among the two or more persons within the one essence of the one true God. How could there be true, transcendent love before creation and in eternity if there is only one person within the single essence of God?

Conclusion: Within the divine essence of God, there exists more than one person. This statement is logically undeniable and rationally inescapable. Since traditional, orthodox Christianity is the first, and only, religion to teach such a doctrine in such a manner, then Christianity must be closer to the full truth about the existence of God than any other religion.

Viewed in this light, Christianity becomes the most rational belief about God, his triune nature, and the universe. Its worldview is more logical and more rationally compelling than that of any other religion. It is more logical, reasonable, and plausible than pantheism, polytheism, deism, or any other form of monotheism. It is more logical, reasonable, and plausible than Judaism, Islam, Buddhism, or Hinduism. And it is certainly more logical than atheism, agnosticism, or pure materialism.

The Moral Argument

There are many ways to express the moral argument, but most of them seem to boil down to one important axiom: Moral absolutes exist; their existence is logically self-evident.

This axiom is perhaps the most controversial idea you can ever proclaim to anyone in our society today. Try doing it sometime and see what kind of reaction you get! Sooner or later, and probably sooner rather than later, you'll run into someone who gets really upset by this idea. Chances are, the person will say something like this: "You're wrong. There are no moral absolutes."

By now, if you have read this book from the beginning, you should know how to reply to such an illogical statement. Simply ask the person, "Is that statement itself an absolute truth about morality and do you believe in it absolutely?" If the person answers yes, then he has contradicted himself, because he has made an absolute statement about morality that says there are no absolute truths about morality. His statement violates the Law of Noncontradiction and is therefore false. If, on the other hand, the person answers no, then his statement is not an absolute truth claim, it is just his opinion, and there is no logically compelling reason you should accept it. Either way, he loses the argument and you have affirmed the original axiom: Moral absolutes exist; their existence is logically self-evident.

Of course, the person may be stubborn and refuse to admit his defeat. He may in fact give you another argument. Perhaps he will say to you, "All moral rules are subjective. They differ from culture to culture and person to person." He might try to back up this argument by adding, "All moral beliefs are also subjective. They are an emotional or psychological, and hence nonrational, reaction to certain environmental stimuli."

Such arguments are logically invalid and therefore false.

To begin with, they confuse moral truths with moral beliefs. Moral truths and moral beliefs do not "have the same logical status and share the same logical fate. . . . Beliefs can logically be false, while truths cannot logically be false." Truth is always "logically independent of what any finite person believes, prefers, or thinks about it."[7] It is also logically independent of what any one culture or society believes, prefers, or thinks about it. Moral rules based purely on one's personal feelings or beliefs can indeed be subjective or false, but they can also be objective and true.

Second, the idea that moral beliefs are emotional and nonrational is also a belief about morality. How do we know whether or not this belief itself isn't purely emotional and nonrational? Either this idea is objective and therefore self-contradictory, or it is subjective and therefore no more valid than any other view of morality.

Finally, it isn't necessarily true that moral beliefs differ so widely from culture to culture or person to person. As we have seen, even Joseph Campbell, despite his inconsistencies, says that all "good" religions teach it is good to "love thy neighbor as thyself."

C. S. Lewis, the brilliant Christian author and defender of the faith, points out in *Mere Christianity* that no matter what any one person believes or thinks about morality, nearly everyone has a basic sense of justice and fairness, of right and wrong. If they didn't, says Lewis, they wouldn't be able to quarrel with one another because "quarreling means trying to show that the other man is in the wrong." They wouldn't try to show that the other person is wrong if they didn't both agree that there exists "some kind of Law or Rule of fair play or decent behaviour or morality."[8]

Many cultures in the past have had similar moral teachings to our own, adds Lewis, and he refers the reader to the appendix in his book *The Abolition of Man,* which gives some of the evidence for this. He also asks the reader to imagine what a completely different moral belief system would be like.

> Think of a country where people were admired for running away in battle, or where a man felt proud of doublecrossing all the people who had been kindest to him. You might as well try to imagine a country where two and two made five. Men have differed as regards what people you ought to be unselfish to—whether it was only your own family, or your fellow countrymen, or everyone. But they have always agreed that you ought not to put yourself first. Selfishness has never

been admired. Men have differed as to whether you should have one wife or four. But they have always agreed that you must not simply have any woman you liked. . . . It seems, then, we are forced to believe in a real Right and Wrong. People may be sometimes mistaken about them, just as people sometimes get their sums wrong; but they are not a matter of mere taste and opinion any more than the multiplication table.[9]

Thus, moral absolutes do indeed exist; their existence is logically self-evident. We can truly believe in this objective moral order, even though we don't always know what it requires of us. We are also objectively required to obey this objective moral order, whether or not we fully accept it.

Moral absolutes not only exist, however, they are also independent of us and they transcend any individual person or culture. If they didn't, they wouldn't be true absolutes, and we have already proven that such absolutes do indeed exist. It is illogical to completely deny the objective, independent, and transcendent quality of these moral absolutes, because at the same time you deny this quality, you set up your own objective, independent, and transcendent moral absolute. This is clearly contradictory and therefore false.

But what is the foundation for the objective, independent, transcendent moral order? On what does it rest? This is the ultimate question, my friends. For if we can answer this question, we can perhaps go a long way toward determining what the objective, transcendent moral order actually requires of human beings.

And therein lies the heart of the whole matter: The objective moral order requires all human beings to obey it. But since human beings are personal, the foundation of the transcendent moral order must, therefore, in some sense also be personal. The foundation must be personal because the moral order requires personal beings to do things. It also must be personal because only personal beings who are self-aware and who can communicate can discuss, debate, and think about the objective, transcendent moral order. It also must be personal because an impersonal moral foundation that requires personal beings to do things is not a consistent and coherent worldview.

Therefore, it is reasonable and logical to conclude that the foundation of the objective, transcendent moral order is itself personal.

Our own inherent value and worth, and the inherent value and worth of "the community of persons"[10] to which we belong, is derived from, and dependent on, the inherent value and worth of the personal and transcendent foundation of the objective moral order.

We have "duties, obligations, and responsibilities"[11] toward ourselves and toward each other. These duties, obligations, and responsibilities not only carry out and express the inherent, objective value and worth of human beings, they also carry out and express the inherent, objective value and worth of the transcendent, personal moral order. All of the absolute moral principles which make up this moral order define these duties, obligations, and responsibilities. They also define the inherent, objective (and personal) value and worth of the limited, or finite, human beings who exist.

This view of an independent, absolute, personal, transcendent, and objective moral order is rationally coherent, however, only if the moral order is grounded in and founded on an independent, absolute, personal, transcendent, and objective being, or God. An independent, absolute, personal, transcendent, objective moral order, in order to exist, logically requires the mutual existence of an independent, absolute, personal, transcendent, and objective God. You may deny the existence of such things, but at the exact same time you deny it, you automatically erect your own independent, absolute, personal, transcendent, and objective moral order.

Conclusion: Moral absolutes exist; their existence is logically self-evident. These moral absolutes are part of an independent, absolute, personal, transcendent, and objective moral order. They define the duties, obligations, and responsibilities that we have toward ourselves and toward each other. They also define our objective value and worth as personal beings. Finally, they are rooted in the essential or fundamental character of the Divine Personhood of God. Moral absolutes exist; they are rationally inescapable; therefore, God exists.

The Problem of Evil, Pain, and Suffering

Over the years, many atheists have asked a valid question: If a completely holy, just, and good God does exist, why does he allow so much evil, pain, and suffering in the world? This question has been distressing to Christians for centuries.

In recent years, however, Christian philosophers have developed definitive answers to this problem and the issues it raises.[12] To begin with, they point out that much of the evil, pain, and suffering around us seems to be man-made. It is possible, therefore, that God has given us free will to choose evil. In order to truly give human beings free will, God logically must also give human beings the ability to do evil. Otherwise, they would not truly have free will. Thus, it is logically possible that it is not within God's power to create a world including morally free agents without also creating a world including evil and suffering. "To demand that God eliminate or reduce the possibility of great evil," argues Ronald Nash in *Faith and Reason,* "is also to ask that God eliminate or reduce the possibility of great good."[13] To allow the *possibility* of evil is not to create evil itself. God is not the author of evil.

It is also logically possible that God's essential goodness moves him to create morally free agents. In fact, the idea that God could have created a world where he foreknows that all morally free agents would always do good does not really make sense. As Christian philosopher Stuart Hackett notes in *The Reconstruction of the Christian Revelation Claim,* if human beings do not really have the ability to choose evil, then God could not foreknow that they would choose goodness because human beings would not really be free moral agents and there would be nothing for God to know.

We live in a physical universe. Some types of physical pleasure, such as swimming and eating cooked food, also involve the possibility of pain, e.g., drowning and burnt fingers. If God eliminated all possibility of physical pain, he would drastically change the nature of this universe. It is possible that such a changed universe would include less physical pleasure than the one we live in now.

Physical pain is often a warning signal. It warns our bodies when they are in danger. The atheist who complains about a God who created the possibility of physical pain should ask people with leprosy if they would like to be able to feel pain again. My guess is that they would answer yes.

God has made this physical universe an orderly, predictable place. Gravity makes objects fall, and handguns fire when people pull the trigger. Since this universe is a predictable one, human beings are often able to measure the consequences of their actions. They can then become accountable to other human beings and to God.

To ask God to intervene constantly in such a universe to prevent evil, pain, and suffering is to ask that God suspend the natural order. This desire has hedonism (the idea that pleasure is the only or main goal in life) as its ultimate aim. Before you make such a request, you should ask yourself, "If not this universe, then what kind of universe should God have created?" While you consider this question, think about these words from Dr. Nash: "Unless humans exist in a regular and predictable environment, they cannot act freely and responsibly. In such a universe, natural evils will occur."[14]

Sometimes it seems that the evil things human beings do are purely gratuitous or unnecessary. It is possible, however, that God has a secret purpose for such evil. It is also possible that God takes such needless evil and helps us to create good things out of it. It seems reasonable to believe that unless human beings have the power to do completely gratuitous evil, they are not really free moral agents. "We live in a world in which there are genuine risks and the threat of real loss; it is a world in which we face real, not imaginary, dangers and challenges."[15] If the world did not include great dangers and huge challenges, then any victory we achieve over the obstacles we face would be that much diminished. Such dangers and challenges help to mold our characters morally, spiritually, emotionally, and intellectually. The existence of gratuitous evil does not make the existence of God improbable.

It is therefore possible that God allows us to encounter evil, pain, and suffering so that we can grow and develop into better human beings. It is also true that evil, pain, and suffering help us to have empathy with and compassion for our fellow human beings when they are themselves the victims of evil, pain, and suffering. It is therefore possible that God helps us to transform the evil, pain, and suffering we undergo into great acts of love, compassion, and empathy.

Although there may be much evil, pain, and suffering in this world, God has allowed only the minimum necessary to achieve a morally perfect world. The Bible, which claims to be the Word of God, tells us that God is doing something to destroy evil. It promises that he will eventually end the evil, pain, and suffering in the world and bring peace, joy, and love to those who serve him and do good.

> To him who is thirsty I will give to drink without cost from the spring of the water of life. He who overcomes will inherit all this, and I will be his God and he will be my son. But the cowardly, the unbelieving, the vile, the murderers, the sexually immoral, those who practice magic arts, the idolaters and all liars—their place will be in the fiery lake of burning sulfur.
>
> Revelation 21:6–8

To ask that God eliminate all evil, pain, and suffering may in fact be asking that God get rid of you! For evil, pain, and suffering are often caused by human beings like you and me. The real question is not "What is God doing to prevent and stop evil, pain, and suffering?" The real question is "What are *we* doing to prevent and stop evil, pain, and suffering?" God permits evil for a season, he brings about some good in its midst, and, most important of all, he will not let it last forever.

Weapons of Faith

When it comes to the existence of God, Christians have better arguments than atheists, agnostics, and other non-Christians. Unfortunately, these arguments are largely unknown because many Christians don't know how to use them. Christians should know and use arguments like the transcendental argument, the cosmological argument, and the moral argument. God has given them these weapons of faith. Only if Christians know and use these weapons will non-Christians be better informed about the Christian faith and its true benefits.

Talk about God is not meaningless. Those who say so contradict themselves because they themselves are making a meaningful statement about God.

Skeptics who assert, "The existence of God is unknowable," cannot answer, "How do you know that it is unknowable? Just because you don't know if God exists today doesn't mean you won't know tomorrow."

Those who contend, "There are no absolute truths," can't face the challenge, "Is that an absolute truth and do you believe it absolutely? If so, then you contradicted yourself again."

Agnostics who pontificate, "We can't logically prove the existence of God," are deflated by, "Can you logically prove that statement? If not, then I am free to reject it and if so, then it seems rather arbitrary to say that we can apply logic to your argument against the proof of God's existence but we can't apply that same logic to prove God's existence."

Such agnostics can't reply, "We can't talk objectively about the existence of God," because to do so is to fall before this challenge: "Is that an objective statement? If so, then you contradicted yourself and your statement is false, and if not, then your statement is purely a subjective statement and I can reject it as an arbitrary one."

The naive atheist who complains, "I can't believe God exists because there is so much evil and suffering in the world. If God existed, he would do something about it," is defeated by, "God *has* done something about it. He sets down rules for behavior and speaks to you through the Bible. In the books of the Bible, he promises us that he will indeed stop evil and suffering some day. If God didn't exist, and if he didn't speak through the Bible, how would you know what is evil and what is good? How would you even decide what is evil and what is good? By what standard do you judge God anyway? If you're going to borrow the standards he sets forth in the Bible, why don't you read the rest of what God says in those books?"

Finally, someone who declares, "There are no moral absolutes. All moral rules are subjective. They differ from culture to culture and person to person. All moral beliefs are also subjective. They are an emotional or psychological, and hence nonrational, reaction to certain environmental stimuli," cannot adequately answer the following questions.

"Is that a moral absolute? Is that an objective statement about morality? Do you personally believe it is absolutely true? How do you know that moral beliefs differ from culture to culture and person to person? What is your evidence for such a statement? Would it be morally right for me to pour boiling water on your head without due cause? Would it be just? What about racism or Nazi Germany? Is it right to hate someone just because of his or her skin color? Was it okay for Adolf Hitler to murder Jews? Would it be fair for me to deny you a job because of your beliefs about morality? If not, why not? If so, then how do you rationally justify that position, especially if you don't think there are any objective, absolute moral truths? Why shouldn't I just consider your own views about God as an emotional desire to deny God because you don't want to accept any personal responsibility for obeying his moral laws? The same psychological argument you use on my beliefs about moral truth can be applied to yours, so why are you convinced by it? Why does it make logical sense to you? If you can't answer these simple questions, then why should I accept your beliefs?"

Ethical monotheism is true. A personal, rational God does indeed exist. This God is "the ultimate standard of moral goodness or worth in an objective sense."[16] Goodness is part of God's nature; there are no independent moral standards outside of his divine person. Out of his goodness, God has established an objective, transcendent moral order. All human beings must obey this moral order. We are without excuse.

The New Testament: Eyewitnesses of His Majesty

y using the basic laws of logic to prove the existence of a personal, rational Creator-God in chapter 11, we also validated a particular worldview called *classical theism.* Classical theism implies at least four important facts:

1. The material universe is, in some significant measure, an orderly place that can be rationally understood by human beings.
2. Human beings can therefore use logic, philosophy, science, history, theology, and even law to help them obtain knowledge about the material universe.
3. Since a personal, rational God does indeed exist, "then there is an objective meaning to all [the] facts in the world" that he created.[1] We can therefore learn the true meaning of those facts, including the facts of history.
4. Because God is a person, he has the ability, like all other persons, to disclose or not disclose facts about himself. It is

possible therefore for us to discover what God has revealed about himself, if anything, and to determine objectively the meaning of that revelation. Hypothetically, such a revelation would, by necessity, take place within the orderly, material universe created by God. Consequently, we should be able to apply the same general tests of truth for the facts of divine revelation as we do for any other possible facts we encounter in this universe. To make an exception for divine revelation in this instance would be arbitrary and unwarranted.

The New Testament documents in the Christian Bible claim that Jesus Christ, the unique Son of God, was born in Israel during the time of the ancient Romans. Jesus came to reveal the truth about God. He also came to "save his people from their sins" (Matt. 1:21). Jesus himself claims in Mark 10:45 that he "did not come to be served, but to serve, and to give his life as a ransom for many," to deliver people from God's penalty for their sins.

"I am the resurrection and the life," proclaims Jesus. "He who believes in me will live, even though he dies; and whoever lives and believes in me will never die" (John 11:25–26). Later, Jesus adds, "I came from God. I came from the Father and entered the world; now I am leaving the world and going back to the Father" (John 16:27–28). Earlier, Jesus claimed, "Anyone who has seen me has seen the Father. . . . I am in the Father, and . . . the Father is in me" (John 14:9–10).

In the opening to his book, the Greek physician named Luke, a close friend of the apostle Paul, writes, "I myself have carefully investigated everything from the beginning" (Luke 1:3). In his sequel, Acts, Luke reports that, after his physical resurrection from the dead, Jesus appeared to his apostles "and gave many convincing proofs that he was alive" (Acts 1:3). The apostle Peter says in 2 Peter 1:16, "We did not follow cleverly invented stories when we told you about the power and coming of our Lord Jesus Christ, but we were eyewitnesses of his majesty."

The Book of John also claims to be written by an eyewitness: "The Word became flesh and made his dwelling among us. We have seen his glory, the glory of the One and Only, who came from the Father, full of grace and truth. . . . No one has ever seen God, but God the

One and Only, who is at the Father's side, has made him known" (John 1:14, 18). In 1 John 1:3, the apostle John declares, "We proclaim to you what we have seen and heard," and in 1 Corinthians 15, the apostle Paul says that "Christ died for our sins" (v. 3) and was buried, but that he rose on the third day and appeared not only to Peter, James, Paul, and all the apostles, but also to over five hundred people at one time (v. 6).

What do we make of all this? Are the books of the New Testament what they claim to be—accurate, reliable records of the life and teachings of Jesus Christ?

In order to answer these questions, this chapter examines two different areas of concern: the legal and historical credibility of the New Testament documents and the personal credibility of the New Testament writers and eyewitnesses.

Judging the Credibility of the New Testament

In a court of law, the burden of proof for denying the credibility of an eyewitness falls on those who wish to undermine that credibility. An eyewitness should be given the benefit of the doubt "unless we have clear evidence to the contrary."[2]

We can apply this rule to the New Testament documents. When discussing the credibility of these documents, the nonbeliever cannot dismiss the reliability of these documents without giving solid reasons why he doubts their credibility. He must give specific evidence to back up any of his own historical claims. The nonbeliever must also present a fair and reliable test that will produce the kind of evidence he needs from Christians in order to change his mind and put his trust in the credibility of the New Testament accounts of Jesus Christ and his apostles. Only a fair investigation of the evidence can provide a firm foundation for judging the credibility of the New Testament documents.

Both lawyers and historians frequently rely on documentary evidence to prove their cases. They have developed excellent rules and tests for such evidence. The legal system, for example, uses a rule called the ancient documents rule,[3] and historians use the bibliographic test and the external sources test to determine the reliability of ancient documents.

The Ancient Documents Test

Under the ancient documents rule, ancient documents like those of the New Testament are admissible as evidence and will be given more credence if it can be shown that, in the ancient past, people who could have contested their authenticity acted upon the information contained in the documents. If they acted upon them, it increases the practical probability that they are true. There still, of course, may be other reasons to reject the authenticity of the ancient documents, however.

Most scholars today accept the fact that, in general, the New Testament books were written between A.D. 40 and 100 (although the dates of one or two books may still be disputed). Historical research shows that the New Testament books clearly had a great influence on the origins of Christianity in the first century A.D. Many Jews and Gentiles born during that century read the books and used the information in those books to run their lives. We have evidence from first and second century documents written by these people that this is true. In a court of law, this fact would give the New Testament more credibility as an ancient historical document.

The Bibliographic Test

The bibliographic test asks three questions: (1) How many copies and fragments of copies do we have? (2) Are the copies basically the same or do they show a wide variety of differences that indicate they may have undergone an extensive amount of editing? (3) What is the time gap between the dates of the copies we have and the approximate date at which the document was probably written? The more copies we have, the more similarities among the copies, and the closer the time gap, the more accurate and reliable the text of the document is.

Using this test, how does the New Testament stack up?

As stated above, the New Testament documents were written between A.D. 40 and, at the latest, A.D. 100. There are in fact good reasons to date *all* of the New Testament books before A.D. 70. Excluding small fragments, the earliest complete copies of these documents have been dated between A.D. 300 and 400, or 260 to 360 years later. In total, we have about 5000 Greek copies and fragments, about 10,000 Latin Vulgate copies and fragments, and about 9000 other versions of the New Testament books dated between A.D. 120 and 1200. Note that the earliest of these copies and fragments are dated within 100 years of the original writings.[4]

In comparison, we have only 643 manuscripts of Homer's *Iliad,* written about 900 B.C., with the earliest complete copy dated about 400 B.C., 500 years later. Also, we have only ten copies of Julius Caesar's *Gallic Wars,* written between 58 and 50 B.C., with the earliest copy dated A.D. 900, a gap of almost 1000 years. Finally, we have only 21 copies of the works of the Roman historian Tacitus, written about A.D. 100, with the earliest copy dated A.D. 1000, a span of 900 years.

Scholars who have compared the copies and fragments of the New Testament documents have found overwhelming agreement among them. These scholars have painstakingly sifted out all of the typical copying mistakes and textual problems. According to New Testament scholar Bruce Metzger, only 40 lines, or about 400 words, of the 20,000 lines in the New Testament books are in doubt as to whether they really were part of the original text as we have them today. In contrast, Homer's *Iliad* contains about 15,600 lines, but 764 lines have been questioned by scholars. Christian scholar and philosopher Norman L. Geisler writes,

> This would mean that Homer's text is only 95 percent pure or accurate compared to over 99.5 percent accuracy for the New Testament copies. The national epic of India [the *Mahabharata*] has suffered even more textual corruption. . . . The *Mahabharata* is some eight times the size of the *Iliad,* of which some 26,000 lines are in doubt. This would be roughly 10 percent textual corruption or a 90 percent accuracy copy of the original. From this documentary standpoint the New Testament writings are superior to comparable ancient writings. The records for the New Testament are vastly more abundant, clearly more ancient, and considerably more accurate in their text.[5]

Copies and fragments of manuscripts are not our only source of knowledge about the text of the New Testament documents. For example, the writings of the church fathers from before the Council of Nicea in A.D. 325 contain about 32,000 citations of the New

Testament text. "Virtually the entire New Testament could be reproduced from citations contained in the works of the early church fathers," says philosopher J. P. Moreland.[6] Furthermore, although every church father does not quote every New Testament book, every book is quoted as authoritative and authentic by some church father. This indicates that the New Testament writings were "recognized as apostolic [originating from Jesus Christ's own appointed church leaders] from the very beginning."[7]

Finally, note the apostle Paul's testimony in his own letters, which are the earliest of all New Testament documents. Paul's letter to the Galatians, for example, has been dated as early as A.D. 48. The dates of his other letters may be established as follows: 1 and 2 Thessalonians, A.D. 50; 1 and 2 Corinthians, A.D. 54–56; Romans, A.D. 57; and Philippians, Colossians, Philemon, and Ephesians, around A.D. 60. Many scholars, including more liberal ones, believe that Paul's description of the resurrection of Jesus Christ in 1 Corinthians 15 can be traced back to an early confession of faith from the early to middle A.D. 30s, within a few years after the death of Jesus Christ!

There is no reason, therefore, to doubt the accuracy and integrity of the New Testament documents. The bibliographic test clearly shows that the text of the New Testament has not been changed by the Christian church.

> The evidence for the text of the books of the New Testament is better than for any other ancient book, both in the number of extant manuscripts and in the nearness of the date of some of these manuscripts to the date when the book was originally written.[8]

We can trust that the translations we now have are essentially the same as the original writings.

External Sources Test

The second test historians use to determine the factual reliability of an ancient document is the external sources test. In this test, historians look at what external sources say about the document and the events described within it. External sources not only include other ancient writings but also archeological and anthropological evidence.

I have already mentioned the testimony of the early church fathers with regard to the bibliographic test. Their testimony also satisfies the external sources test. For instance, several second century fathers affirm that the Book of John in the New Testament was written by the apostle John. These writers include Irenaeus, Clement of Alexandria, Theophilus of Antioch, and Tertullian of Carthage.

The testimony of Irenaeus is important "because he had been a student of Polycarp, bishop of Smyrna (martyred in 156 A.D. after being a Christian for eighty-six years), and Polycarp in turn had been a disciple of the apostle John himself."[9] Not only does Irenaeus affirm the authorship of John's Gospel, he also reports that Matthew produced his Gospel for the Jews while Peter and Paul were founding the Christian church in Rome (about A.D. 58). Irenaeus also writes that Mark, Peter's disciple, set down his Gospel after Peter's death, sometime around A.D. 65, and that Paul's friend Luke wrote his Gospel sometime thereafter. In a letter to his colleague Florinus, quoted by church historian Eusebius two hundred years later, Irenaeus mentions how both he and Florinus had heard Polycarp talk about what John and other witnesses had told Polycarp about Jesus.

According to a second century document by Papias, the Christian bishop of Hierapolis, who wrote between A.D. 130 and 140, the apostle Matthew compiled a collection of Jesus Christ's sayings. Papias also testifies that the apostle John, before he died in about A.D. 95, told Papias that Mark composed his record of Jesus on the basis of information supplied by the apostle Peter himself. Finally, Papias adds that John dictated his own account of the life of Christ to people in the Christian church.

The New Testament documents are also consistent with the textual evidence from ancient non-Christian external sources. This evidence shows that the life and death of Jesus Christ was not just some crazy story dreamt up by some ancient religious cult.

The Jewish Talmud itself, for example (compiled between A.D. 200 and 500), refers to Jesus Christ and five of his disciples. These references claim that Jesus was a sorcerer who led the Jewish people astray and who came to add things to the Mosaic Law. Eventually, they claim, Jesus was executed on the eve of Passover for heresy and for misleading the people. Following his death, the disciples of Jesus healed the sick in his name.[10]

Although the accuracy of portions of his text are questioned, Jewish historian Josephus, who wrote about A.D. 90, mentions John the Baptist, Jesus Christ, and James, the brother of Jesus. Josephus confirms the dates of Christ's ministry, his reputation for practicing "wonders" of some kind, his kinship to James, his crucifixion by Pilate, his messianic claim, and the fact that his disciples reported Jesus rose from the dead.[11]

Roman historian Cornelius Tacitus, who probably had access to official Roman records, refers to Jesus Christ's execution under Pontius Pilate and relates Roman Emperor Nero's persecution of Christians after the great fire ravaged the city of Rome in A.D. 64. In A.D. 112, C. Plinius Secundus (Pliny the Younger), governor of Bithynia in Asia Minor, wrote to Emperor Trajan asking for advice about how to deal with troublesome Christians. In his letter, Pliny reports that the Christians meet on a fixed day to pray to Christ as God and promise each other to follow certain moral standards. He also says they refuse to curse the name of Jesus.

The New Testament books are filled with references to secular history in the first century. Archeological evidence has confirmed many of these references to historical events and persons and to political factions, geographical areas, and social and cultural differences. For instance, the apostle John in his book on the life of Jesus displays accurate knowledge about buildings and landscapes in Jerusalem and the surrounding countryside before A.D. 70, when Jerusalem suffered massive destruction by the Roman Empire. Archeological findings have also confirmed the existence of Pontius Pilate, the Roman ruler who ordered Jesus Christ's execution, and the family of Caiaphas, the Jewish high priest who opposed Jesus. As a whole, the New Testament documents display a remarkable degree of familiarity with many areas of Jewish life and Jewish thought in the first century A.D.

In addition, Luke, the author of the third Gospel and the Acts of the Apostles, is often cited for his accuracy about the history and geography of those ancient times about which he wrote. His books contain many references to the imperial history of Rome and a detailed chronicle of the Herod family. Luke is also accurate in his use of various official titles in the Roman Empire, no small feat considering the fact that such titles often changed in a short period of time during changes in the administration of the empire. Luke's description of the founding and rise of the Christian church in Acts matches what we know from other historical writings and archeology. The Book of Acts itself contains several instances where the apostles and various local churches receive reports from other Christians about events taking place over a wide geographic area. There is no reason to doubt that the events reported in the New Testament documents were not widely disseminated throughout the Roman Empire and beyond. As Paul notes in Acts 26, these things were not done in a corner, they were *common knowledge.*

Thus, not only do the New Testament writings pass the ancient documents rule and the bibliographic test, they also pass the external sources test. The weight of the evidence affirms the legal and historical credibility of the New Testament documents.

Judging the Credibility of the Writers and Eyewitnesses

There are at least three ways to judge the personal credibility of an eyewitness, author, or expert.

The first way to judge someone's personal credibility is to find out if the person has a reputation for being a truth teller or a liar. Such a reputation is not the one and only deciding factor—sometimes even liars tell the truth—but it does affect the amount of credibility you can give someone's testimony.

The next way to judge is to ask whether or not the person displays an obvious or undue bias. In evaluating this level of credibility, it is good to remember that we aren't judging whether the person has no bias whatsoever. A person can have a bias but still tell the truth. Instead, we are just trying to evaluate whether the person's bias is so obvious or excessive that it warps his testimony.

A third and final way to check someone's personal credibility is to see if his testimony is consistent. Here, we are mostly looking for major inconsistencies. Minor ones may be simply a matter of different interpretation.

Truth Tellers or Liars?

Neither the apostles who wrote some of the books in the New Testament, nor any of the other writers and eyewitnesses, ever displayed the kind of character that would lead them to invent such an incredible story as the historical, physical resurrection of Jesus Christ. After Jesus allegedly rose from the dead, these men were not afraid to come forth to speak boldly and publicly about the things they witnessed. They did this in spite of the incredible pressures put upon them to retract their claims. Their faith and moral strength remained unshakable in the face of bigotry, torture, and death, and their lives became a model for the early church, as many of the early church fathers testify. A man may die for what he believes, but a man will not die for something he *knows* to be a lie.

Although he does not affirm the complete historical reliability of the New Testament writings, Robin Lane Fox in *Pagans and Christians* speaks eloquently about the authentic faith evidenced by Christians who suffered persecution as part of the early church. Fox believes that the apostle Paul was probably executed by the Romans in A.D. 62 and that Paul's execution set the precedent for the later persecution of Christians not only by Emperor Nero in A.D. 64 but also by other Romans later. Writes Fox:

> The intransigence of the braver Christians made a great impression on their brethren and also impressed itself on pagans. . . . the entire theology of martyrdom sustained and animated many Christians under arrest. They believed their Gospel's promises and warnings, and to those who believe, martyrdom needs no justification.[12]

The New Testament writers never hesitate to reveal serious character flaws and mistakes made by the disciples around Jesus or the leaders of the early church, even though they would have had no reason *not* to if they were "inventing" Christianity. Just read Luke 22:54–62, Acts 8:1–3, and Galatians 2:11–21. Even Paul, despite his strong convictions, does not glorify his own role but perceives himself as merely a humble servant of Jesus Christ, a lowly man and a great sinner who was saved only by the divine grace of God. If the New Testament writers and eyewitnesses were liars, why didn't they cover up these flaws?

In essence, the character of the New Testament writers and eyewitnesses is one of self-sacrifice in pursuit of truth and appeal to historical evidence, not one of personal gain through conscious deceit. Honesty and sacrifice was what Jesus taught and how they lived and died. Their faith was based on the physical resurrection of Jesus Christ which they repeatedly claim to have witnessed with their own eyes, ears, and hands.

Bias

In *McCormick's Handbook of the Law of Evidence*, three main types of undue or obvious bias are listed: favor or prejudice, hostility, and self-interest.[13] Is there any evidence that these types of bias distorted the testimony of the New Testament writers and eyewitnesses?

Although it is true that the New Testament writers and eyewitnesses have an extremely high view of Jesus Christ, they were taken completely by surprise when they found his tomb empty and when Jesus appeared to them after his death. In fact, they were at first inclined to disbelieve the resurrection despite their leader's previous predictions and despite Jewish belief in a physical resurrection. Three short days before the resurrection of Jesus Christ, they fled in fear and sorrow after witnessing his horrible arrest, punishment, and death. The apostles themselves did not become convinced of his physical resurrection until he showed himself to them and gave "many convincing proofs that he was alive" (Acts 1:3). These proofs convinced them that Jesus was indeed more than just a man. They may have held a high view of Jesus, but they were not at all prepared to invent a fantastic story about a corpse coming back to life, unless it was true.

The New Testament writers and eyewitnesses at times display anger and frustration with the Jewish leaders who helped condemn Jesus to death and who continued to persecute his followers, but they also expressed unsolicited forgiveness and openness toward them. Not only did they ask their enemies to become brothers with them in Christ, they also followed the example set by Stephen who, while being brutally stoned to death by Jewish authorities in Jerusalem, nevertheless asked God not to "hold this sin against them" (Acts 7:60). It is highly unlikely that any hostility the Christians may have felt toward their fellow Jews or toward the Romans would have led them to invent stories and beliefs that could only result in further persecution, misery, and scorn. The New Testament writers and eyewitnesses preached the resurrection of Jesus

Christ not because they hated the Jewish and Roman authorities; they preached the resurrection because they witnessed it.

The New Testament writers and eyewitnesses didn't preach the resurrection of Jesus Christ for any motives of self-interest or self-ishness. Many of them were terribly persecuted for their testimony and beliefs. Some of them were physically tortured and sometimes killed. The Christian lifestyle called for a daily existence of self-denial and sacrifice. Self-interest as a reason for obvious or undue bias would actually cause them to deny the resurrection and recant their testimony. It certainly wouldn't lead them to preach it openly in the Jerusalem temple and in the synagogues, much less in the very courts of Rome. But this is exactly what they did.

As we have seen, the New Testament writers and eyewitnesses had a strong motive to obey the warnings of the Jewish authorities and stop preaching about the resurrection of Jesus Christ. Instead, these men did the opposite, risking their lives to preach the good news of his resurrection. They preached repeatedly and openly in the Jewish synagogues, leaving themselves vulnerable to an increasingly hostile religious leadership.

"The disciples could not afford to risk inaccuracies," says Dr. John Warwick Montgomery, "which would at once be exposed by those who would be only too glad to do so."[14] Yet they never hesitated to confront Jewish leaders, hostile pagan forces, and even the Roman authorities. They endured rejection by their own ethnic community, persecution, torture, and death because of their testimony. If their testimony was so full of holes, how could they have gotten away with such bad testimony? If they lied about the resurrection, if their testimony was unduly biased, how do we account for reports of the empty tomb? The Jews and pagans who opposed them had the means, motive, and opportunity to *completely refute* the evidence for Jesus Christ's resurrection, yet these hostile witnesses never could shake the testimony of these first evangelists. They failed to produce the kind of solid evidence that would at the time disprove the testimony of the New Testament writers and eyewitnesses.

Consistency of Testimony

Contrary to popular opinion among non-Christians, and even the misconceptions of some Christians, the testimony of the New Testament writers and eyewitnesses is not full of contradictions and inconsistencies. Many books and articles have been written that resolve these alleged contradictions and inconsistencies. Among the best ones are John W. Haley's *Alleged Discrepancies of the Bible* and Gleason Archer's *Encyclopedia of Bible Difficulties.*

Archer, for instance, answers the charge about inconsistencies among the four New Testament books (Matthew, Mark, Luke, and John), which describe the disciples' discovery of the empty tomb. He resolves one of the apparent contradictions by concluding that the three women who went to the tomb (Mary Magdalene, Salome, and Mary the wife, or perhaps mother, of the apostle called James) did not actually see the angel who had rolled away the heavy stone from the tomb's entrance until *after* they had entered the empty tomb. Thus, he argues, Matthew 28 doesn't give a description of the women entering the tomb but instead skips right to the angel speaking to the women.

After this, the women returned to the disciples to tell them that Jesus Christ's body was gone, whereupon Mary Magdalene specifically took pains to tell Peter and John first. Peter and John ran to the tomb but were followed separately by Mary Magdalene, who was alone, and then by Salome and the other Mary. At this point, Peter and John discovered for themselves the empty tomb and the heavy burial shroud of Jesus lying undisturbed but empty "as if the body had simply passed right out of the headcloth and shroud."[15]

On her way back to the tomb, Mary Magdalene met the resurrected Jesus, who ordered her to tell the disciples that he was going to see his Father in heaven before he met with them. Shortly thereafter, Jesus met the other two women and told them similar things. According to Luke 24:34, Jesus also had a short private meeting with Peter, a fact confirmed by Paul in 1 Corinthians 15:5.

Archer's brief synopsis here resolves all of the major inconsistencies in the four Gospels' accounts of the discovery of the empty tomb. The only differences between these accounts is that each book mentions details or omits details that the other books do not.

If you examine the texts, you will find that the New Testament writers and eyewitnesses agree on the following major points: Jesus underwent a public execution. His death was certified by the Roman authorities. He was placed in a private tomb, the location of which was known. Jesus then appeared to some of his female disciples and to his male apostles. People touched him and talked with him. He ate with them. He also commanded them to lead all people everywhere into repentance toward God, belief in him, and forgiveness of sins in his name.

The internal consistency of the New Testament documents is beyond reproach. There is "no good ground for concluding, as some biased scholars mistakenly do, that the differences between the Gospels involve genuine discrepancies and unresolvable contradictions."[16]

The evidence for the historical resurrection of Jesus Christ is better than the evidence for the actions of Julius Caesar or any other historical figure in the ancient world. F. F. Bruce writes,

> We are confronted with a hard core of historical fact: (a) the tomb was really empty; (b) the Lord appeared to various individuals and groups of disciples both in Judea and Galilee; (c) the Jewish authorities could not disprove the disciples' claim that He had risen from the dead.[17]

Adds Bruce Metzger,

> The evidence for the resurrection of Jesus Christ is overwhelming. Nothing in history is more certain than that the disciples believed that, after being crucified, dead, and buried, Christ rose again from the tomb on the third day, and that at intervals thereafter he met and conversed with them.[18]

The personal credibility of the New Testament writers and eyewitnesses can be verified objectively by the historical and textual evidence. The New Testament documents are an accurate and reliable description of the lives and teachings of Jesus Christ and his apostles. The resurrection of Jesus Christ fits the facts. It really did happen. Only God, as the creator and sustainer of life, has the power of resurrection. As Jesus notes in John 2:19 and 5:21, both he and the Father have that power. There is no good reason, therefore, for anyone to doubt that Jesus Christ was indeed God in the flesh, that he died for all our sins, not just the sins of Gentiles, pagans, atheists, and agnostics, but the sins of Jews as well.

For God so loved the world that he gave his one and only Son, that whoever believes in him shall not perish but have eternal life.

John 3:16

Conclusion

The Book of Genesis in the Old Testament tells us that God created the heavens and the earth out of nothing. God is the founder and sustainer of creation. He creates order out of nothing. He is the source of rationality, personality, and consciousness. He is the root of all reason and all logic. He is the ultimate source of all goodness. He sets the moral standards by which we should live.

If all of this is not true, then we cannot rely on our own reasoning ability, because it is through our minds that we perceive the material universe. If logic has no ultimate, objective, and absolute foundation, then even language and science become unreliable. We wouldn't even be able to say, "language and science are unreliable," because it is through our personal, rational minds that we say such things. And, if there is no ultimate, objective, and absolute basis for goodness and morality, then we wouldn't be justified in telling anyone else that he or she ought to do or believe anything. Thus, Carl Sagan wouldn't be able to honestly say, "Creation science is wrong," and the judges at the Nuremberg trials would have had no right whatsoever to condemn and execute any Nazi war criminals. Without God, all thought, all logic, all science, and all morality become pure chaos. It takes more faith to believe in a universe without a personal God than to believe in a universe with a personal God.

Although we are not infinite beings like God but are instead limited beings, we are like God because we have personal, rational minds with the ability to communicate with other personal, rational minds. In that sense, we are indeed made in the image of God, as the Bible clearly states in Genesis 1:27.

Since man is created in the image of God, then God can take on our own image, without losing his other divine capabilities. The New Testament claims that, in the person of Jesus Christ, God assumed human nature, but never ceased being God. Jesus Christ is thus both fully human and fully divine. As such, he represents man to God and

God to man. He also reveals the nature of God to mankind and, when we accept him as he historically claimed himself to be—the Lamb of God who takes away the sin of the world (John 1:29)—he welcomes us as brothers and sisters in the kingdom of God. In this way, he brings us the fullness of God's love.

That love, however, does not contradict God's truth or God's justice. As the apostle Paul writes in 1 Corinthians 13:6, "Love does not delight in evil but rejoices with the truth."

"I am the way and the truth and the life," proclaims Jesus in John 14:6. "No one comes to the Father except through me." Unless you believe that he was who he claimed to be, "you will indeed die in your sins" (John 8:24). You will remain forever separated from the holy and just almighty living God.

When people asked Jesus what they should do to do the works that God commands, he answered, "The work of God is this: to believe in the one he has sent" (John 6:29). Consequently, he informed his disciples after his bodily resurrection that "repentance and forgiveness of sins will be preached in his [Christ's] name to all nations, beginning at Jerusalem" (Luke 24:47). This is indeed what the apostle Peter preached in Acts 2:38–39 when he instructed people gathered in Jerusalem:

> Repent and be baptized, every one of you, in the name of Jesus Christ so that your sins may be forgiven. And you will receive the gift of the Holy Spirit. The promise is for you and your children and for all who are far off—for all whom the Lord our God will call.

Earlier, Jesus gave his apostles the divine power of the Holy Spirit, who gave them the ability to remember "everything" that Jesus said to them (John 14:26). The Holy Spirit "will guide you into all truth," added Jesus.[19]

The New Testament documents ask us all to repent and confess our sins, to turn our hearts and minds away from evil and toward God. When God the Father enables us to do this (John 6:65) and we are baptized in the name of Christ, our sins are forgiven and we receive the power of the Holy Spirit. This divine power transforms our lives morally. It restores our broken relationship with God. It gives us the gift of eternal life.

To those who believe in his authority, Jesus gives "the right to become children of God—born not of natural descent, nor of human decision or a husband's will, but born of God" (John 1:12–13). Through Jesus Christ, the apostle Paul asserts in Romans 8:35–37, we are "more than conquerors" when faced with trouble, hardship, persecution, famine, nakedness, danger, or war.

> For I am convinced that neither death nor life, neither angels nor demons, neither the present nor the future, nor any powers, neither height nor depth, nor anything else in all creation, will be able to separate us from the love of God that is in Christ Jesus our Lord.
>
> Romans 8:38–39

As Dr. John Warwick Montgomery wisely notes, "The servant of Christ is slave to no man . . . [but] is free to develop his capacities to the fullest, under God."[20]

It is time to decide what you believe.

"The kingdom of God is near," declares Jesus in Mark 1:15. "Repent and believe the good news!"

Here is the good news: Jesus Christ died for your sins. Yield to the power of the kingdom of God. Confess with your mouth, "Jesus is Lord" and believe in your mind and heart that God raised him from the dead, and you will be saved by the grace of God and the work of Christ on the cross.

Conclusion

Kaboom!

Imagine yourself an American soldier on a battlefield. The enemy is shelling your outpost. The cold steel of death is raining down heavily on your position.

The troop commander, however, has assembled his officers. He gives them the order to start returning the enemy fire. One of the officers refuses to obey the order.

"What do you mean, 'I refuse to fire'?!!" screams the commander.

"How do we know that's really the enemy out there, sir?" he replies. "After all, there are no absolute truths. I believe there's a verse in Sanskrit, sir, which says, 'He who thinks he knows, doesn't know.'"

"That's crazy," the commander objects.

"Not really, sir," a second officer insists. "Many great philosophers have indeed remarked that ultimate reality is beyond all of our limited categories of thought. Pardon me for saying so, sir, but your attitude smacks of two-dimensional thinking. Why must you always think in terms of opposites—us versus them, good guys versus bad guys? Let go of your narrow interpretation, sir, and get in touch with that part of you which lies below your rational mind."

"Jones is right, Commander," declares a third officer. "If you think of the universe and everything in it as being just connected parts of the same life force or consciousness, then we'd really be killing ourselves if we fired at the enemy, sir."

"Yeah," answers a fourth officer, "everything in the universe arises in mutual relation to everything else, so you can't really blame anybody for anything. Each person should be free to follow his own destiny, sir, to find his own happiness. What was proper fifty years ago is not proper today."

The commander is still angry, but he tries to reason with his men.

"Your country is depending on you, men," he exhorts. "Stand up and defend your country. It's your patriotic duty to fight for freedom and justice."

"Excuse me, sir," replies a fifth officer, "but the world has changed. We live in a global village. Your view of patriotism is narrow minded. The freedom and justice you speak about has been built on five hundred years of slavery, racism, sexism, economic exploitation, and blood. Our heritage is something we should be ashamed of, not something we should defend."

In desperation, the commander, a religious man, responds, "In the Bible, Jesus Christ says, 'Give to Caesar what is Caesar's, and to God what is God's.' This is a volunteer army, boys. You made a pledge when you joined. Now's the time to honor that pledge. Your soul belongs to God, but your patriotic duty belongs to Uncle Sam."

"You can't trust anything you read in the Bible, sir," proclaims a sixth officer. "It's been touched and retouched by the Christian church. The people who edited the Bible also borrowed many ideas from pagan myths. There is no divine authority any more that we have to recognize, sir. There are no more 'Thou shalts.' We don't *have* to believe or do anything."

"That's right," a seventh officer agrees, "and science has completely refuted the Bible's view of the universe. The earth is not the center of the universe. Man is not a descendent of two people named Adam and Eve; he evolved from the animals. That old man up there has been blown away."

At that very moment, the enemy forces breach your camp. Like the fourth officer in our story, they believe that everything arises in mutual relation to everything else and that you can't really blame anybody for anything. So they kill everybody in the camp and move on.

And the last words you hear as you die are those of the troop commander who exclaims (with apologies to Joseph Conrad's novel

Heart of Darkness and Francis Ford Coppola's Vietnam War film *Apocalypse Now*), "The horror! The horror!"

***

This nightmare scenario is written partly in jest, but it is the kind of nightmare that lies hidden within the worldview of Joseph Campbell, like a poisonous snake coiled under a rock. Such a nightmare is implicit in the seven major themes permeating Campbell's worldview. These themes play an important role in the nightmare story.

Many other people in our world today are trying to spread these seven ideas. Some of these people are even admirers of Campbell and his work. They are active in our schools, our government, our mass media, our work places, and even our churches and temples. In many ways, we are engaged in a massive culture war over these issues. We can see this war taking shape in the recent debates over traditional family values, political correctness on campus, and the pros and cons of western culture.

Joseph Campbell is one of the generals in this culture war. Despite his death, the shadow of his work lies heavily over it. His mystical worldview of intellectual and moral relativism, pantheism, religious emotionalism, evolutionary fables, knee-jerk reactions against western civilization, and hysterical attacks against the Bible and those who trust in it are shared by many people in the culture war.

The new sacred cows these people espouse can, however, be refuted. As this book has shown, there *are* absolute truths and moral values on which we can rely. We also have good ways to test these values and truths. If you deny these tests, truths, and values, you end up making your own tests, truths, and values in order to reject the other ones. Sometimes, you even use these tests, truths, and values at the same time you deny them. Whatever position you take on these issues, you still have to justify or validate your beliefs. That is what this book has tried to do with the tests, truths, and values it has proposed.

Using these tests, truths, and values, this book has shown that Campbell's mysticism, pantheism, and spiritual emotionalism are internally inconsistent and self-contradictory, unduly biased, illogical, and overly vague. Campbell's worldview contains a self-defeating mysticism contrary to reality, a contradictory or inconsistent view of man and his environment, an improper view of logic, and an incoherent view of God. It includes a radical, unsound moral relativism leading inevitably to a total breakdown in moral values. It also includes an unduly biased and factually inaccurate view of western civilization and an unwarranted faith in science and theories of human macroevolution and the evolution of religion. Finally, his bitter, vicious attacks on the Bible and its historical reliability reflect a great ignorance of the historical record as well as an inaccurate and unduly biased outlook on the text itself. Even his view of "myth" is distorted. As we showed in chapters 2 and 3, there are other myth scholars who have deeper views on the subject and who usually, though not always, prevent their own religious beliefs from influencing their research, especially to the high degree Campbell does.

Joseph Campbell's worldview is filled with logical contradictions and fallacies, factual errors, and an undue bias. His reputation as a great thinker and competent scholar is undeserved. Worst of all, he borrows ideas from the Bible and distorts them to fit his own worldview. This is, at the very least, unintentionally dishonest if not intentionally so.

Contrary to what Campbell teaches in his books, lectures, and interviews, the existence of the Christian God is rationally inescapable, and the New Testament documents are historically reliable, internally consistent, honest reports of the life and teaching of Jesus Christ and his personally appointed apostles. These documents provide us with a way to God and a moral lifestyle that are true and good. Throughout the centuries, these documents have improved countless lives and produced much good in many nations. They have been a beacon of light to the world even when people in the world have failed to live by them. Indeed,

> all Scripture is God-breathed and is useful for teaching, rebuking, correcting and training in righteousness, so that the man of God may be thoroughly equipped for every good work.
>
> 2 Timothy 3:16–17

In affirming these facts and rejecting most of what Campbell says, we have used tests, principles, procedures, and arguments that are logically sound and factually reliable. Christianity does not command us to put our minds on hold. It does not require us to remain gullible fools. It does not require us to follow the show business antics of the money-hungry evangelist or the faith-healing con man.

The Christian worldview is a reasonable one. It makes sense of the world around us. It does not violate the basic laws of logic. These laws are in fact a part of the nature of God. It seems reasonable to believe that God enables us to use logic more properly when he restores our fellowship with him through the blood sacrifice of Jesus Christ, who is both fully divine and fully human and is therefore the perfect mediator between the human and the divine. How can we truly love God with all our mind (Matt. 22:37) unless God enables us to use the basic laws of logic, the key to all rational thought? Jesus Christ is indeed "the true light that gives light to every man" (John 1:9).

The Christian worldview also fits the facts, not only the facts concerning the historical reliability of the Bible and the resurrection of Jesus Christ but also the facts concerning the anthropology of man and the cosmology of the universe. Human beings seem to have a natural tendency toward evil and violence, a sinful nature if you will. Yet from the earliest records we have, they have also held a consistent belief in a benevolent, moral, just, and holy God who created the universe. This God has progressively revealed himself to sinful human beings, as recorded in the Bible, the most unique set of documents ever written.

The Gospel of John in the New Testament warns us,

> This is the verdict: Light has come into the world, but men loved darkness instead of light because their deeds were evil. Everyone who does evil hates the light and will not come into the light for fear that his deeds will be exposed. But whoever lives by the truth comes into the light, so that it may be seen plainly that what he has done has been done through God.
>
> John 3:19–21

Come out of the darkness and into the light. Recognize Joseph Campbell for what he was: an articulate, charismatic literary critic and dedicated mystic/pantheist who spent his life dabbling in certain kinds of research, writing books, and giving lectures and interviews supporting his own moral and religious theology.

Recognize Jesus Christ for who and what he is—not a clown in charge of some circus, as Campbell implies at one point, nor a madman in charge of an asylum, nor a fool leading his followers the way to dusty death. No. Jesus is the only begotten Son of the Most High, Living God, the Son who died for our sins and who redeems us from those sins. He is the God of truth and justice, as well as love, who is the source of all goodness and who gives eternal life to all those who believe on his holy name.

We can all recognize these truths simply by looking at the logical and factual evidence for and against them. This means we must avoid, with all our strength, the false worldview of Joseph Campbell, who cast unfounded aspersions against those who disagreed with him and who frequently made mystical, emotional declarations that tickle the ears of those untrained in the basic rules of logic and the basic rules of evidence. Campbell had an ax to grind. That ax was not only aimed at the head of Jesus Christ but also at all the truly decent standards of truth and goodness.

We must accurately perceive truth so that we can proceed righteously *in truth.* For it is only when we can see truth correctly that we are truly able to love our neighbors as ourselves and find the real bliss that God has waiting for us.

Christians who firmly believe that Jesus Christ is the purest reflection of all truth have nothing to fear from an honest investigation of truth. As the apostle Paul declares in 1 Corinthians 13:6, "Love does not delight in evil but rejoices with the truth."

Let us therefore rejoice!

Appendix: Worldviews

veryone has a worldview, "a way of viewing or interpreting all of reality," "an interpretive framework through which or by which one makes sense out of the data of life and the world."[1]

The Bible has a worldview. Films, books, plays, songs, TV programs, and public speeches can also have a worldview. Sometimes a particular worldview is unified, clear, and straightforward. Other times, it is hidden or mixed.

There are only a few basic worldviews you can hold. Some scholars like Norman Geisler claim there are only seven basic worldviews. Other scholars like Greg Bahnsen hold that there are really only two: Christian and non-Christian. I propose a compromise and say there are really only five basic worldviews: nihilism, theism, atheism, polytheism, and pantheism. Below is a brief description of them.

Nihilism

Nihilism says everything is meaningless. It denies the possibility of any objective truth or knowledge. It asserts that the universe is meaningless and without purpose, that human life lacks all value and significance, and that moral values are totally arbitrary and worthless.

Theism

Theism affirms that the world or universe is real but finite or limited. It also says that the material universe was created by an eternal, nonmaterial, personal, and infinite Supreme Being, or God, who exists outside of or separate from the material universe, but who has ultimate control over the universe and who can therefore act within that universe. This God has established a set of absolute moral principles which all people are required to obey. In this worldview, all men have a unified soul and body, but the soul survives the physical death of the body, whereupon the person will be judged by God according to some specific criteria.

Prime examples of theism: Christianity, Judaism, and Islam. (Note: Deism, which says that God does not or cannot act within the universe, is a weak form of theism.)

Atheism

Although some atheists admit they cannot disprove the existence of God, atheism says people should conduct their lives as if God does not exist. Most atheists believe the material universe is real and declare that people are really only composed of matter. They deny there is a spirit or soul apart from our physical bodies. Finally, they believe that people create their own moral laws, which emerge by trial and error.

Prime examples of atheism: Secular humanism, classical Marxism, the work of Friedrich Nietzsche, existential atheism (Jean-Paul Sartre), psychological atheism (Sigmund Freud), capitalistic atheism (Ayn Rand and some members of the Libertarian Party), and scientific atheists like Isaac Asimov. (Note: Agnosticism, the belief that human beings do not, and sometimes even cannot, know whether a God or gods exist, is a weak form of atheism.)

Polytheism

Polytheism claims there are two or more finite, personal gods. These gods are usually changing. Some of them are good, some of them are evil, and some of them are both good and evil. They often compete for power with one another and with human beings whose souls are immortal but whose bodies are not. Polytheism also usually contends that the material universe is eternal. The universe "is a great multifaceted, expanding organism that contains opposites which often war against each other, causing conflict and temporal states of chaos."[2] The universe as we know it now was created out of some kind of pre-existent matter by the gods or by itself. The gods do not exist outside of this material cosmos but only act within it. According to polytheism, there are no absolute or universal ethics; moral laws are relative and local.

Prime examples of polytheism: Mormonism, some forms of Hinduism, Confucianism, some primitive religions, Shinto Buddhism, Taoism, some UFO religions, ancient Greek writers like Homer and Hesiod, the Church of Scientology, and religious scholar David L. Miller *(The New Polytheism).* Psychologist James Hillman *(Re-Visioning Psychology)* also takes a polytheistic approach toward life, though he believes that the gods exist only within our minds as ideas and images fraught with conflicting emotions.

Pantheism

Pantheism asserts that what we call God is an infinite, impersonal energy, force, or even consciousness that, because the material universe flows out of God, is really one with the universe. Miracles are impossible in this worldview, and man's immortal soul must eventually unite with God in this world or in the next, often after being reincarnated countless times in various physical bodies, sometimes even animal and insect bodies, throughout history. Unlike theism, pantheism proclaims that people must transcend or go beyond good and evil, especially when they unite with God. Until that time, people are encouraged to live relatively moral lives in order to attain ever higher levels of spiritual growth, though an ethical life is never the ultimate goal.

Prime examples of pantheism: Zen Buddhism, Hinduism, some primitive religions, New Age believers like Shirley MacLaine and Joseph Campbell.

All of these worldviews seem to share five things: (1) they have a cosmology, a view of the universe; (2) they have a metaphysics, a view of what might or might not lie beyond the universe; (3) they have an anthropology, a view of human beings and their culture; (4) they have a psychology, a view of the human soul and the interior life of human beings; and (5) they have an axiology, a philosophy of values.

Each of these worldviews can be mixed with the others. For instance, there is a special worldview called panentheism, which says that God is actually finite at the present time but is becoming or growing toward infinity and that the material universe is a part of God who still has some kind of existence beyond the universe. This worldview is a combination of theism and pantheism. Also, some forms of weak theism can seem quite atheistic when you examine their worldview, and some forms of atheism borrow ideas from pantheism, polytheism, and theism. The modern view of pluralism seems to be a combination of atheism and polytheism because it sets up a world where everyone is allowed to create his or her own gods, as long as those gods are secular.

In general, a good worldview must have at least three things: **internal consistency, explanatory power,** and **empirical adequacy** or **sufficiency**. These are something the theistic Christian worldview definitely has.

For instance, the Christian worldview affirms the existence of an ordered, physical universe created by an eternal, transcendental God. This God has instilled in people the ability to engage in rational thought and empirical observation. Thus, the Christian worldview actually affirms the general validity, but not the infallibility, of science.

The Christian worldview also accepts the idea that truth exists and can be known by finite human beings like you and me. This truth is objective, transcendent, and absolute. It is perfectly proper, therefore, for human beings to spend their lives searching for truth.

Third, the Christian worldview proclaims that there is an objective, transcendent moral order (or set of essential moral values and principles), which every person must obey. These moral values and principles are part of God's character. In this way, the Christian worldview provides a rational justification for judging what is good and evil, right and wrong, and proper and improper. Without a worldview such as Christian theism, we could not claim that murder is wrong or that the war against Nazi Germany in World War II was the right thing to do. Thus, the Christian worldview has a compelling moral philosophy.

The Christian worldview is also a superior one because it gives human beings a meaningful love. The love that God has for human beings is rooted in the loving relationship that exists eternally between the Father, Son, and Holy Spirit—the three persons of the Triune God.

Finally, the Christian worldview, because it is based on a set of historical documents—the books of the Bible—can be empirically verified by using basic rules of evidence. There is sufficient evidence that the biblical documents are internally consistent and factually true. The Bible clearly states that all human beings are sinful (Gen. 8:21; Ps. 14:1–3; John 3:19; Rom. 3:9–18, 23), but that Jesus Christ died for their sins and rose from the dead (Mark 10:45; 16:6; Luke 24:45–48; 1 Cor. 15:1–8). Human beings can receive forgiveness from God for their sins by believing in Jesus Christ and the work he has done (John 8:12; 11:25–26; Acts 2:38; 26:15–18; Eph. 1:17; 1 John 2:12).

Notes

Introduction: *Storytelling and Mythmaking*

1. *The American Heritage Dictionary,* New College Edition, 1989.

2. Joseph Campbell, in conversation with Michael Toms, *An Open Life* (Burdett, N.Y.: Larson, 1988), 21.

3. A worldview is a comprehensive theory of reality, "a way of viewing or interpreting all of reality." Norman L. Geisler and William D. Watkins, *Worlds Apart: A Handbook on World Views* (Grand Rapids: Baker Book House, 1989), 11. See the appendix on worldviews.

4. Joseph Campbell with Bill Moyers, *The Power of Myth* (New York: Doubleday, 1988), 10.

5. Robert A. Segal, *Joseph Campbell: An Introduction,* rev. ed. (New York: Penguin, 1990), 14.

6. Segal, 15.

7. Campbell, *An Open Life,* 123.

8. Segal, 18.

9. Mysticism is "the experience of mystical union or direct communion with ultimate reality," or with God (*Webster's Seventh New Collegiate Dictionary,* 1971).

10. Pantheism is the belief that the whole universe, and everything in it, are part of a divine, impersonal force or consciousness.

11. Campbell, *The Power of Myth,* 155.

12. John Warwick Montgomery, *Where Is History Going?* (Minneapolis: Bethany House, 1969), 74.

Chapter 1: *Tests for Truth*

1. Campbell, *The Power of Myth,* 55.

2. J. P. Moreland, *Christianity and the Nature of Science: A Philosophical Investigation* (Grand Rapids: Baker Book House, 1989), 60.

3. Metaphysics is the study of the nature of reality and the nature of being.

4. Philosophy is the study of the intellectual foundations of all knowledge and experience.

5. Larry Laudan, "The Demise of the Demarcation Problem," in *Physics, Philosophy and Psychoanalysis,* R. S. Cohen and Larry Laudan, eds. (D. Reidel, 1983), 125. See also John Kekes, *The Nature of Philosophy* (Totowa, N.J.: Rowman and Littlefield, 1980), 148–62.

6. Norman L. Geisler and Paul D. Feinberg, *Introduction to Philosophy* (Grand Rapids: Baker Book House, 1980), 110.

7. Antony Flew, *Thinking Straight* (Buffalo: Prometheus, 1977), 15.

8. Norman L. Geisler, *Christian Apologetics* (Grand Rapids: Baker Book House, 1976), 239.

9. Edward W. Cleary, ed., *McCormick's Handbook of the Law of Evidence* (St. Paul: West Publishing Co., 1972), 66. See also Marcus Stone, *Proof of Fact in Criminal Trials* (Edinburgh: W. Green & Son, 1984) and Simon Greenleaf, "The Testimony of the Evangelists" in *The Law Above the Law* by John W. Montgomery (Minneapolis: Bethany House Publishers, 1975), 91–140.

10. A. J. Ayer, *Philosophy in the 20th Century* (London: Weidenfeld and Nicolson, 1982), 16.

11. Campbell, *The Power of Myth*, 55.

12. Campbell, *The Power of Myth*, 55.

13. "Pluralism," *Webster's Seventh New Collegiate Dictionary*, 1971.

Chapter 2: *Close Encounters with the Sacred*

1. Campbell, *An Open Life*, 22.

2. Campbell, *Power of Myth*, 49.

3. Campbell, *Power of Myth*, 62.

4. Campbell, *Power of Myth*, 49.

5. Norman Geisler and Winfried Corduan, *Philosophy of Religion*, 2nd ed. (Grand Rapids: Baker Book House, 1988), 17.

6. Mircea Eliade, *Rites and Symbols of Initiation: The Mysteries of Birth and Rebirth* (New York: Harper, 1975), 102.

7. Campbell, *An Open Life*, 53.

8. Campbell, *The Power of Myth*, 39.

9. Stuart C. Hackett, *The Reconstruction of the Christian Revelation Claim: A Philosophical and Critical Apologetic* (Grand Rapids: Baker Book House, 1984), 29.

10. Hackett, 39.

11. Montgomery, *Where Is History Going?* 204.

12. Hackett, 129.

13. Joseph Campbell, *The Hero with a Thousand Faces,* 2nd ed. (Princeton, N.J.: Princeton University Press, 1968), 30.

14. Campbell, *Hero,* 391.

15. *The American Heritage Dictionary,* New College Edition, 1989.

16. Geisler and Corduan, 16–17.

17. Mircea Eliade, *Myths, Dreams, and Mysteries* (New York: Harper & Row, 1960), 16.

18. Mircea Eliade, *The Sacred and the Profane: The Nature of Religion* (New York: Harcourt, 1959), 9.

19. See Kenneth L. Gentry Jr., *Before Jerusalem Fell: Dating the Book of Revelation* (Tyler, Tex.: Institute for Christian Economics, 1989). Although his view is controversial, Gentry argues convincingly for this early date for Revelation.

20. James Hillman, *Re-Visioning Psychology* (New York: Harper & Row, 1975), 112.

21. Hillman, 158.

22. Eliade, *The Sacred and the Profane,* 95.

Chapter 3: *Kinds of Myth and Principles of Interpretation*

1. Eliade, *Rites and Symbols,* 134–35.

2. Eliade, *Rites and Symbols,* x.

3. Eliade, *Rites and Symbols,* xii.

4. Eliade, *Rites and Symbols,* 135–36.

5. Eliade, *Rites and Symbols,* 127–28.

6. Victor W. Turner, *The Forest of Symbols: Aspects of Ndembu Ritual* (Ithaca, N.Y.: Cornell University Press, 1967), 91.

7. Victor W. Turner, "Myth and Symbol," *The International Encyclopedia of the Social Sciences,* vol. 10, David L. Sills, ed. (New York: Macmillan, 1968), 577.

8. Victor W. Turner, *Dramas, Fields, and Metaphors: Symbolic Action in Human Society* (Ithaca, N.Y.: Cornell University Press, 1974), 241.

9. Arnold van Gennep, *The Rites of Passage* (Chicago: University of Chicago Press, 1960), 20.

10. Turner, "Myth and Symbol," 581.

11. Michael Osborn, "Responding to Rowland's Myth or In Defense of Pluralism—A Reply to Robert Rowland," *Communications Studies* 2 (1990), 123.

12. Osborn, 123.

13. Osborn, 123.

14. Campbell, *Hero,* 35.

15. *Webster's Ninth New Collegiate Dictionary,* 1989.

16. Frank McConnell, *Storytelling and Mythmaking: Images from Film and Literature* (New York: Oxford University Press, 1979), 6.

17. McConnell, 3.

18. Peter Cotterell and Max Turner, *Linguistics & Biblical Interpretation* (Downers Grove, Ill.: InterVarsity Press, 1989), 60.

19. Cotterell and Turner, 61.

20. Vern S. Poythress, *Understanding Dispensationalists* (Grand Rapids: Zondervan, 1987), 46.

21. A. Berkeley Mickelsen, *Interpreting the Bible* (Grand Rapids: Eerdmans, 1963), 100.

22. Cotterel and Turner, 61.

23. Poythress, 46.

24. Milton S. Terry, *Biblical Hermeneutics: A Treatise on the Interpretation of the Old and New Testaments* (Grand Rapids: Zondervan, 1974), 17.

25. Campbell, *An Open Life*, 22.

Chapter 4: *Campbell's Pantheism: All Is One, One Is All*

1. Campbell, *Power of Myth,* 228.

2. Campbell, *Power of Myth,* 228.

3. Campbell, *Power of Myth,* 31.

4. Campbell, *Power of Myth,* 13.

5. Joseph Campbell, *Myths to Live By* (New York: Bantam Books, 1973), 17.

6. Campbell, *Myths to Live By,* 256.

7. Campbell, *Power of Myth,* 21.

8. Campbell, *Myths to Live By,* 5.

9. Campbell, *Power of Myth,* 49.

10. Campbell, *Power of Myth,* 211.

11. Campbell, *Power of Myth,* 132.

12. Campbell, *Power of Myth,* 14.

13. Campbell, *Myths to Live By,* 253.

14. Campbell, *Power of Myth,* 53.

15. Campbell, *Power of Myth,* 208.

16. Campbell, *Power of Myth,* 148.

17. Campbell, *Occidental Mythology,* vol. 3 of *The Masks of God* (New York: Penguin, 1964), 523.

18. *The American Heritage Dictionary.*

19. *The American Heritage Dictionary.*

20. *Webster's Ninth New Collegiate Dictionary.*

21. Geisler and Watkins, 11.

22. The meanings of these terms are not necessary at this point. See the appendix on worldviews.

23. David K. Clark and Norman L. Geisler, *Apologetics in the New Age: A Christian Critique of Pantheism* (Grand Rapids: Baker Book House, 1990), 13.

24. Clark and Geisler, 93.

25. Campbell, *Power of Myth,* 231.

26. Campbell, *Power of Myth,* 220.

27. Clark and Geisler, 177, 180.

28. Geisler and Watkins, 104.

29. Clark and Geisler, 169.

30. Hackett, 49.

31. Warren C. Young, *A Christian Approach to Philosophy* (Grand Rapids: Baker Book House, 1954), 67.

32. J. P. Moreland, *Scaling the Secular City: A Defense of Christianity* (Grand Rapids: Baker Book House, 1987), 86, 87.

33. Moreland, *Scaling the Secular City,* 89.

34. Moreland, *Scaling the Secular City,* 96.

35. Moreland, *Scaling the Secular City,* 102–3.

36. Geisler and Watkins, 105.

37. Campbell, *Power of Myth,* 53.

38. Geisler and Watkins, 104.

39. "Mysticism," *The New International Dictionary of the Christian Church,* J. D. Douglas, gen. ed. (Grand Rapids: Zondervan, 1978).

40. "Mysticism," *The New International Dictionary of the Christian Church.*

41. "Mysticism," *The New International Dictionary of the Christian Church.*

Chapter 5: *Myth Interpretations*

1. Joseph Campbell, *The Flight of the Wild Gander: Explorations in the Mythological Dimension* (South Bend, Ind.: Regnery/Gateway, 1979), 168. For Campbell, the word "immanent" means that the "transcendent ground of all being" actually lives inside all living things. For orthodox Christians, however, the word means that although God exists outside of and apart from the material universe, he can act within that universe. God also sustains everything in the universe with his power, and everything in the universe is immediately in his presence. Campbell used the word

"immanent" in order to try to prove Christianity has a hidden pantheism, but his definition is a misuse of the term.

2. Campbell, *Flight of the Wild Gander,* 111.

3. Campbell, *Primitive Mythology,* vol. 1 of *The Masks of God* (New York: Viking Press, 1959), 150.

4. Campbell, *Primitive Mythology,* 150.

5. Campbell, *Primitive Mythology,* 150.

6. Campbell, *Primitive Mythology,* 148.

7. Campbell, *Primitive Mythology,* 149–50.

8. Alexander Goldenweiser, "The Diffusion Controversy," in G. Elliot Smith, Bronislaw Malinowski, Herbert J. Spinden, and Alexander Goldenweiser, *Culture: The Diffusion Controversy* (New York: W. W. Norton & Co., Inc., 1927), 103.

9. Bronislaw Malinowski, "The Life of Culture," in *Culture: The Diffusion Controversy,* 30.

10. Campbell, *Flight of the Wild Gander,* 46–48.

11. Campbell, *Flight of the Wild Gander,* 45.

12. Campbell, *Flight of the Wild Gander,* 49.

13. Melville Jacobs and Bernhard J. Stern, *General Anthropology,* 2nd ed. (New York: Barnes & Noble, 1955), 125. See also "Anthropology," *The New Encyclopaedia Britannica Macropaedia* (Chicago: Chicago University Press, 1989), and articles on Frobenius, Malinowski, Goldenweiser, and Fritz Graebner in the *Encyclopaedia Britannica Micropaedia.*

14. Sir E. E. Evans-Pritchard, *Theories of Primitive Religion* (New York: Oxford University Press, 1966), 43–44.

15. Evans-Pritchard, 44.

16. Evans-Pritchard, 44–46.

17. Evans-Pritchard, 112.

18. See Chester G. Starr, *A History of the Ancient World,* 4th ed. (New York: Oxford University Press, 1991); Moses I. Finley, *The Ancient Greeks* (New York: Viking Press, 1964); and "Hinduism" and "Buddhism" in *The Encyclopaedia Britannica Macropaedia.*

19. Finley, 16.

20. Finley, 21.

21. Eliade, *The Sacred and the Profane,* 38–39.

22. Eliade, *The Sacred and the Profane,* 64–65.

23. Campbell, *Power of Myth,* 45.

24. Walter C. Kaiser, *Toward an Old Testament Theology* (Grand Rapids: Zondervan, 1978), 77.

25. Campbell, *Myths to Live By,* 96–97.

26. For a proper reading of the Greek text of John 10:30, see R. C. H. Lenski's *The Interpretation of St. John's Gospel* (Minneapolis: Augsburg Publishing House, 1943), 759–61. The verse actually says, "I and the Father we are one"—two persons, one essence.

27. Campbell, *Power of Myth,* 57.

28. Campbell, *Occidental Mythology,* 370.

29. Campbell, *Power of Myth,* 56.

30. Richard N. Longenecker, "The Acts of the Apostles," *The Expositor's Bible Commentary,* vol. 9 (Grand Rapids: Zondervan, 1981), 258.

31. Campbell, *Power of Myth,* 106.

32. Campbell, *Power of Myth,* 106–7.

33. Campbell, *Power of Myth,* 108.

34. Campbell, *Power of Myth,* 180.

35. Campbell, *Power of Myth,* 179.

36. Campbell, *Power of Myth,* 182.

Chapter 6: *Campbell's Morality*

1. Luke 10:25–37, my own paraphrase based on *New International Version.*

2. Campbell, *Power of Myth,* 225.

3. See Leviticus 19:18 and Mark 12:31.

4. Campbell, *Power of Myth,* 13.

5. Campbell, *Power of Myth,* 148.

6. Campbell, *Power of Myth,* 211.

7. Campbell, *Power of Myth,* 211.

8. Campbell, *Myths to Live By,* 253.

9. Douglas R. Groothuis, *Unmasking the New Age* (Downers Grove, Ill.: InterVarsity Press, 1986), 48.

10. Groothuis, 121.

11. See Robert M. Bowman Jr., "Strange New Worlds: The Humanist Philosophy of Star Trek," *Christian Research Journal* (Fall 1991), 20–27.

12. Campbell, *Power of Myth,* 32.

13. Campbell, *Power of Myth,* 229.

14. Hackett, 154.

15. Hackett, 155.

16. Hackett, 155.

17. Paul Johnson, *Modern Times* (New York: Harper & Row, 1983), 11.

Chapter 7: *The Traditional Values of Western Civilization*

1. Campbell, *Power of Myth,* 199.

2. Campbell, *Power of Myth,* 197.

3. For an excellent insight into the attack against western civilization at American universities, see Dinesh D'Souza, *Illiberal Education: The Politics of Race and Sex on Campus* (New York: The Free Press, 1991); Charles J. Sykes, *The Hollow Men: Politics and Corruption in Higher Education* (Washington, D.C.: Regnery Gateway, 1990); Allan Bloom, *The Closing of the American Mind* (New York: Simon & Schuster, 1987); "The New Fascism: Political Correctness on Campus," *Campus* (Winter 1991), 3–7; and "The Feminist Assault on the University," *Campus* (Spring 1991), 2–3, 5.

4. Montgomery, *Where Is History Going?* 95.

5. Jeff Florer, history instructor at Orange Coast College in Costa Mesa, California, telephone interview, January 18, 1992. Also see Starr, *A History of the Ancient World;* Kenneth Scott Latourette, *A History of Christianity,* rev. ed. (New York: Harper & Row, 1975); Earle E. Cairns, *Christianity through the Ages,* rev. and enlarged ed. (Grand Rapids: Zondervan, 1981); J. M. Roberts, *The Penguin History of the World,* rev. ed. (London: Penguin Books, 1990); and Russell Kirk, *The Roots of American Order,* 3rd ed. (Washington, D.C.: Regnery Gateway, 1991).

6. Cairns, 57.

7. Mircea Eliade, *A History of Religious Ideas,* vol. 2 (Chicago: University of Chicago Press, 1982), 413.

8. Florer.

9. Cairns, 127.

10. Cairns, 219–20.

11. Paul Johnson, *A History of the Jews* (New York: Harper & Row, 1987), 205–22.

12. Cairns, 243.

13. Cairns, 243.

14. Morris Bishop, *The Middle Ages* (Boston: Houghton Mifflin, 1968), 64.

15. Johnson, *History of the Jews,* 245–58, 284–87, 352–53.

16. Johnson, *History of the Jews,* 226.

17. Cairns, 311–12.

18. Cairns, 355.

19. Elizabeth Chesley Baity, *Americans before Columbus* (New York: Viking Press, 1963), 207. See also Roberts, 597–98, and John Eidsmoe, *Columbus & Cortez, Conquerors for Christ* (Green Forest, Ark.: New Leaf Press, 1992).

20. Baity, 234.

21. See S. L. A. Marshall, *Crimsoned Prairie: The Indian Wars* (New York: De Capo Press, 1972).

22. Robert Royal, "1492 and Multiculturalism," *The Intercollegiate Review* (Spring 1992), 5, 6. See also Robert Royal, *1492 and All That: Political Manipulations of History* (Washington, D.C.: Ethics and Public Policy Center, 1992).

23. See John Eidsmoe, *Christianity and the Constitution: The Faith of Our Founding Fathers* (Grand Rapids: Baker Book House, 1987), and M. E. Bradford, *Original Intentions* (Athens, Ga.: University of Georgia Press, 1993).

24. Latourette, 1470.

25. W. E. H. Lecky, *History of Morals from Augustus to Charlemagne*, II, 2nd ed. (London: Longmans, Green, 1861), 88. See also Christopher Dawson, *Religion and the Rise of Western Culture* (New York: Doubleday, 1991), originally published 1950.

26. Hackett, 113.

Chapter 8: *Origins*

1. Campbell, *Myths to Live By,* 1–2.

2. Campbell, *Myths to Live By,* 6.

3. Campbell, *Myths to Live By,* 76.

4. Hugh Ross, *The Fingerprint of God,* 2nd ed. (Orange, Calif.: Promise Publishing, 1991), 22–23. Dr. Ross is an astronomer. His book is one of many that show how the biblical text can be reconciled to current scientific thinking about the origin of the universe.

5. Laudan, 125.

6. J. P. Moreland, *Christianity and the Nature of Science,* 60.

7. Kekes, 148.

8. "Inductivism is the view of the scientific method wherein scientists are seen as progressively piling up more and more facts by observations, generalizing them by enumerative induction into laws, combining these generalizations into broader and broader generalizations by piling up more facts, and, finally, arriving at various levels of scientific laws whose contents are nothing but the facts." Moreland, *Christianity and the Nature of Science,* 61.

9. Moreland, *Scaling the Secular City,* 198.

10. Gleason L. Archer, *Encyclopedia of Bible Difficulties* (Grand Rapids: Zondervan, 1982), 58.

11. Archer, 58.

12. Archer, 58.

13. Henri Blocher, *In the Beginning: The Opening Chapters of Genesis,* trans. by David G. Preston (Downers Grove, Ill.: InterVarsity Press, 1984), 50.

14. Bernard Ramm, *The Christian View of Science and Scripture* (Grand Rapids: Eerdmans, 1954), 149.

15. Ronald F. Youngblood, *The Book of Genesis: An Introductory Commentary*, 2nd ed. (Grand Rapids: Baker Book House, 1991), 26.

16. Youngblood, 45.

17. Youngblood, 45.

18. Kaiser, 75.

19. Robert C. Newman and Herman J. Eckelmann Jr., *Genesis One and the Origin of the Earth* (Downers Grove, Ill.: InterVarsity Press, 1977), 74.

20. Newman and Eckelmann, 74.

21. Newman and Eckelmann, 84.

22. Newman and Eckelmann, 83.

23. Newman and Eckelmann, 85.

24. Blocher, 50.

25. Blocher, 50.

26. See also Leland Ryken, *Words of Delight: A Literary Introduction to the Bible* (Grand Rapids: Baker Book House, 1987).

27. Archer, 60.

28. James Oliver Buswell Jr., *A Systematic Theology of the Christian Religion*, 2nd ed. (Grand Rapids: Zondervan, 1975), 139.

29. *The Holy Bible*, New International Version (Grand Rapids: Zondervan, 1978). See footnote f, page 6, and footnote c, page 11.

30. Gleason L. Archer, *A Survey of Old Testament Introduction*, rev. ed. (Chicago: Moody Press, 1985), 204.

31. Archer, *Encyclopedia of Bible Difficulties*, 64.

32. Archer, *Encyclopedia of Bible Difficulties*, 64.

33. Kaiser, 75–76.

34. Archer, *Encyclopedia of Bible Difficulties*, 64.

35. Archer, *Encyclopedia of Bible Difficulties*, 65.

36. John H. Sailhamer, *Genesis*, in vol. 2 of *The Expositor's Bible Commentary*, Frank E. Gaebelein, gen. ed. (Grand Rapids: Zondervan, 1990), 72.

37. Campbell, *Myths to Live By*, 257.

Chapter 9: *Evolution and the Great High God*

1. Reed Wicander and James S. Monroe, *Historical Geology: Evolution of the Earth and Life through Time* (St. Paul: West Publishing Company, 1989), 16–17.

2. Michael Denton, *Evolution: A Theory in Crisis* (Bethesda, Md.: Adler & Adler, 1986), 105.

3. Denton, 286.

4. Denton, 306.

5. Phillip E. Johnson, *Darwin on Trial* (Downers Grove, Ill.: InterVarsity Press, 1991), 36.

6. Phillip E. Johnson, 98.

7. Campbell, *Myths to Live By*, 30.

8. Campbell, *Myths to Live By*, 31.

9. Wicander and Monroe, 538.

10. Stanley M. Garn, ed., "Human Evolution," *The New Encyclopaedia Britannica Macropaedia*, 1989.

11. Wicander and Monroe, 538.

12. "Neanderthal Man," *The New Encyclopaedia Britannica Micropaedia*, 1989.

13. Garn, 965.

14. Jared Diamond, *The Third Chimpanzee: The Evolution and Future of the Human Animal* (New York: HarperCollins, 1992), 44.

15. Diamond, 51.

16. Sarunas Milisauskas, *European Prehistory* (New York: Harcourt Brace Jovanovich, 1978), 32.

17. Campbell, *Primitive Mythology*, 311.

18. Eliade, *A History of Religious Ideas*, vol. 1, 7.

19. Ross, 160.

20. C. Simon, "Stone-Age Sanctuary, Oldest Known Shrine, Discovered in Spain," *Science News* 120 (1981), 357.

21. Archer, *Encyclopedia of Bible Difficulties*, 65.

22. Campbell, *Power of Myth*, 71.

23. Christopher B. Stringer, "The Emergence of Modern Humans," *Scientific American* (December 1990), 103.

24. Roger Lewin, *Bones of Contention: Controversies in the Search for Human Origins* (New York: Simon & Schuster, 1987), 26.

25. Animism is the belief that all objects contain spirits.

26. Totemism is the belief that you share a special kinship with an object, usually a plant or an animal, which becomes a religious emblem for your family or clan.

27. Fetishism is the belief that certain objects have a magical or spiritual power to protect or aid you.

28. Mana is an impersonal, nonmaterial spiritual essence that can manifest itself in all things and is a source of power.

29. Jacobs and Stern, 202 (emphasis mine).

30. Eliade, *Myths, Dreams, and Mysteries*, 135.

31. Eliade, *Myths, Dreams, and Mysteries*, 136.

32. Wilhelm Schmidt, *The Origin and Growth of Religion: Facts and Theories* (New York: Cooper Square Publishers, 1972), 168, 172.

33. Schmidt, 261.

34. Schmidt, 264.

35. Schmidt, 265.

36. Schmidt, 266.

37. Schmidt, 274.

38. Schmidt, 276.

39. See Charles Joseph Adams, "Religions, the Study and Classification of," *The New Encyclopaedia Britannica Macropaedia,* 1989, 554, 561; and Edward Evans-Pritchard, *Theories of Primitive Religion* (New York: Oxford University Press, 1987), 104.

40. Adams, 554.

41. Schmidt, 211.

42. Ernest Brandewie, *Wilhelm Schmidt and the Origin of the Idea of God* (Lanham, Md.: University Press of America, 1983), 244.

43. Brandewie, 251.

44. Brandewie, 44.

45. Brandewie, 119.

46. Jacobs and Stern, 202.

47. Evans-Pritchard, 104–5.

48. See Campbell, *Primitive Mythology,* 318–23, 351, 362, 363, 447.

49. Although I lean toward the view that the earth may be billions of years old, not every Christian scientist agrees with me. If you are interested in finding out more about a young earth view, contact the Institute for Creation Research, P.O. Box 2667, El Cajon, CA 92021. If you want more information that supports my viewpoint, contact Reasons to Believe, P.O. Box 5978, Pasadena, CA 91107.

50. J. P. Moreland, *Scaling the Secular City,* 221.

Chapter 10: *The Great Bible Debate*

1. Such as Isaac Asimov, Carl Sagan, atheist Madelyn Murray O'Hair, New Age Catholic theologian Matthew Fox, and others.

2. Such as chapter 34 of Deuteronomy, which describes Moses' death.

3. Campbell, *Myths to Live By,* 6–7. See also *Occidental Mythology,* 95–140.

4. Archer, *A Survey of Old Testament Introduction,* 110.

5. See Josh McDowell, *Evidence That Demands a Verdict,* vol. 1 and 2, rev. ed. (San Bernardino, Calif.: Here's Life Publishers, 1979 and 1981), for extensive quotes from Albright and many other archeologists that

support the historical reliability of the Old Testament and the New Testament documents.

6. Archer, *Survey of Old Testament Introduction,* 115.

7. Archer, *Survey of Old Testament Introduction,* 116.

8. Archer, *Survey of Old Testament Introduction,* 121–23.

9. Campbell, *Power of Myth,* 173.

10. Campbell, *Power of Myth,* 174.

11. See Campbell, *Primitive Mythology,* 101; and *Occidental Mythology,* 27.

12. See Campbell, *Primitive Mythology,* 101, 143, 176–90, 212, 350–51, 368; and *Occidental Mythology,* 14–16, 27–28, 43–44, 138, 147, 234, 237, 254–71, 334, 362, 481.

13. Campbell, *Occidental Mythology,* 516.

14. Campbell, *Power of Myth,* 106.

15. Campbell, *Power of Myth,* 107.

16. Evans-Pritchard, 51–52.

17. Evans-Pritchard, 52.

18. Evans-Pritchard, 42.

19. Walter Burkert, *Ancient Mystery Cults* (Cambridge: Harvard University Press, 1987), 75.

20. J. Gresham Machen, *The Origin of Paul's Religion* (Grand Rapids: Eerdmans, 1973 reprint of 1925 edition), 234–35.

21. See Ronald H. Nash, *Christianity and the Hellenistic World* (Grand Rapids: Zondervan, 1984), 172–73.

22. Nash, 147.

23. Burkert, 111.

24. Machen, 283.

25. Nash, 171–72.

26. Campbell, *Occidental Mythology*, 27.

27. Eliade, *Rites and Symbols of Initiation,* 118–19.

28. Eliade, *Rites and Symbols of Initiation,* 115. To back up his claims, Eliade cites several sources, the latest one dating from 1955. See his footnote 34 on page 115.

29. Machen, 9.

30. Machen, 284.

31. Machen, 289.

32. When Paul says "Lord" here, he uses the word *kyrios,* which is the Greek translation of the Hebrew name for God, Yahweh. Thus, when Paul says "Jesus is Lord," he is "proclaiming that Jesus is the Yahweh of the Old Testament" (Nash, 169).

33. Burkert, 101.

34. Burkert, 51–52.

35. Nash, 220.

36. Nash, 218, 219.

37. Campbell, *Power of Myth,* 57.

38. Campbell, *Occidental Mythology,* 370.

39. Bentley Layton, *The Gnostic Scriptures: A New Translation with Annotations and Introductions* (Garden City, N.Y.: Doubleday, 1987), 377.

40. Nash, 227.

41. Campbell, *Flight of the Wild Gander,* 225.

42. See F. F. Bruce, *The New Testament Documents: Are They Reliable?* 5th ed. (Downers Grove, Ill.: InterVarsity Press, 1987); Donald Guthrie, *New Testament Introduction,* 3rd ed. (Downers Grove, Ill.: InterVarsity Press, 1970); and Gary R. Habermas, *The Verdict of History: Conclusive Evidence for the Life of Jesus* (Nashville: Thomas Nelson, 1988).

Chapter 11: *Cosmos or Theos: Does God Exist?*

1. Flew, 15.

2. Joseph Leighton, as quoted in Young, 133.

3. Geisler, *Christian Apologetics,* 239.

4. Hackett, 102.

5. Hackett, 101.

6. Hackett, 111.

7. Hackett, 155.

8. C. S. Lewis, *Mere Christianity* (New York: Macmillan, 1952), 17.

9. Lewis, 19–20.

10. Hackett, 113.

11. Hackett, 113.

12. See, for example, Alvin Plantinga, *God, Freedom and Evil* (Grand Rapids: Eerdmans, 1974); Ronald Nash, *Faith and Reason: Searching for a Rational Faith* (Grand Rapids: Zondervan, 1988); Norman Geisler, *The Roots of Evil,* 2nd ed. (Dallas: Word, 1989); and Michael Peterson, *Evil and the Christian God* (Grand Rapids: Baker Book House, 1982).

13. Nash, *Faith and Reason,* 219.

14. Nash, *Faith and Reason,* 219.

15. Nash, *Faith and Reason,* 219.

16. Hackett, 89.

Chapter 12: *The New Testament: Eyewitnesses of His Majesty*

1. Geisler, *Christian Apologetics,* 292.

2. Bob Passantino, "Contend Earnestly for the Faith: How Far Can We Trust the Bible?" (Costa Mesa, Calif.: Answers In Action).

3. See Cleary, *McCormick's Handbook of the Law of Evidence.*

4. See Norman L. Geisler and William E. Nix, *A General Introduction to the Bible* (Chicago: Moody Press, 1975), 285; Bruce M. Metzger, *The Early Versions of the New Testament* (Oxford: Clarendon Press, 1977), 293; and Josh McDowell, *The Best of Josh McDowell: A Ready Defense* (San Bernardino, Calif.: Here's Life Publishers, 1990), 43.

5. Geisler, *Christian Apologetics,* 308.

6. J. P. Moreland, *Scaling the Secular City,* 136.

7. Norman L. Geisler and William E. Nix, *From God to Us: How We Got Our Bible* (Chicago: Moody Press, 1974), 108.

8. American Bible Society, "Preface," *The Bible,* Revised Standard Version (New York: 1971), vi.

9. Montgomery, *Where Is History Going?* 48.

10. Bruce, 100–102.

11. Bruce, 112. Also see Habermas, 90–93.

12. Robin Lane Fox, *Pagans and Christians* (New York: Knopf, 1987), 421, 441.

13. See Cleary, *McCormick's Handbook of the Law of Evidence.*

14. Montgomery, *Where Is History Going?,* 51.

15. Archer, *Encyclopedia of Bible Difficulties,* 349.

16. Archer, *Encyclopedia of Bible Difficulties,* 341.

17. Bruce, 65.

18. Metzger, 126.

19. If this sounds too miraculous for you, all I ask is that you think about the creation of this universe and the gift of life that happens every day. Aren't these every bit as miraculous? Brain surgeons have the power to trigger long forgotten memories when they probe your brain. Why can't the one true God who created the universe and who gave life to brain surgeons have such power?

20. Montgomery, *Where Is History Going?* 51.

Appendix: *Worldviews*

1. Geisler and Watkins, 11.

2. Geisler and Watkins, 246.

Bibliography

By and about Joseph Campbell

Campbell, Joseph. *The Flight of the Wild Gander: Explorations in the Mythological Dimension.* South Bend, Ind.: Regnery/Gateway, 1979.

———. *The Hero with a Thousand Faces.* Princeton, N.J.: Princeton University Press, 1968.

———. *The Masks of God.* 4 vols. New York: Penguin Books, 1964.

———. *Myths to Live By.* New York: Bantam Books, 1973.

———. *The Power of Myth.* New York: Doubleday, 1988.

Maher, John M., and Dennie Briggs, ed. *An Open Life: Joseph Campbell in Conversation with Michael Toms.* Burdett, N.Y.: Larson Publications, 1988.

Segal, Robert A. *Joseph Campbell: An Introduction.* New York: Penguin Books, 1990.

Mythology and Comparative Religion

Bettelheim, Bruno. *Freud and Man's Soul.* New York: Random House, 1984.

Brandewie, Ernest. *Wilhelm Schmidt and the Origin of the Idea of God.* Lanham, Md.: University Press of America, 1983.

Burkert, Walter. *Ancient Mystery Cults.* Cambridge: Harvard University Press, 1987.

Edinger, Edward F. *Ego and Archetype: Individuation and the Religious Function of the Psyche.* Baltimore: Penguin Books, 1974.

Eliade, Mircea. *Cosmos and History: The Myth of the Eternal Return.* New York: Harper & Row, 1959.

———. *A History of Religious Ideas.* 3 vols. Chicago: University of Chicago Press, 1982.

———. *Myth and Reality.* New York: Harper & Row, 1975.

———. *Myths, Dreams, and Mysteries: The Encounter Between Contemporary Faiths and Archaic Realities.* New York: Harper & Row, 1960.

———. *Rites and Symbols of Initiation: The Mysteries of Birth and Rebirth.* New York: Harper & Row, 1975.

———. *The Sacred and the Profane: The Nature of Religion.* New York: Harcourt, 1959.

Evans-Pritchard, E. E. *Theories of Primitive Religion.* New York: Oxford University Press, 1966.

Freud, Sigmund. *Totem and Taboo.* New York: W. W. Norton, 1950.

Frye, Northrup. *Anatomy of Criticism: Four Essays.* Princeton: Princeton University Press, 1957.

Hillman, James. *The Dream and the Underworld.* New York: Harper & Row, 1979.

———. *Re-Visioning Psychology.* New York: Harper & Row, 1975.

Jung, C. G. *The Archetypes and the Collective Unconscious,* vol. 9, pt. 1 of *The Collected Works of C. G. Jung.* New York: Pantheon Books, 1953–1979.

———. *The Undiscovered Self.* New York: The New American Library, 1958.

Jung, C. G. et al. *Man and His Symbols.* New York: Dell, 1978.

Leach, Edmund. *Claude Levi-Strauss.* New York: Penguin Books, 1980.

Levi-Strauss, Claude. *Myth and Meaning: Five Talks for Radio.* Toronto: University of Toronto Press, 1978.

McConnell, Frank. *Storytelling and Mythmaking: Images from Film and Literature.* New York: Oxford University Press, 1979.

Montgomery, John Warwick, ed. *Myth, Allegory, and Gospel.* Minneapolis: Bethany House Publishers, 1975.

Osborne, Michael. "Responding to Rowland's Myth or In Defense of Pluralism—A Reply to Robert Rowland." *Communications Studies 2,* 1990.

Propp, V. I. *Morphology of the Folktale.* Austin: University of Texas Press, 1968.

Richardson, Don. *Eternity in Their Hearts.* Ventura, Calif.: Regal Books, 1981.

Schmidt, Wilhelm. *The Origin and Growth of Religion: Facts and Theories.* New York: Cooper Square Publishers, 1972.

Slater, Philip E. *The Glory of Hera: Greek Mythology and the Greek Family.* Boston: Beacon Press, 1968.

Slotkin, Richard. *Regeneration through Violence: The Mythology of the American Frontier.* Middletown, Conn.: Wesleyan University Press, 1973.

Turner, Victor W. *Dramas, Fields, and Metaphors: Symbolic Action in Human Society.* Ithaca, N.Y.: Cornell University Press, 1974.

———. *The Forest of Symbols: Aspects of Ndembu Ritual.* Ithaca, N.Y.: Cornell University Press, 1967.

———. *From Ritual to Theatre.* New York: Performing Arts Journal Publications, 1982.

———. "Myth and Symbol," *The International Encyclopedia of the Social Sciences,* vol. 10, David L. Sills, ed. New York: Macmillan, 1968.

———. *The Ritual Process: Structure and Anti-Structure.* Chicago: Aldine Publishers, 1969.

Van Gennep, Arnold. *The Rites of Passage.* Chicago: University of Chicago Press, 1960.

Wilber, Ken. *No Boundary: Eastern and Western Approaches to Personal Growth.* Boulder, Colo.: Shambhala Publications, 1979.

Science and Evolution

Denton, Michael. *Evolution: A Theory in Crisis.* Bethesda, Md.: Adler & Adler, 1986.

Diamond, Jared. *The Third Chimpanzee: The Evolution and Future of the Human Animal.* New York: HarperCollins, 1992.

Garn, Stanley M., ed. "Human Evolution." *The New Encyclopaedia Britannica Macropaedia.* 1989.

Geisler, Norman L., and J. Kerby Anderson. *Origin Science: A Proposal for the Creation-Evolution Controversy.* Grand Rapids: Baker Book House, 1987.

Jaki, Stanley L. *God and the Cosmologists.* Washington, D.C.: Regnery Gateway, 1989.

Johnson, Phillip E. *Darwin on Trial.* Downers Grove, Ill.: InterVarsity Press, 1991.

Lewin, Roger. *Bones of Contention: Controversies in the Search for Human Origins.* New York: Simon & Schuster, 1987.

Moreland, J. P. *Christianity and the Nature of Science: A Philosophical Investigation.* Grand Rapids: Baker Book House, 1989.

Newman, Robert C., and Herman J. Eckelmann Jr. *Genesis One & the Origin of the Earth.* Downers Grove, Ill.: InterVarsity Press, 1977.

Poythress, Vern S. *Science and Hermeneutics: Implications of Scientific Method for Biblical Interpretation.* Grand Rapids: Zondervan, 1988.

Ramm, Bernard. *The Christian View of Science and Scripture.* Grand Rapids: Eerdmans, 1954.

Ratzsch, Del. *Philosophy of Science: The Natural Sciences in Christian Perspective.* Downers Grove, Ill.: InterVarsity Press, 1986.

Ross, Hugh. *The Creator and the Cosmos: How the Greatest Scientific Discoveries of the Century Reveal God.* Colorado Springs: NavPress, 1993.

————. *The Fingerprint of God.* 2nd ed. Orange, Calif.: Promise Publishing, 1991.

Stringer, Christopher B. "The Emergence of Modern Humans." *Scientific American.* December 1990.

Wicander, Reed, and James S. Monroe. *Historical Geology: Evolution of the Earth and Life through Time.* Rev. ed. St. Paul: West Publishing Company, 1989.

Wilder-Smith, A. E. *Man's Origin, Man's Destiny: A Critical Survey of the Principles of Evolution and Christianity.* Minneapolis: Bethany House, 1975.

————. *The Natural Sciences Know Nothing of Evolution.* Costa Mesa, Calif.: T.W.F.T. Publishers, 1981.

————. *The Scientific Alternative to Neo-Darwinian Evolutionary Theory.* Costa Mesa, Calif.: T.W.F.T. Publishers, 1987.

Interpretation

Boice, James Montgomery. *Standing on the Rock: The Importance of Biblical Inerrancy.* Grand Rapids: Baker Book House, 1994.

Buswell, James Oliver. *A Systematic Theology of the Christian Religion.* 2nd ed. Grand Rapids: Zondervan, 1975.

Cotterell, Peter, and Max Turner. *Linguistics & Biblical Interpretation.* Downers Grove, Ill.: InterVarsity Press, 1989.

Fee, Gordon D., and Douglas Stuart. *How to Read the Bible for All It's Worth: A Guide to Understanding the Bible.* Grand Rapids: Zondervan, 1982.

Kaiser, Walter C. *Back toward the Future: Hints for Interpreting Biblical Prophecy.* Grand Rapids: Baker Book House, 1989.

————. *Toward an Old Testament Theology.* Grand Rapids: Zondervan, 1978.

Longman III, Tremper. *Literary Approaches to Biblical Interpretation.* Grand Rapids: Zondervan, 1987.

Mickelsen, A. Berkeley. *Interpreting the Bible.* Grand Rapids: Eerdmans, 1963.

Mickelsen, A. Berkeley, and Alvera Mickelsen. *Understanding Scripture.* Ventura, Calif.: Regal Books, 1982.

Osborne, Grant R. *The Hermeneutical Spiral: A Comprehensive Introduction to Biblical Interpretation.* Downers Grove, Ill.: InterVarsity Press, 1991.

Ramm, Bernard. *Protestant Biblical Interpretation: A Textbook of Hermeneutics.* 3rd ed. Grand Rapids: Baker Book House, 1970.

Ryken, Leland. *Words of Delight: A Literary Introduction to the Bible.* Grand Rapids: Baker Book House, 1987.

Silva, Moises. *Biblical Words and Their Meaning: An Introduction to Lexical Semantics.* Grand Rapids: Zondervan, 1983.

―――. *Has the Church Misread the Bible? The History of Interpretation in the Light of Current Issues.* Grand Rapids: Zondervan, 1987.

Sire, James W. *Scripture Twisting: 20 Ways the Cults Misread the Bible.* Downers Grove, Ill.: InterVarsity Press, 1980.

Terry, Milton S. *Biblical Hermeneutics: A Treatise on the Interpretation of the Old and New Testaments.* Grand Rapids: Zondervan, 1974.

Books Defending the Bible and Christianity

Allis, Oswald T. *The Five Books of Moses.* Phillipsburg, N.J.: Presbyterian and Reformed Publishing Company, 1949.

Ankerberg, John, John Weldon, and Walter C. Kaiser Jr. *The Case for Jesus the Messiah: Incredible Prophecies that Prove God Exists.* Eugene, Ore.: Harvest House, 1989.

Archer, Gleason L. *Encyclopedia of Bible Difficulties.* Grand Rapids: Zondervan, 1982.

―――. *A Survey of Old Testament Introduction.* Chicago: Moody Press, 1985.

Beisner, E. Calvin. *Answers for Atheists, Agnostics, and Other Thoughtful Skeptics: Dialogs about Christian Faith and Life.* Rev. ed. Wheaton, Ill.: Crossway Books, 1993.

―――. *God in Three Persons.* Wheaton, Ill.: Tyndale, 1984.

Bruce, F. F. *The New Testament Documents: Are They Reliable?* Downers Grove, Ill.: InterVarsity Press, 1987.

Bush, L. Russ. *Classical Readings in Christian Apologetics: A.D. 100–1800.* Grand Rapids: Zondervan, 1983.

Carson, D. A., and John D. Woodbridge, eds. *God and Culture: Essays in Honor of Carl F. H. Henry.* Grand Rapids: Eerdmans, 1993.

Chemnitz, Martin. *The Two Natures in Christ.* St. Louis: Concordia, 1971.

Clark, David K., and Norman L. Geisler. *Apologetics in the New Age: A Christian Critique of Pantheism.* Grand Rapids: Baker Book House, 1990.

Custance, Arthur C. *The Doorway Papers.* Grand Rapids: Zondervan, 1976.

Geisler, Norman L. *Christian Apologetics.* Grand Rapids: Baker Book House, 1989.

————. *False Gods of Our Time.* Eugene, Ore.: Harvest House, 1985.

Geisler, Norman L., and Ronald M. Brooks. *Come, Let Us Reason: An Introduction to Logical Thinking.* Grand Rapids: Baker Book House, 1990.

Geisler, Norman L., and William D. Watkins. *Worlds Apart: A Handbook of World Views.* Grand Rapids: Baker Book House, 1989.

Geisler, Norman L., and William E. Nix. *From God to Us: How We Got Our Bible.* Chicago: Moody Press, 1974.

————. *A General Introduction to the Bible.* Chicago: Moody Press, 1975.

Geisler, Norman L., and Winfried Corduan. *Philosophy of Religion.* Grand Rapids: Baker Book House, 1988.

Groothuis, Douglas. *Confronting the New Age: How to Resist a Growing Religious Movement.* Downers Grove, Ill.: InterVarsity Press, 1988.

————. *Unmasking the New Age.* Downers Grove, Ill.: InterVarsity Press, 1986.

Habermas, Gary. *The Verdict of History: Conclusive Evidence for the Life of Jesus.* Nashville: Thomas Nelson, 1988.

Hackett, Stuart C. *The Reconstruction of the Christian Revelation Claim: A Philosophical and Critical Apologetic.* Grand Rapids: Baker Book House, 1984.

Haley, John W. *Alleged Discrepancies of the Bible.* Springdale, Pa.: Whitaker House, n.d.

Lewis, C. S. *Mere Christianity.* New York: Macmillan, 1952.

Linneman, Eta. *Historical Criticism of the Bible: Methodology or Ideology?* Grand Rapids: Baker Book House, 1990.

Little, Paul E. *Know What You Believe.* Rev. ed. Wheaton, Ill.: Victor Books, 1987.

————. *Know Why You Believe.* 3rd ed. Downers Grove, Ill.: InterVarsity Press, 1988.

Machen, J. Gresham. *Christianity and Liberalism.* Grand Rapids: Eerdmans, 1990.

————. *The Origin of Paul's Religion.* Grand Rapids: Eerdmans, 1973.

————. *The Virgin Birth of Christ.* Grand Rapids: Baker Book House, 1985.

Martin, Walter. *Essential Christianity.* Rev. ed. Ventura, Calif.: Regal Books, 1980.

McDowell, Josh, and Don Stewart. *Answers to Tough Questions Skeptics Ask about the Christian Faith.* Wheaton, Ill.: Tyndale, 1986.

McDowell, Josh, and Bill Wilson. *He Walked among Us: Evidence for the Historical Jesus.* San Bernardino, Calif.: Here's Life Publishers, 1988.

Milne, Bruce. *Know the Truth: A Handbook of Christian Belief.* Downers Grove, Ill.: InterVarsity Press, 1982.

Montgomery, John Warwick. *The Law above the Law.* Minneapolis: Bethany House, 1975.

————. *Where Is History Going?* Minneapolis: Bethany House, 1969.

Moreland, J. P. *Scaling the Secular City: A Defense of Christianity.* Grand Rapids: Baker Book House, 1987.

Nash, Ronald H. *Christianity and the Hellenistic World.* Grand Rapids: Zondervan, 1984.

————. *Faith and Reason: Searching for a Rational Faith.* Grand Rapids: Zondervan, 1988.

Packer, J. I. *Knowing God.* Downers Grove, Ill.: InterVarsity Press, 1973.

Phillips, J. B. *Your God Is Too Small.* New York: Macmillan, 1961.

Sproul, R. C. *Basic Training: Plain Talk on the Key Truths of the Faith.* Grand Rapids: Zondervan, 1982.

Young, Warren C. *A Christian Approach to Philosophy.* Grand Rapids: Baker Book House, 1954.

Index

275